BECOMING
JIMI
HENDRIX

BECOMING
JIMI
HENDRIX

From Southern Crossroads to
Psychedelic London, the Untold
Story of a Musical Genius

STEVEN ROBY and **BRAD SCHREIBER**

DA CAPO PRESS
A Member of the Perseus Books Group

Editorial production by the Book Factory.
Designed by Anita Koury.
Set in 10 point Prensa by the Perseus Books Group

Library of Congress Cataloging-in-Publication Data
Roby, Steven.
Becoming Jimi Hendrix : from Southern crossroads to psychedelic London, the untold story of a musical genius / Steven Roby and Brad Schreiber. — 1st Da Capo Press ed.
    p. cm.
  Includes bibliographical references and index.
  ISBN 978-0-306-81910-0
1. Hendrix, Jimi. 2. Rock musicians—United States—Biography. I. Schreiber, Brad, 1978- II. Title.
ML410.H476R62 2010
787.87'166092--dc22
[B]

                                        2010016644

First Da Capo Press edition 2010
ISBN: 978-0-306-81910-0

Published by Da Capo Press
A Member of the Perseus Books Group
www.dacapopress.com

Da Capo Press books are available at special discounts for bulk purchases in the U.S. by corporations, institutions, and other organizations. For more information, please contact the Special Markets Department at the Perseus Books Group, 2300 Chestnut Street, Suite 200, Philadelphia, PA 19103, or call (800) 810-4145, ext. 5000, or e-mail special.markets@perseus-books.com.

10 9 8 7 6 5 4 3 2 1

Contents

Acknowledgments

FOR THEIR INTERVIEWS AND VALUABLE TIME, WE'D LIKE TO EX-tend our thanks to Keith Altham, Brian Auger, William Bell, Marion Booker, David Brigati, Rosa Lee Brooks, Freeman Brown, Clifford Burks, Reggie T. Butler, Randy California, Danny Casey, Lester Chambers, Willie Chambers, Jimmy Church, Joe Conzo, Dean Courtney, Don Covay, Billy Cox, Steve Cropper, Dick Dale, Billy Davis, Joey Dee, Walter DeVanne, Tim Dulaine, Cornell Dupree, Robert Fisher, Earl Gaines, Grady Gaines, John Goddard, Dobie Gray, Kim Fowley, Richie Havens, Leon Hendrix, Chris Hillman, Herman Hitson, Samuel Hooker, Frank Howard, Moogy Klingman, Bob Kulick, Art Laboe, Arthur Lee, Bob Levine, David MacDonald, Joe Marra, Chas Matthews, Jimmi Mayes, Ellen McIlwaine, Buddy Miles, Billy Mitchell, Art Neville, Jeremiah Newman, James Nixon, Jimmy Norman, Gorgeous George Odell, Deanie Parker, Larry Perigo, Charles Pope, Linda Porter, Lithofayne Pridgon, Bernard Purdie, Eddie Purell, Chuck Rainey, Alexander Randolph, Kenny Rankin, Little Richard, Monti Rock III, Tom Rush, Pete Sando, John Sebastian, Stella Shapiro, Ray Sharpe, James T. Shaw, Carol Shiroky, Percy Sledge, Robert Lee Smith, Melvin Sparks, Bobby Taylor, Chip Taylor, Dewey Terry, Danny Toan, Buddy Travis, Rick

Vito, Charles Walker, Alan Wauters, Mary Willix, Glen Willings, Frank Wood, Oscar Wright, Sandra Wright, George Yates, Alphonso Young, and Lonnie Youngblood.

Special thanks are due to photographer John Goddard for digging out his 1965 calendar and documenting the two dates he saw Jimi perform with Little Richard and for the wonderful photos he took. And a sincere thank-you to Kees de Lange, who went beyond the call of duty with his research and suggestion assistance.

We are also very indebted to the following, who further assisted us in our research with documents, interviews, and advice: Nico Bauer, Doug Bell, Mary-Ann Brandon, Michael Fageros, David Ferguson, Chris Fry, Ray Rae Goldman, Chris James, Fred James, Christy Howard, Victor Kahn, Jeff Kaliss, David Kirby, Pete Hoppula, Lee Housekeeper, Oscar Jordan, Preston Lauterbach, Martin Lewis, Paul MacPhail, Megan McFann, Jim O'Neal, Bev Moore, Elizabeth Pepin, Brian Poust, Domenic Priore, Joel Selvin, Gary Serkin, Tom Shaw, Roy Simonds, Francine Szymanoski, Allan Taylor, Jon Tiven, Gloria Torrence, Lewis Watts, Narada Michael Walden, Don West, Thomas Yeates, and all the hep cats and kittens at CTT.

The authors wish to sincerely thank renowned Hendrix historians Ken Voss and Caesar Glebbeek for vetting the manuscript.

We need to praise countless research librarians, especially Jodie Fenton at the Seattle Public Library, for their patience and for their ability to answer many requests for books and newspapers on micro-film. During the process of compiling interviews, we sadly lost three important figures shortly after speaking to them. We especially want to acknowledge Johnny Jones, Teddy Acklen Jr., and Kenny Rankin for their fond memories of Jimi.

We also extend our gratitude to our literary agent, Matthew Car-nicelli, and Da Capo Press editor Ben Schafer for their advice and en-couragement and for their help in making this book a reality.

IN 1967, A RECORD REVIEWER USED THE WORDS "ROBUST AND HELL-ish" to describe the unusual sound he heard on Jimi's debut LP, *Are*

You Experienced, yet he did not describe how the previously unknown artist coaxed such unworldly vibrations from his guitar. Forty years later, on the anniversary of that timeless recording, I decided to develop an idea I had about Jimi's R&B apprentice years into an article. The period always fascinated me, and as far as I was concerned, not enough time was spent in most biographies on the early development of this musical genius.

The spark that ignited the story was reporter Keith Altham's un-published account of Jimi's first New York encounter with Chas Chandler, a little over a year before Chandler decided to become his manager. When an article on Jimi's 1965 tour with Little Richard blossomed into seven thousand words, I realized it had morphed into a chapter, and I decided to write this book instead.

Next, I set out to interview as many surviving band members, concert eyewitnesses, and Jimi's friends and lovers I could find from this time period; surprisingly, many were still around. I'd already compiled a fair amount of interviews, but when fellow Hendrix archivist Kees de Lange assisted me, the list grew immensely. Music author/historian Peter Guralnick graciously assisted with his input on the timeline for Jimi's R&B years, and we often discussed how and where Jimi joined multiple act tours in the early 1960s. We also owe a great deal of grat-itude to Hendrix documentarian David Kramer, Jacob McMurray at Experience Music Project, and Michael Gray at the Country Music Hall of Fame for their enduring support and help in locating many key people for interviews.

Other major breakthroughs came when both Lithofayne Pridgon and Dean Courtney agreed to be interviewed for this book. Faye was Jimi's friend and lover from 1963 to 1970 and hadn't discussed Jimi in great detail for many decades. Dean became Jimi's close friend shortly after Jimi arrived in New York in 1963, and the two were roommates when the situation called for it. After many face-to-face interviews, e-mails, and lengthy phone calls, their help and assistance filled in many gaps of Jimi's time in New York.

Writing a biography on Jimi's formative years was no simple task, and I was appreciative when Brad Schreiber decided to come on board as coauthor. Brad has been a valuable writing coach to me over the years, and it's been an honor to work with him on this exciting project.

My e-mail contact for any sources with additional information for future updates is lostarchives@yahoo.com. The interested reader can also visit www.steveroby.com to view a schedule of readings and lectures and to sign up for the course I teach on Jimi's life and music.

For Francine, A Love Supreme

—Steven Roby, February 2010

MY UNDERSTANDING OF WHAT THE ELECTRIC GUITAR COULD DO—and what popular music could be—changed the day I first heard "3rd Stone from the Sun" and "Are You Experienced" come out of my AM radio.

I'm grateful to my friend Steve Roby for giving me the opportunity to cowrite this exploration of Jimi's early years and how it made him the person and musical legend he became. It is one thing to work with a preeminent scholar on a biography. It is entirely another thing to find that this expert possesses a deep well of generosity and compassion. Steve made our journey together all the more pleasurable and fulfilling, professionally and spiritually.

Andrea Blackman, when she was in charge of the Civil Rights Room of the main branch of the Nashville Public Library, was indispensable in detailing the early civil rights sit-ins in that city as they related to Jimi's participation in them.

I have always felt that the most stirring biographical writing somehow finds a deeper path into the psychology of the subject, and to that end my conversations with three people in particular, David Kramer, Richie Havens, and Jimi's brother Leon Hendrix, led me to a more profound understanding.

On a personal note, my longtime literary guru, Jim Parish, again gave me great advice, and considering his vast experience with biographies, I was fortunate to have his counsel.

Our man in London, Richard Edwards, gave us valuable insights regarding British phraseology and Jimi's forays into England.

Brian Schindele, one of my oldest and dearest friends, was a source of continual support and strength as I dove headfirst into the life of Jimi.

With love to Jennifer and to Dr. Andrew J. Schreiber, Julie, Robin, and the memory of Ruth Elizabeth Davis, "Miss Ruthie," whose energy, intelligence, and wit far outran her considerable years.

—*Brad Schreiber, February 2010*

Preface

HE WAS BORN JOHNNY ALLEN HENDRIX. BUT WHEN HIS FATHER, Al, returned from World War II and saw his son for the first time, he renamed him James Marshall Hendrix.

As a little boy, he earned the nickname "Buster," because his hero was the actor who played Flash Gordon, Buster Crabbe.

In his Seattle band The Rocking Kings, his innocent face and quiet demeanor made others call him "Cupcake."

Because he slept with his guitar and brought it everywhere he went, other band members in Nashville referred to him as "Marbles," as if he had lost his.

He told Little Richard that his name was "Maurice James."

When he toured with Joey Dee and the Starliters, he was known as "Jimmy James."

In Harlem, his friend Dean Courtney named him after an animated, soft-spoken mountain lion on TV, "Snagglepuss."

Singer Etta James called him "Egg Foo Yung," because this is what he ate every night in Harlem.

He was called "the Creeper" when he lived with the Isley brothers in Englewood, New Jersey, because he moved so quietly around their house.

He changed the spelling of his first name during his breakthrough run at Greenwich Village's Cafe Wha?, becoming "Jimi James."

A New York ad referred to him as "the Blue Flame."

When he lived in London, members of his group called him "the Bat," because he wore capes and always had the curtains closed.

But for those who knew him best and for those who came to embrace his music, spirit, and vision, he will always be known as Jimi Hendrix.

Introduction
SEATTLE—THE CHILDHOOD THAT NEVER WAS

JIMI HENDRIX CLAIMED HIS EARLIEST MEMORY WAS BEING TAKEN out of his crib by a nurse. "And then she held me up to the window. This was in Seattle. And she showed me something up against the sky. And it was fireworks and all that."

His first Fourth of July saw him battling pneumonia, struggling for life, taken care of by a nurse.

Jimi's first memory was connected to an astonishing sonic and visual display, filling his young ears and eyes. His fascination with the mystical, the spiritual, the science fictional, flowered in the wildly imaginative drawings he made as a schoolboy and, inevitably, in the music he created, which transcended genres and expanded the horizon of rock music.

Women found him adorable as a child and irresistible as a man. His mother, her sisters, Delores Hall and Ernestine Benson, and her friend Dorothy Harding all helped when the beautiful, caramel-skinned Lucille was out running around, drinking, and nowhere to be found.

James Marshall Hendrix was originally named Johnny Allen Hendrix, and while his presumed biological father, Al, was away in the military, Lucille sought out the company of other men, including John

Page. A shipyard worker who hailed from Kansas City, Missouri, he lived with Lucille, wanted to become her pimp, and was at times violent toward her. The name change from Johnny to James reflected Al's resentment of Page's murky influence in his son's early life.

When Al Hendrix returned from World War II and could not find Lucille, he learned that his son Jimi, whom he had never seen, was with Mrs. Champ, a family friend in Berkeley. The boy did not recognize Al as his father and threw a toddler's temper tantrum on the train ride back to Seattle, which earned him a spanking.

Page's continued pursuit of Lucille after Al's return resulted in Page being punched out by Al, a former Golden Gloves competitor. The fight happened at the Atlas Cinema near the Rainier Vista housing project, where the Hendrixes lived, in front of Lucille, Delores, and other releatives. Lucille's sister Delores and her mother eventually had Page arrested and imprisoned for the time he transported a minor, Lucille, across state lines. When released, Page went to the door of the Hendrix house and threatened to kill the family. A family friend produced a gun and finally drove Page away.

Jimi and Leon had one younger brother, Joseph, and two sisters, Cathy and Pamela. All three younger siblings had health problems and were given up to foster care. When Jimi's parents divorced in December 1951, Al received custody of the two older boys but then had to send Leon to a nearby foster home. Leon would often be taken away from his older brother in foster care, and the threat of a permanent separation was an ongoing and very present possibility.

Al struggled to make a living as a landscaper, and he collected and sold scrap glass and discarded cans to add to his meager income. He asked his sons to collect bottles—clear, brown, or green glass—and bring them home. Sometimes, the boys watched their father burn the coating off of copper wiring he had found and planned to resell.

Like Lucille, Al's drinking and pursuit of the opposite sex caused him to be absent from the house for days on end. His chronic under-employment, coupled with gambling, kept the three male Hendrixes enmeshed in poverty, and Jimi took the responsibility for the care of his younger brother.

This almost Dickensian struggle for survival included the boys scrounging meals where they could from understanding, kind neighbors. Sometimes, unpaid bills meant Jimi and Leon woke up alone in a cold, dark house.

The shy, soft-spoken Jimi, who stuttered at an early age, once walked with his little brother into a Seattle Safeway supermarket. He surreptitiously opened a package of white bread, took out two pieces, and resealed the bag. He led Leon to the cold cuts section, opened a package of bologna, took out one slice, placed it between the two pieces of bread, and closed the package. Jimi walked him cautiously outside, under the store's harsh, revealing light, as Leon ate his first meal of the day,

Years later, after Jimi had attained worldwide fame, he was living a block away from the home of his music producer friend Alan Douglas and his wife, Stella, in Manhattan. He called Stella, telling her he'd been up late the night before in the recording studio and was starving.

"He asked if I would bring him a sandwich from a nearby deli," Stella recalled. "I said: 'Are you kidding? Let me make you something.' I was a really good cook. He said, 'No, I just want a bologna sandwich on white bread with mayonnaise.'"

Jimi not only helped raise Leon, but he also shared his own passion for music and art with his little brother. Jimi's artistic ability was exceptional. His drawings of soldiers fighting, cowboys and Indians clashing, and distant planets orbiting in space showed skills well beyond average. Jimi fell in love with the science fiction world of *Flash Gordon* and earned the nickname "Buster," after the serial's star, Buster Crabbe. Jimi often wore a homemade cape and once jumped off the roof of his house, trying to fly like his hero.

As a toddler, Leon interrupted Jimi's fantasy of playing guitar— the term "air guitar" did not yet exist—and Jimi tied a pencil to his little brother's hand and urged him to draw instead. Eventually, Leon won an art award among all Seattle high school students and became a technical draftsman for the Boeing Corporation.

Jimi, who with Leon had seen Elvis Presley at Sicks Stadium in 1957 with 15,000 other screaming, joyous fans, helped Leon fall asleep on certain difficult nights by softly singing to him, "You ain't nothing but a hound dog, crying all the time."

But there were some things in their hardscrabble existence that were beyond any comfort Jimi could provide. Lucille was admitted to a hospital twice in 1957 for cirrhosis of the liver. In early 1958, she was again hospitalized, this time with hepatitis. Jimi and Leon were stunned by how wan and frail she looked as she sat in a wheelchair and warmly but briefly welcomed them. Jimi brought handmade cards and huddled close to his mother, speaking little.

They never saw her alive again. On February 1, 1958, Lucille Jeter Hendrix was found unconscious in the back alley of a bar on Yesler Street. Delores Hall found her later at the hospital, untreated, in a hallway. She died of a ruptured spleen, a treatable condition and one that was more likely to have been caused by violence than alcohol consumption. She was only thirty-three.

Al Hendrix did not take the boys to Lucille's funeral. Instead, he gave the children shots of his Seagram's 7 whiskey and told them that was how men dealt with their grief.

Because of Al's refusal to let the boys attend their mother's burial, Dorothy Harding, furious, never spoke to him again.

Jimi rarely discussed the trauma of growing up in Seattle. He expressed love to his father in the letters he wrote and idealized his mother, especially in his emotionally raw, at times falsetto-voiced "Angel," in which he wrote of a silver-winged angel who, against "the child's sunrise," encourages him to persevere.

Silver wings silhouetted
Against the child's sunrise
And my angel she said unto me
Today is the day for you to rise.

But a rare expression of resentment about his childhood upbringing came out in his song "51st Anniversary." In it, a couple have been married for ten years, with hungry, unattended children running around the house.

Ten years they've been married
And a thousand kids run around hungry
'Cause their mama's a louse
Daddy's down at the whiskey house.

In 1967, Jimi did a survey for the British publication *New Musical Express*. The profundity of his reply summed up the importance of his mother's loss and his need to write and perform music beyond all things in life: "Personal ambition: Have my own style of music. See my mother again."

Jimi was so desperate to play guitar that when he was at Horace Mann Elementary School in Seattle, he brought a broom to school regularly, keeping it close to him, as a younger child might cling to a blanket. A social worker tried, after a year of this pitiable behavior, to get funds to buy Jimi a guitar. She wrote a note, insisting that not providing the boy a guitar might result in psychological damage. But the school did not think a boy humming and treating a broom like a guitar in a public school indicated any kind of mental imbalance. Al, typically tightfisted about money, contended he did not have the money to buy one.

But Al found a discarded ukulele with one remaining string while he was clearing out a neighborhood garage, and he gave the little, damaged instrument to Jimi. Jimi's imagination had to fill in all the sounds he wished he could make on that one string.

He did not realize it, but Jimi was following in the path of other great blues guitarists, such as Elmore James and B. B. King, who as children played what was called the "one strand on the wall." A single wire that held a broom together would be removed, straightened with a rock or other hard object, and then nailed to a wall or a back porch. The neck of a bottle became the slide, which produced a limited range of notes while the wire was plucked.

Jimi's desire to play guitar was so great that before the ukulele, he, as other blues guitarists had done as boys, constructed a makeshift guitar. It was made out of an empty cigar box with a hole cut out and a sheet of plastic wrap stretched across the supposed sound hole, held taut with a rubber band. Other scraps made a false neck, and finally Jimi had his first guitar. It replaced his imaginary friend, "Cessa," whom Jimi claimed he spoke to between the ages of four and six, although he never described Cessa when others asked.

Although Lucille was absent so often in Jimi's life, the other women around him intervened when Al seemed incapable of handling sole support. One night, Al was playing cards with a male friend who had an acoustic guitar. Jimi sometimes quietly brought it out onto the front porch and carefully explored its strings and neck. On that night, Al's friend drunkenly decided to sell it for five dollars to satisfy the boy who was so fascinated by it. But Al again cried poverty and said he could not spare the money, waving away the offer.

But Ernestine Benson, who was present, sprang to Jimi's defense. It was Ernestine who played old 78 rpm records that captivated Jimi, including the blues of Muddy Waters (McKinley Morganfield), Howlin' Wolf (Chester Arthur Burnett), Robert Johnson, and others.

Ernestine laid into Al, yelling, finally demanding, "Al Hendrix, you're going to buy this guitar for five dollars!" That acoustic guitar, Jimi's first real guitar, would be so dear to him that he carried it everywhere, played it constantly, even slept with it on his chest. It provided him the comfort his mother could not.

Being left-handed, he had to reverse the order of the strings on a right-handed guitar because left-handed models were hard to find and more expensive. His father disapproved of Jimi playing left-handed, calling it the Devil's work. So Jimi simply chose the most logical solution to the problem: He learned to play right-handed guitars upside down without changing the strings.

By his late teens, Jimi was playing in local bands. First, it was the Velvetones and the Rocking Kings, followed by Thomas and the Tomcats. He practiced every spare moment he had, even if some of his strings were broken. When he didn't have his guitar with him, he pretended he did.

"One day I was walking down the hall," recalled his Garfield High School classmate Mike Tagawa, "and here was Hendrix coming in the other direction playing air guitar." Tagawa asked Jimi where his books were. "He gave me that nice warm smile of his and said . . . 'I don't need my books. I've got my guitar.'"

Jimi, introverted, fearful of his future, never able to bring friends over to his house, was bullied by some of boys, who saw him as peculiar and aloof. Once, friends saw Jimi chased across a football field by a boy he would not let hold his guitar. Eventually, Jimi was knocked to the turf, punched, and kicked. He suffered the blows, rather than releasing the guitar and risking damage to it.

In spite of the indignities Jimi faced, his mind craved new musical experiences. He listened to Seattle's two black radio stations, KFKF and KZAM. They played many of the top R&B and soul hits. Jimi's early interest in John Lee Hooker, B. B. and Albert King, and other bluesmen now incorporated rock-and-roll acts such as Fats Domino, Chuck Berry, and Little Richard.

As if an omen of Jimi's musical future, he and Leon one day spotted a shiny Cadillac parked outside the house of their neighbor, Mrs. Penniman, whom they knew through their church, Goodwill Baptist, at 14th and Spring. Richard Penniman, aka Little Richard, was there visiting his mother. He had left show business to preach the gospel and invited the boys to come. Jimi and Leon went both nights. Jimi could never have predicted that in a few short years he would be playing guitar in Little Richard's re-formed band, battling with the singer for the spotlight.

HENDRIX'S FIRST ELECTRIC GUITAR WAS A WHITE SUPRO OZARK. After it was stolen at a dance, Jimmy got a cheaper, green Danelectro, which his father bought him at Myers Music Store in downtown Seattle. His school friends nicknamed it the "Chiang Kai-shek guitar" because it had been made in China. It was cheap and had a tinny sound, and to compensate for the instrument's limitations, he painted it different colors: red one week, purple another, and then back to green.

At dances, Jimi used it to play popular songs such as "Rockin' Robin," "Do You Want to Dance," and "Yakety Yak." As his style improved, he composed an original tune in the key of C called "Jimmy's Blues."

As Jimi got older, he played a club south of Seattle by the name of the Spanish Castle, which he later reminisced about in a song he titled "Spanish Castle Magic":

> *It's very far away*
> *It takes about half a day*
> *To get there*
> *If we travel by my, uh, dragonfly.*

The dragonfly was metaphorically the old, green Plymouth Fury with pronounced wings that one of the bands Jimi sat in with drove, when it wasn't broken down, to gigs. Leon tagged along with Jimi and looked forward to the shows at the Spanish Castle, its external square turrets and neon light cutting through the mist of Pacific Northwest nights. Jimi's little brother also looked forward to a free hot dog and French fries while the band played. On certain late nights, Leon slept under the stage.

But once at Birdland, another local club, the girlfriend of a Rocking Kings band member was very taken by Jimi's quiet, loner persona. During a break, Jimi was invited into the men's room for a band meeting. He exited, his face puffy and slightly bloody, beaten up by his jealous bandmate. Jimi quit the Rocking Kings. The band broke up shortly thereafter. Fred Rollins, the group's leader, was scheduled to join the army.

The next time Jimi saw him, Rollins was on furlough, wearing his paratrooper's uniform. Many of his friends, including Jimi, were impressed by the "Screaming Eagle" patch prominently displayed on Rollins's arm.

Jimi's early bands recognized his brilliance, but in a pattern that would repeat itself, he was unable to contain his need to create new sounds while playing cover songs. He was continually fired for cutting loose with screeching, whirring, fuzzy, or wailing sounds that hardly fit the songs being played.

No one understood what he was trying to do, and his compulsion to branch out sonically puzzled his fellow musicians and audiences. Once, an amplifier had been partially busted by Jimi's excessive volume.

The metallic sound from the damaged speaker excited Jimi, but when he brought it to another musician's attention, all he got was a strange stare.

Jimi had played Birdland numerous times. Despite Garfield High's ethnic mix of black, white, Asian, and Hispanic students, despite Jimi's home at the Yesler Terrace projects—one of the most ethnically diverse in the United States—Birdland was the furthest a Negro band could possibly go in the Seattle music scene of 1961. He was trapped in his fragmented family, in the region, in poverty, and in the music of the time.

Not surprisingly, Jimi eventually dropped out of high school. He stole moments and kisses with his first steady girlfriend, Betty Jean Morgan, a sweet, uncomplicated girl whose family had moved to Seattle from the Deep South.

But Jimi's father, a child of the Depression, bitter about his fate with Lucille, pushed Jimi to work in his landscape business, making him do the physical work of mowing grass and hauling heavy stones.

According to Leon, Al rejected Jimi's playing guitar, saying, "You need to work with your hands." Jimi, his sense of humor his partial salvation, once shot back while holding his guitar, "I am working with my hands!" At night, tired of his father's daily demands, Jimi pursued any activity that would take him out of the world in which he found himself.

Jimi and a friend robbed the clothing store of one of Al's clients, but the young robbers were so naïve and nervous, they tried to return the goods and were caught. Instead of a fine or jail for his son, Al was ordered to give free landscaping to the victim. When Jimi objected to his own participation in this compensation, Al snapped and punched Jimi full in the face. Jimi ran to a friend's house, but Al, now calmer, brought him back home.

When Jimi later joined the army, it required a written statement of his misdeed when he was fifteen:

A friend and I were playing around in an ally [*sic*] and we noticed a broken window in the back of a clothing store. We then got a clothes hanger which was lying on the ground and unbent it so we could stick it through the window and hook some clothes, which we did. The clothes didn't fit us. We gave it [sic] to a Christmas fund at school, and that's how we got caught.

IN MAY 1961, THE SEATTLE POLICE DEPARTMENT WAS INVESTI-gating black youths during a crime wave that involved seventeen homes and $2,500 worth of goods and cash stolen. On May 2, police spotted a car full of young Negroes having too good a time on a Tuesday night. Jimi was arrested, along with three other boys, for riding in a stolen car. As a result, he spent the day confined in the Rainier Vista 4-H Youth Center and then was released to his father. As a young man, Al had been arrested in a similar incident. So when Jimi claimed he had no idea the car was stolen, his father was very understanding. However, just three days later, Jimi was arrested again under the same circumstances. This time, after seven days locked up in Rainier Vista, he faced a judge.

During Jimi's incarceration, Seattle police nabbed six teens who were part of the home burglary ring. Still, during his hearing on May 16, Jimi had a tough choice to face. After listening to the plea bargain from the public defender assigned to Jimi's case, the judge suspended Jimi's two-year sentence with the stipulation that the young man im-mediately enlist for military duty. The two "taking and riding" charges, however, remained on his permanent record.

ON MAY 29, JIMI DEPARTED SEATTLE ON A SOUTHBOUND TRAIN headed toward Fort Ord, near Monterey, California, for eight weeks of basic training. He had signed up to be part of the U.S. Army's 101st Airborne, to wear a Screaming Eagle patch like Fred Rollins's.

Days before his departure, Jimi went to a street dance with Betty Jean Morgan, giving her a rhinestone engagement ring, although he was in no position to support the two of them in a marriage. There, in her bobby sox, saddle shoes, and long skirt, Morgan kissed him, not realizing that, although she would see him again, it was the beginning of the end of their relationship.

Jimi's confusion about leaving those he cared about coexisted with his eagerness to put his nightmarish existence in Seattle behind him. He addressed that uncertainty later in his career in a powerful blues number, "Hear My Train A Comin." A definitive performance of the song appears in the documentary *A Film About Jimi Hendrix*, during which Jimi, picking up a Zemaitis twelve-string guitar—an instrument he had not often played—gave a stirring rendition of the song. Significantly, Jimi also referred to the song as "Getting My Heart Back Together." With Delta blues mournfulness, he sang about buying an unnamed town and putting it all in his shoe.

I'm gonna buy this town
And put it all in my shoe
Might even give a piece to you
That's what I'm gonna' do.

Jimi caught the train out of Seattle, eager to go, yearning to musically express himself fully, now headed for the military, an institution that would tolerate his free-spiritedness even less than his father, his schoolmates, and his previous bands had.

1

The Case Against
Private Hendrix
(JANUARY–JUNE 1962)

IN JUNE 1961, JIMI BEGAN HIS ARMY BASIC TRAINING AT FORT ORD, California. It seemed very likely that Jimi would eventually see military action when he completed his training as a paratrooper and member of the 101st Airborne.

His choice to join the military rather than go to jail came at a time when the United States was committed to stopping the spread of communism in the world and strongly reacting to perceived threats to itself and its allies in numerous global hotspots.

The House Armed Services Committee voted in 1961 to increase production of Boeing B-52 bombers, in response to growing tensions between Cuba and the United States after the Bay of Pigs invasion. (President John F. Kennedy had been intimidated by the Pentagon into undertaking that failed mission.) There were still 50,000 American troops in South Korea after that war. The Berlin Wall was being built. Both the Soviet Union and the United States resumed nuclear weapons testing despite talks in Geneva. And the United States tripled its military advisers in a Southeast Asian country most Americans were still unfamiliar with: Vietnam.

Once he completed the eight weeks of training, Jimi was dispatched to Fort Campbell, home of the Screaming Eagles Air Assault Division. Fort Campbell, Kentucky, borders Hopkinsville, Kentucky, and Clarksville, Tennessee. Its more than 100,000 acres, including a large airfield and transportation infrastructure, made it a prime location in the early 1960s for a top-secret nuclear weapons storage and modification facility. Four electrified fences separated 5,000 acres in the southeast corner of the camp, and underground tunnels leading to storage areas were burrowed into the limestone.

Jimi's arrival at Fort Campbell on November 8 was followed by a letter to his father detailing how physically challenging the army proved to the new recruit: "There's nothing but physical training and harrasement [sic] here for two weeks, then when you go to jump school, that's when you get hell. They work you to DEATH, fussing and fighting."

On January 11, 1962, Major General C. W. G. Rich awarded Jimi the famed 101st Division Screaming Eagles patch he desired. "I made it in eight months and eight days," Jimi handwrote his father. But Jimi was quickly developing a sense of homesickness. He later wrote to Al: "You know, I've been having dreams of coming home and seeing you and everybody. It seems kind of funny. I must really want to come home for a while."

JIMI, WHO HAD DROPPED OUT OF GARFIELD HIGH, WAS REQUIRED to take General Education Development (GED) tests, and by the end of the month he was promoted to private first class (PFC). What still mattered most to PFC Hendrix were his music and the guitar that was over 2,400 miles away at Betty Jean Morgan's house in Seattle. The beat-up instruments he could check out from the music room on the base couldn't satisfy his restless, talented, self-taught hands.

"Send my guitar as soon as you can," Jimi pleaded in his next letter home. "I really need it now." The red, electric Danelectro Silvertone guitar arrived safely at the base, with its rosewood neck that fit so comfortingly between his long fingers and "Betty Jean" written on the body.

Jimi could not keep up with Morgan's letters, and she became jealous and concerned when he did not reply fast enough for her. He wrote to Al that Morgan expressed her fury in a letter, saying: "You're fooling with someone else down there. California girls are tuff [*sic*]. . . . You better write and leave those 'saphires' [*sic*] alone or you better not come up here to see me." Morgan's reference to Sapphire, one of the black characters on the long-running *Amos 'n' Andy* radio and TV series, suggested her insecurity about Jimi gravitating toward more aggressive women.

Morgan was prescient in that Jimi's first love was music, and he would later use his status as a musician and his natural shyness to attract women to him. But while he was at Fort Campbell, Jimi scraped together the money to buy Morgan a double wedding band and mail it to her. Presumably, the additional fifty-five dollars he earned per month for parachuting jumps helped pay for it. But Betty Jean eventually returned the wedding ring. In moments of vulnerability and desperation, near the end of his life, Jimi would propose to other women. But after Morgan refused his marital pledge, he set out on a path of sexual voraciousness that would become unparalleled in the liberated world of rock music sexual mores. At the apex of his career, various eyewitnesses entered hotel rooms where three or four women were in his bed, recuperating from the previous night's activities.

PRIVATE HENDRIX'S ARMY DUTIES BECAME OBLIGATORY INTER-ruptions taking him away from practicing on the Danelectro. He told his army pals that he wanted to capture "air sounds" on his guitar like the ones he heard in jump school training: the droning roar and rumble of the plane's engines, the rush of wind cascading past the ears on the journey back to solid ground.

Jimi annoyed his fellow soldiers with his constant strumming and, at times, the eerily bent notes emanating from his guitar. The calluses on his fingers were not from his assigned duties but from his nonstop practicing. The recruits snubbed him and made snide comments about his sleeping with and talking to the instrument. It was, in essence, a replay of his experience at Garfield High: His withdrawn personality and obsession with his guitar made him a source of ridicule. As in Seattle, the scorn sometimes turned physical, and some of his fellow paratroopers, as a prank, hid his guitar. He was forced to beg before they returned it to him.

IN SEATTLE, JIMI HAD FOUND MANY MUSICIANS TO JAM WITH, although most rejected his sonic experimentations. But at Fort Campbell, one soldier in particular discovered Jimi. His staggering inventiveness brought them together for life.

One rainy night, Private Billy Cox and a friend, after seeing a John Wayne movie, waited for the downpour to ebb. Through an open window of Service Club 1, Cox heard a solo guitar played in a wildly unique manner. He later claimed it was as if Beethoven and John Lee Hooker had merged.

"It was something the human ear hadn't heard," Cox reported. "I said, 'That's incredible!' And the guy I was with said, 'Sounds like shit to me.' I went in and introduced myself to him and said I played a little upright bass, and I checked out the Danelectro he was playing."

Billy Cox, one year older than Jimi, was educated in Pittsburgh, and his mother was a classically trained pianist. At an early age, Cox decided to pursue a musical career. He attempted the violin, piano, and various horns, but became fixated with the electric bass sound he heard in Lloyd Price's R&B band. Cox possessed Jimi's rebellious streak. He was kicked out of a symphony for the unorthodox way he played the bass. "They wanted me to play with a bow," he stated in a 2009 radio interview.

Cox, like Jimi, enlisted in the army to avoid complications.

"At that time, they would draft you," Cox remembered bitterly. "It was incarceration. If they did that, they could send you wherever they wanted. And I have claustrophobia. I went in and got it over with."

Their special association began with songs they both knew, by King Curtis, Booker T. & the MGs, and others. "We were gigging on base at all the functions. We practiced all day, every day. We would play all over Clarksville, Tennessee: the Elks Club, the D.A.V. [Disabled

American Veterans] hall, until we got a regular job at the Pink Poodle. . . . We did steps and everything. We had a lot of energy."

Jimi and Cox had a third player in their army ensemble for a brief while; he was, oddly enough, a superior officer. Major Charles Washington, who played saxophone in his off hours at Fort Campbell, formed a small rehearsal group with them and noticed the guitarist's occasional lack of concentration while performing.

"It really appeared that Jimi in many cases was never really with us," Washington told the makers of a 1973 documentary. "We'd look over at him occasionally and there he is, staring . . . on Cloud Nine. You didn't really get to know him that closely, as far as the exact line of thinking."

Washington resented Jimi's absentmindedness, as he often pawned the guitar before a gig at a dance or club, and then there would be a scramble to get the Danelectro out of hock because Jimi refused to use another instrument.

But Cox saw past Jimi's casual and introverted demeanor and recognized his serious commitment to music. Cox terminated his jump status so that they could dedicate even more time to practicing. They also worked out a clever scheme to avoid work detail and get in more practice time. After reveille, Jimi would "ghost" out of his company area and work out tunes with Cox until just before 3:00 p.m., when they would sneak back into their respective companies before the director from the USO could catch them. The routine worked until the army got suspicious.

Before joining the service, Cox took part in regular Saturday afternoon jam sessions at King Studios in Nashville, just fifty-five miles from the base. Typically, disc jockey Bill "Hoss" Allen, from the 50,000-watt powerhouse WLAC-AM, would let the tape run over the course of five hours, and within the music that emerged, he might find something worth using and sell it to a local label.

WLAC's signal in the early 1960s blasted rhythm and blues and gospel music to a wide audience all over the East, the South, and parts of the Midwest. Some say it could be heard in the Caribbean and Canada as well. The station had switched to all-black programming in 1946, shortly after a group of black college students showed up with of a stack of 78s, demanding, "Why don't you play some of *our* music?"

In the 1950s, Allen played hot new releases by Chuck Berry, Jimmy Reed, (Sam) Lightnin' Hopkins, and Etta James for fans listening to their transistor radios under their pillows as part of his "Under the Covers Club." With this new exposure, more rhythm and blues records appeared in the 1960s pop charts than in any previous decade. The hip approach used by "the Hossman" was of a piece with the station's other black-sounding jocks. It was a shock for some to learn that the DJs who used "jive talk" to pitch hairdressing products like White Rose Petroleum Jelly and Royal Crown Pomade were really good ole southern white boys.

Cox convinced Allen to listen to his new and extraordinary guitarist. So Jimi arrived at the studio, his fatigues newly laundered, pressed, and starched.

"So I got him plugged into the board," said Allen, "and said I just wanted him to play a New Orleans rhythm, a simple 4/4. Someone had just brought in a tune they'd written that week and we kicked it off. The next thing I heard in the headphones is BLLAAMM WEEE WOO. I stopped and said, 'Hey, man, just give me a good straight four. We've already got a guy playing lead.' He never looked up and we started again. Same thing. BLAAMM WEEE WOO. I yelled to the engineer, 'Cut that mother off. Cut him off the board.'"

After the session was finished, Allen played it back. Jimi knew his burst of improvisation had been left out. Used to this lack of acceptance, he said nothing.

Jimi's refusal to play guitar lines that were "normal" would cause him trouble time and again. Similarly, in almost comical fashion, everything he did while in the army was either substandard or outside of regulations. It was as if he were trapped and, short of desertion, wanted to find a way out of his forced conscription. After late-night gigs, Private Hendrix was caught napping the next day. He was also a terrible marksman, labeled "unqualified" and ranked lowest on the list of recruits during his basic training.

On Friday, February 16, 1962, Captain Gilbert Batchman requested a physical and psychiatric examination of Hendrix. Batchman's report concluded:

"Individual is unable to conform to military rules and regulations. Misses bed check; sleeps while supposed to be working; unsatisfactory duty performance. Requires excessive supervision at all times. Was caught masturbating by member of the platoon."

Board proceedings were then ordered for Jimi, who signed a statement declining counsel. He did not submit any statement on his own behalf. Private First Class Hendrix was advised that he might receive a discharge as a result of the board's findings. It's likely he considered this good news.

Jimi continued parachute practice and in March sent home a photo he had taken of other jumpers back in December. He referred to the experience as "dreadful."

"I can laugh at it now," wrote Jimi to his father, "but if I laughed, I would've been pushing Tennessee around all with my hands . . . push ups. See how that poor soul is almost choking half to death? That's the way [the cable] snaps you, like a whip!"

Cox and Jimi formed a group billed as both the Casuals and the Kasuals. The band featured Gary Ferguson on drums and, for a very short time, Major Washington on sax. They played Service Clubs 1 and 2, the EM (the enlisted men's club at Fort Campbell), and occasionally the Pink Poodle Club in Clarksville, Tennessee, about fourteen miles away from base.

The Pink Poodle was, by the standards of the early 1960s, a dive. The "stage" was a wooden riser, barely inches above the floor. The College Street club's owners came to the attention of the local police department for allowing minors to loiter where alcohol was sold and for selling liquor after hours. To keep the cops at bay and stay in business, the Pink Poodle instituted a new rule: To get in, you had to have a membership card.

Jimi wandered in one night and immediately felt a bit better upon seeing another left-handed guitar player on stage, George Yates. But Jimi became entranced with another guitarist's style. Johnny Jones enjoyed a steady six-night gig at Nashville's New Era Club with his regular group, the Imperials. They played Tuesdays with a local pick-up band in Clarksville, mostly to soldiers who bummed a ride from Fort Campbell.

Jones was six years Jimi's elder. He was born in Edes, Tennessee, and traveled to Memphis at age thirteen to take in his first blues show. In the early 1950s in Chicago, Jones was greatly affected by seeing blues greats of the era, including Muddy Waters and Howlin' Wolf. By 1961, Jones was living in Nashville and working as a studio guitarist, along with his regular club dates.

Jimi mustered up his courage and approached the seasoned guitarist when Jones went to take a break. "He had sat there all night and watched the show," remembered Jones. "He wanted to know where I was from, and then he asked to hold my guitar. I was kind of skeptical about letting anybody hold my guitar because you can easily drop one if you didn't know how to hold it right. I didn't know he played.

"Jimi said, 'I'll just sit a few feet from the stage.' So I left my amp on low and went over to the bar to take a break. During those thirty minutes, the jukebox was playing, people were dancing, and Jimi was up there picking away on my guitar. When he flipped it around and put it on upside down, that's when I got a cold chill."

Jones played a cherry red Gibson ES 335, and this was the first time Jimi had a chance to hold and play a decent guitar, let alone have a front-row seat in front of a player who spun off authentic blues licks learned from watching the masters.

"You know Jimi came from out there in Seattle," said Jones. "He didn't have much black on him when he got here. No, he'd talk like a white boy. His diction was real good. He was kind of shy but once you got to know him and watched him play, there was some kind of fire inside him, man."

THE YEAR 1962 WAS A FORMATIVE ONE FOR JIMI AND COINCIDED with great changes afoot in pop music. In England, the Beatles auditioned for Decca Records while the Rolling Stones played their first club dates. In the United States on the R&B side, Otis Redding, Isaac Hayes, and Booker T. & the MGs began their musical careers.

Chubby Checker's 1960 number one hit, "The Twist," reentered the pop charts and returned to the number one position in 1962. The dance craze showed no signs of abating. Joey Dee and the Starliters, King Curtis, Sam Cooke, and the Isley Brothers had Twist hits as well. Amazingly, not far into the future, Jimi would find himself playing on the same tour with Cooke and in the three other groups.

For an ambitious young guitar slinger like Jimi, there were two major black rock-and-roll guitar idols in 1962. Bo Diddley and Chuck Berry both had successfully crossed over into the white pop music world in the 1950s. Diddley exemplified Jimi's desire to manipulate tone, using the tremolo to fluctuate the volume at pulsating intervals. Not satisfied with available technology, Diddley built his own device from an old clock. He later described the apparatus to *Guitar Player* magazine: "I found you could bend one part of the clock to get a slow sound and bend it again to get a faster sound."

Chuck Berry accented his guitar work with provocative body language. Back in the 1956 film *Rock, Rock, Rock!* DJ Alan Freed introduced Berry, who performed one of his fast-car tribute songs, "You Can't Catch Me." When he reached the lyric "Sweetest little thing I've ever seen," Berry affectionately kissed the neck of the guitar. He concluded the song with his famous "duck-walk": knees bent, side profile, and guitar in a low and somewhat phallic position. Jimi had to be encouraged by Diddley and Berry's expansion of technical and showmanship boundaries, and their growing audience.

POPULAR GUITAR INSTRUMENTALS IN THE KASUALS' CLUB SETS gave Jimi a chance to step forward. Duane Eddy's "Peter Gunn," Santo and Johnny's "Sleep Walk," or Link Wray's "Rumble" coaxed even the shyest wallflower to the dance floor, as the Kasuals built a reputation. The local girls were taking notice of the flashy young guitar player with the shy smile.

A late Saturday night gig on March 31, however, caused Jimi to miss bed check, resulting in a demotion to the rank of general private. The excuse he entered on a report was vague and amusing: "Delay due to payday activities and weekend."

Jimi's flagrant disregard for the military's rules grew. "Failure to pay overdue laundry expenses" was now added to his list of infractions. After another weekend gig on Saturday, April 14, General Private Hendrix once again failed to report for bed check. This time, his superiors gave him a fourteen-day restriction in Building 6781 from April 16 through 29.

When a weekend furlough came around, Jimi and Cox came up with a plan to achieve a little out-of-town recognition. They'd heard about a talent competition in Indianapolis that offered a $100 first prize.

Jimi and Cox piled into Cox's beat-up '55 Plymouth and set off on the four-hour drive north. Like the Plymouth that had plagued Jimi during Spanish Castle gigs in Seattle, this car was unreliable. It did not go into reverse. Their impulsive scheme lacked a drummer and a singer, so they hoped to find some local players willing to split the prize money. After spending Friday night in a cheap hotel awaiting the competition, the little money they brought nearly ran out, so they decided to "move in" to Cox's cramped Plymouth.

There was a possible offer to play with the house band at the Brass Rail Tavern and back up Ophelia Hoy, a bawdy blues singer known for her risqué act. Unfortunately, things didn't go as planned, and the club didn't hire them. To make matters worse, Cox's car wouldn't start, and their last hope of raising cash was to win the competition. Stranded and hungry, they survived the next day on twenty-five-cent chili and all the free crackers they could eat.

Bedraggled and exhausted, Jimi and Cox entered George's Bar in Indianapolis on Saturday afternoon before the evening competition. They still did not have a full band. One of the most popular R&B bands in Indianapolis at the time was the Presidents. Founder Alphonso Young had the top group in Louisville when he took the Presidents to Indianapolis, on the way to Detroit, to record a demo at the new label known as Motown. When the Presidents didn't agree with their producer's direction, they headed back to Indianapolis and became the house band at George's.

After the Presidents impressed the crowd with one of their scorching forty-five-minute sets, Jimi and Cox approached and asked if the Presidents would be their backup band during the competition. At first, Young and his bandmates exchanged looks, then slyly nodded to each other, thinking they'd have some fun with the misguided out-of-towners.

"They looked kind of scruffy to me," Young admitted, "but we let them sit in anyway."

Jimi asked if they knew "Soldier Boy," a 1962 hit by the Shirelles, a tune that was sweetly simple. Instantly, Jimi made it his own, bringing deep sentiment to a song that ironically reflected his own mixed feelings about being in the army. "He started off that song like I've never seen anyone play before," recalled Young, "so we backed them up."

Jimi and Cox signed up for the competition. "We played pretty good, and the girls cheered and hollered," recalled Cox, "but unfortunately, they cheered and hollered louder for the Presidents."

Young proudly acknowledged: "After we got off the stage, Jimi came up to me and complimented me on my guitar playing. Back then, I was a backup man. I knew all my chords, diminished chords, and knew how to play country and western. My uncle was a white man, and he taught me how to play hillbilly when I was a little boy."

Even in defeat, Jimi was quietly confident, almost preternaturally composed. Although he had signed up for the service for three years, he told Young that he would be out of the army soon. He informed Young, the winner of the competition, the hottest act in town, that he should look Jimi up in Clarksville and join Jimi's band.

And this time, Young did not exchange knowing glances with his band members.

Out of gas and money, Jimi and Cox were eventually rescued by their girlfriends and got a ride back to Clarksville and their military life.

ABOUT A WEEK LATER, FORT CAMPBELL PLANNED A FULL WEEK OF activities in Clarksville in observance of Armed Forces Week (May 14–19) with a "Power for Peace" message. It was the annual opportunity for Clarksville to express its gratitude to the military for its dedication and service to the nation. There were parades and hand-to-hand combat shows. Jimi took part in two skydiving exhibitions. Much of the town was represented: the Boy Scouts, the Girl Scouts, the local fire department, and the highway patrol.

When Jimi and Cox finished up on Saturday afternoon, they headed down to Nashville, where the Kasuals, expanded to include local, nonmilitary musicians, had a show at the Club Del Morocco. The lineup was now Jimmy Hendrix on guitar, Billy Cox on bass, Harry Batchelor on vocals, Frank Sheffield on drums, Tee Howard Williams and Tommy Lee Williams on saxophones, and Alphonso "Baby Boo" Young on guitar. Young had received the nickname "Baby Boo" because he had cried all the time when he was little.

"I was the youngest boy in the family," Young explained, "and would get picked on. My father gave me that name."

Jimi managed to get back in time for bed check after he returned from the Nashville gig, but on May 22 he received a "mental hygiene consultation" at Fort Campbell to determine if he was mentally stable for his board hearing. Lieutenant Lanford DeGeneres reported: "There are no disqualifying mental defects sufficient to warrant disposition through medical channels. . . . The individual . . . has the mental capacity to understand and participate in the board proceedings."

Squad Leader Gerd H. K. Klepper also filed a report against Jimi: "Private Hendrix has been found sleeping on duty several times, he has been given extra training as a corrective action on numerous occasions but to no avail. . . . In my opinion, Private Hendrix is unadaptable to military service and should be eliminated from the service."

Once again, Jimi failed to report for bed check on May 23 and was given another fourteen-day base restriction, from May 24 through June 6.

Six other soldiers turned him in or were encouraged to do so. Private James Mattox filed a report May 23 about Jimi's self-pleasuring activities: "On the 26th of April, I was in charge of a detail to wash the ceiling in the squad bay," wrote Mattox.

There was six of us working pairs. . . . Every once in a while, I would catch Hendrix setting down on his footlocker or laying down on his bunk trying to get some sleep. Around 1000 hours, I looked all over the squad bay for Hendrix but couldn't find him. . . . I then went into the latrine and saw Hendrix sitting in the last commode. I thought he was sitting there sleeping so I stood on the stool in the commode next to his and looked into his commode, there sat Hendrix masturbating himself. At that time, [Private] Stroble came into the latrine and I motioned him to come over and witness what was happening. He took a look and then went back into the squad bay and started working again.

The following day, Jimi's platoon sergeant, James C. Spears, filed another damning report: "He has no interest whatsoever in the Army. . . . It is my opinion that Private Hendrix will never come up to the standards required of a soldier. I feel that the military service will benefit if he is discharged as soon as possible."

Jimi's days in the army were numbered. The papers in his file were overflowing.

Exactly one year after Jimi enlisted, Captain Gilbert Batchman filed a request for discharge to the commanding officer of the 101st Airborne Division. The request included seven signed statements, a record of previous convictions, a record of time lost, a request for physical and psychiatric examination, and Jimi's punishment record in his unit.

It has been erroneously reported that Captain John Halbert, a medical officer, recommended that Jimi be discharged primarily for admitting to having homosexual desires for an unnamed soldier. But in the ninety-eight pages of documents the National Personnel Records Center has on Jimi's military history, the word "homosexual" is not mentioned.

There are also references in Halbert's unauthenticated report of Jimi losing fifteen pounds, experiencing chest pains, and having sleep trouble and personal problems, yet there are no official indications of these conditions in his records. Jimi himself muddied the waters by later claiming in the press that in the army he had had a bad back and had broken an ankle during an earlier jump while a paratrooper.

On June 29, 1962, Jimi was approved for an honorable discharge from the army for "unsuitability." Years later, a reporter for the *New Musical Express* asked Jimi why he had left the army so early. He stretched the truth a bit: "Bored to death at 16, I joined the Army Airborne. A little less than a year of screaming 'Ahhhhh!' and 'I'm falllli-iiing' all the time, I squeezed my way out by breaking my ankle and hurting my back. . . . Anyway I was lucky to get out when I did. Vietnam was just coming up."

Psychologically, Jimi was unprepared to cope with the military, yet he never lost respect for those in the armed services. He studiously avoided public discussions of Vietnam, opting instead for general comments on peace and unity.

Jimi's antiwar song "Machine Gun," a live performance on his album *Band of Gypsys*, is considered one of his most visceral works. It was the favorite of his friend Miles Davis. Performed January 1, 1970, at the Fillmore East in New York City, the song came in the wake of the continuing violence in Southeast Asia, as well as in America's inner cities.

In the introduction to the song, Jimi tells the audience: "I'd like to dedicate this one to the 'draggy' scene that's going on. All the soldiers that are fighting in Chicago, Milwaukee and New York. Oh, yes, and all the soldiers fighting in Vietnam."

Alphonso Young provided additional insight into the case against Private Hendrix: "His friend Billy Cox was getting out soon, and Jimi didn't want to stay in the Army alone, so Jimi said he broke his ankle to get out. Jimi wore a cast for about two weeks after he was out, and then it came off. He faked that one. I used to ask him how it was doing, and he said, 'Oh, just fine.' He knew I was teasing him. He'd figured a way to get out and be with Billy."

He was free from the yoke of the military and his father, but at this point in his life Jimi had no idea where he was destined to go.

2

I Can Hear the Blues Callin' My Name

(JULY–DECEMBER 1962)

STANDING OUTSIDE THE GATES OF FORT CAMPBELL ON JULY 2, discharge papers in hand and about $400 in his pocket, James Marshall Hendrix was at another crossroads in his life. He could buy a bus ticket back to Seattle, reunite with Betty Jean Morgan, and possibly resume a career in his father's landscape business, while continuing his pursuit of music there. But the greatest enjoyment Jimi had experienced in live music was playing with Billy Cox, who was still serving and would not be out for three more months.

Also, Jimi had sold the Danelectro guitar he painted red with the white letters "Betty Jean," though at one point their relationship had seemed quite serious.

"Jimi and I were engaged to be married, but I was too young," explained Morgan in the book *Voices from Home*. "I was still in school and my mom wanted me to finish school."

On his last furlough home, Betty Jean was a barely a memory. Emotionally, Jimi wanted to avoid her at all costs, like he wanted to avoid dwelling on the loss of his mother. Al Hendrix asked what was happening with Betty Jean.

"Betty who?" Jimi responded.

Back at the base, in one of the letters he regularly wrote to his father, Jimi told of various musicians he had worked with in different places while he'd been in the army and how much he had enjoyed each adventure. Despite the closing of Jimi's letters expressing love to his father, Al knew the conflict going on in Jimi, the exultation of being away from Seattle, tempered with exhaustion and unfamiliarity.

Jimi's father wrote back: "There's nothing going on back here in Seattle in the music world. If you come back here, you'll just be sitting around idle. There's always a home for you, but I understand your situation. You want to go out there and see what's happening. That's the way I was."

So when he was discharged, Jimi decided to take one day of freedom, one day neither in the army nor back at his father's house, to see how it felt to have more money in his pocket than he had ever had. From Fort Campbell, he returned to Clarksville, Tennessee, the town where his gigs at the admittedly cramped Pink Poodle had so energized him.

The sounds of jazz music from a small club captured his ears as Jimi arrived off the bus in Clarksville. He went inside, had a drink, and found himself enjoying the sounds.

Years later, Jimi went on the record about what happened in that jazz joint in Clarksville. Alcohol would later be the scourge of his existence, driving him to fits of pique, even rare bursts of atypical, physical violence. But on that first day, when he had finally wriggled his way out of the 101st Airborne, the alcohol loosened him up in an entirely different way: "I went in this jazz joint and had a drink. I liked it and I stayed. People tell me I get foolish, good-natured sometimes. Anyway, I guess I felt real benevolent that day. I must have been handing out bills to anyone who asked me. I came out of that place with sixteen dollars left."

Jimi bought drinks for others, celebrating his newfound freedom, enjoying the company of those who welcomed his generosity. Never having had much money and often eating at friends' houses because there was no food at home meant Jimi had no conception of how to handle money. When most of the money in his pocket was gone in that Clarksville juke joint, Jimi did not call his father for the money to get back to Seattle. He could easily surmise what the answer would be, based on experience.

Jimi's day in the jazz club in Clarksville sealed his decision to stay in town and wait for Cox so that they could play in a group again. But he found himself in a town that still lived under the shadow of racial prejudice, in stark contrast to the racial demographics of Seattle.

Clarksville was a quiet little town of about 22,000 people. In 1862, during the Civil War, Union troops took over the town. Rebels regained it without a shot and lost it again, and Clarksville remained under federal control. In the legendary battle of Gettysburg, a regiment of more than nine hundred men from Clarksville fought for the Confederacy. Only three returned to a city that was occupied by the Union Army.

Freed slaves in the surrounding area formed black regiments in Clarksville to fight the Confederates. Black shantytowns sprang up on the bank of the Cumberland River. When Jimi began living in Clarksville a century later, the antebellum separation was still present in the economic difference between white and black neighborhoods.

An ordinance called the Sunday Blue Law had recently passed, and practically all businesses, except for gas stations, restaurants, and drugstore prescription counters, were closed on Sundays. There was not much entertainment to be found compared to what Jimi saw in Nashville. In honor of Chubby Checker's new movie, *Don't Knock the Twist*, Coca-Cola sponsored a "Twist Party" with a $25 prize at a Clarksville movie theater. Stock car races, square dances, and a Flatt & Scruggs hootenanny at the Dunbar Cave were other options, but these were intended for white people.

"Whites Only" signs were commonplace in Montgomery County, but a small section in the *Clarksville Leaf Chronicle* titled "Happenings Among the Colored People" announced funeral services, baptisms, and barbeque chicken dinners at the Faith Temple Church of God in Christ.

Jimi rented a room on 411 Glenn Street, in the black neighborhood, just a short walk from the College Street location of the Pink Poodle. He worked a few odd jobs while Cox served his final months at Fort

Campbell. One agency, W&W, represented Jimi and a band he formed in the interim. It was anything but a major career move.

"Man, they paid us so little," Jimi remembered, "that we decided that the two Ws stood for Wicked and Wrong." According to Jimi, a so-called music agent had the audacity to come up on stage during the middle of a song and slip payment for the gig into the players' pockets, knowing good and well they could never count it during their set. When it came time for a break, the players found their envelopes contained only two or three dollars and the agency rep had disappeared, avoiding any questions.

On October 18, Billy Cox was discharged from the army, and he and Jimi reunited and became roommates. Because their repertoire was limited, they kept to mostly blues songs. "We'd sit around, pass the Jell-O or strawberry upside-down cake, and pull out an Albert King or B. B. King record and get a lick or two," Cox reminisced. Jimi had no way of knowing at the time that he would soon meet, play with, and learn from these two blues masters.

Shortly after Jimi and Cox were reunited and began playing together again, guitarist Alphonso Young reappeared in their lives. The band he had fronted, the Presidents, was arguing regularly, and finally after a heated disagreement with his bass player, Young, remembering Jimi's offer to play together, left his own group in Indianapolis. The three musicians decided to reform the Kasuals and, using Young's suggestion, added "King" to the front of the band name.

Young's rationale for the name change: "I said to Jimi, 'The Kasuals? That don't sound right. We always got suits and ties on.'"

The King Kasuals brought in Tee Howard Williams on sax, Freeman Brown on drums, and Harry Bachelor on vocals. Jimi had always been shy about singing, thinking he did not have a good voice. However, his shy, sensitive demeanor was bringing him much female attention. He even had his own unofficial fan club, known as the Buttons. Sandra Matthews and her friends took care of his stage clothes, because Jimi was in the habit of shearing off shirt buttons during many of his wild stage acrobatics.

The band moved into a small, rented house with a flat roof at 610 Ford Street in Clarksville. The band members were unaware of the house's dark past, which eventually reminded them that at the time in Tennessee the color of their skin was still an issue and they could therefore find themselves in danger.

An undertaker living in the house before them had left town so quickly that not all the local residents knew it. According to Young, the undertaker, who owned the house, had "killed a white guy. He had to move out of his private home because they were after him. When we were there, we wondered why guys were running by and throwing bottles and throwing rocks at the house. We couldn't figure it out." The group, not about to endure hurled refuse and racial epithets, moved out shortly thereafter.

The King Kasuals managed to find gigs, to attract a faithful following, and to be ready when opportunity knocked. The musicians were told in Clarksville that there was a club in Nashville that could use a new house band. The King Kasuals auditioned for the job and were hired at a club that would provide Jimi with a home to hone his rapidly developing skills. It was called the Club Del Morocco, known to those in the music scene as "the Del."

Jimi's greatest period of learning—not experimenting with sound but simply learning styles and techniques—was in Nashville, not only because of his own innate curiosity but also because of the competition for musical dominance. Nashville was "one of the hardest audiences in the South," Jimi insisted. "Everybody knows how to play guitar. You walk down the street and people are sitting on their porch playing more guitars. . . . That's where I learned to play, really, in Nashville."

Nashville's music industry emerged as a considerable force in the early 1960s. Every major label and scores of small companies set up recording studios in town and attracted big names. Elvis Presley cut his RCA hits in Nashville, as did Les Paul and Mary Ford. Four professional studios handled the majority of acts, while six successful smaller studios took up the slack, producing demos and advertising agency jingles.

Two hundred seventeen BMI publishers also did business in Nashville in 1962 and collected license fees on behalf of songwriters, composers, and music publishers, distributing the royalties to their members. There were 1,100 musicians, 350 songwriters and 110 publishing houses. One-half of all American recordings were issued from Nashville when Jimi and his bandmates arrived there.

Nashville's black population stood at 43 percent in 1962, and its entertainment was segregated in the northern part of town, as it had been since the 1940s, along Fourth Avenue North and Jefferson Street. At 2417 Jefferson Street stood the new home base for Jimi and the King Kasuals.

The Del Morocco had been founded by Theodore "Uncle Teddy" Acklen in 1943, refurbishing a hotel for Pullman porters into a club packed every night with soldiers from Fort Campbell. The club was about 150 feet long by 50 feet across, and capacity was approximately two hundred people. The bar, situated in the back behind the tables, was brick, with glass and colored lights that flashed on and off. Upstairs at the Del Morocco was an elegant dinner club called the Blue Room, a piano bar that seated about one hundred. Acklen also ran gambling in an upstairs back room for a select few.

Uncle Teddy was so impressed with the King Kasuals that he gave the band a one-year contract and bought Jimi and Cox new gear to pump up their sound. Cox received a Silvertone amp and Jimi a forty-watt Fender Band Master.

Acklen also provided the King Kasuals with a place to live, for free. In addition to the Del, he owned a local barbershop, a restaurant specializing in fried chicken called the Golden Bird, and a beauty school/salon just down the street from the Del called Joyce's House of Glamour, named after his daughter. Downstairs were six or so rooms, and upstairs, where Jimi, Cox, and Young lived, were about eight more.

Teddy Acklen Jr., the owner's son, admitted that the performers and those who paid for rooms lived rather simply: "These were single rooms. Ain't nothing in them but a bed and a chair, and there was one bathroom everybody shared. Nothing fancy like a hotel, just the bare essentials."

But despite the less than palatial surroundings, it was a time of rambunctiousness and joyful exuberance for Jimi and his bandmates. Young and Jimi ran into the likes of Aretha Franklin and Etta James getting their hair done downstairs at the House of Glamour in preparation for upcoming Del Morocco gigs.

And often, upstairs resembled an out-of-control college dormitory. Cox had a pet monkey who was, unfortunately, not house broken and caused Cox and others to yell angrily at the hairy little troublemaker, though Young remembered that Cox was less than kind to the animal.

Young recalled the chaos quite clearly: "Billy Cox was mean. He'd upset that monkey so much, it would come down and stay with Jimi and me. He'd beat that monkey, and it would be running down the hall, making noise with its little chain around its neck. Jimi kept him half the time because he and Billy would fight."

The King Kasuals took whatever gigs were available during the week and performed at the Del on the weekends. The band did its set and remained on stage playing behind guest singers. On Sunday afternoons, until the club closed at 2 a.m., the Del Morocco had a regular and rather gargantuan jam session, with as many as fifteen bands showing up.

On those Sundays, the Del Morocco often featured organist Ironing Board Sam with Jimi and Cox backing him up. Sam's Hammond B3 organ had sustained superficial burns in a club fire, but he had managed to salvage the keyboard and mount it on top of an ironing board. Sam worked a foot pedal from his setup: A blue light meant it was a slow number; a red light meant the music was hot.

Acklen's wife, Ehrai "Muffy" Walker, a former dancer, convinced her husband to book Vegas-style lounge acts and the occasional stripper, although bands like the King Kasuals drew bigger crowds and generated more bar sales. But the diversity of acts was remarkable. One was a comedian named Raymond Belt, whose wife made him outfits so he could dress in drag, imitating pioneering black comedian Jackie "Moms" Mabley, telling outrageously vulgar jokes.

The King Kasuals' manager, Uncle Teddy, handled the Imperials as well. Those band members had their hair processed at his barbershop and were locally respected for their slick lead guitarist, Johnny Jones. Like Jimi, Jones couldn't read music, but he could play almost anything by ear. He still remembered the night Private Hendrix had patiently sat in the front row at the Pink Poodle in Clarksville and how Jones had cautiously let the youngster hold his guitar. But the youngster had matured.

One night in Nashville, all the top black musicians in town witnessed a memorable showdown at the Club Baron. Local guitarist and friend Larry Lee, representing Jimi, challenged Jones to a guitar dual on Jimi's behalf. Jones was not only technically brilliant but also physically imposing, at six foot four, with a gravelly voice to boot, compared to Jimi, humble, soft-spoken, five foot nine, and as skinny as a rail.

"He come at me one night during intermission. I was sitting at the bar enjoying my second drink," remembered Jones, "and Larry Lee came in the door pushing Jimi's little amp with wheels on it. They'd walked about two blocks. Jimi carried a guitar on his shoulder because he never had a case for it. Larry was doing all the talking. 'Yeah, he's coming at you tonight, Johnny Jones.' I looked up. There was Jimi standing right behind him, head down, not saying a word."

Jimi, always broke and in need of a decent guitar of his own, borrowed one from George Yates, the fellow lefty who played rhythm in Jones's band. Jimi patiently set up his gear and waited to be called to the stage.

Red McMillan, the MC for the evening, announced, "Ladies and gentlemen, now we're going to have the battle of the guitars, featuring Johnny Jones and Jimmy Hendrix," and the duel began. Jimi used a small Fender Reverb concert amp, while Jones was plugged into a dual Showman amp with two fifteen-inch JBL speakers, easily pumping out one hundred watts of fat, nasty tone.

Jimi and Jones traded licks, both being as furiously inventive as possible. But Jones's guitar could be heard more clearly, and he got all the applause during the competition.

After it was over, Lee grabbed Jimi and demanded to know: "What happened up there? You let that man kick your butt all over the place."

Jimi, in his articulate, soft voice, mumbled, "I was trying to get that B. B. King sound."

"To hell with B. B. King. Come on here," urged Lee, and they left the Club Baron quickly. To his credit, Jones saw Jimi the next night and assured him that he was not bad. It was just that Jones was louder.

One quality that came to mark Jimi as a performer was his anger or shame when he had technical problems onstage. It broke his composure and depressed him. And Jones getting the best of him in their guitar duel was a major lesson for Jimi. He would, in the future, do everything in his power to be loud enough to be heard and appreciated. And when his talents eventually catapulted him from New York to instant stardom in London, it was due not only to Jimi's skill but also to the fact that he was playing louder than anyone had ever heard a guitar played in a Greenwich Village club.

The King Kasuals started working a series of black music clubs a few hundred miles outside of Nashville. These joints held about fifty people, often had potbellied stoves, and served chitlins (slang for chitterlings, the intestines of pigs). These small southern clubs, as a group, were known as the Chitlin' Circuit, which Jimi would increasingly play after the King Kasuals.

For this King Kasuals tour, the band added Nashville singer-songwriter Jimmy Church, who'd worked with Johnny Otis's band, and singer-songwriter Bobby Hebb ("Sunny").

"I remember when we played Clarksville," said Church, "and Jimi busted his amp's speaker. He came up to me and said, 'Hey, Church, listen to this sound, man.' I looked at him kind of funny and said, 'Your speaker's busted.' He said, 'Yeah, but listen to that tone, man.' He was so far away from reality, compared to what we were playing, hearing stuff that nobody else could hear."

But Jimi still could not officially play what he heard in his head. The King Kasuals' set list now included a mix of blues and popular cover songs such as Booker T. & the MGs' "Green Onions," the Isley Brothers' "Twist and Shout," and Jimmy Reed's hit "Bright Lights, Big City." They covered King Curtis, Bill Doggett, and Bobby "Blue" Bland as well. Jimi and Cox created some pieces of their own, but during rehearsals Jimi would look at Cox and say of their outrageous compositions, "Man, if we played that, they would lock us up."

Even in the comfortable confines of the Del Morocco, Jimi got odd looks and catcalls when he experimented with the sounds from his guitar. But one thing southern audiences did encourage was physical showmanship.

Alphonso Young was one of the first people to impress Jimi with onstage flash: "Jimi's eyes lit up when he first saw me play the guitar with my teeth and behind my back. I was always a show-off. The girls loved it." George Yates from Johnny Jones's group did the same two tricks.

To make their stage act more outrageous, Cox purchased Jimi a long guitar cord and attached quarter-inch plugs on both ends. The lengthy cord enabled Jimi to leap off the stage and take his theatrics directly into the audience, but the cord had its limitations, depending on the dimensions of certain clubs.

"At a length of eighty feet, we lost 1/1000 of a second, causing an unwanted echo," Cox remembered. "At seventy feet, it still echoed. Finally, at fifty feet, it didn't echo, but it wouldn't let him get out the door." Jimi wanted to play outside the front door of clubs.

Jimi also knew of his stylish guitar predecessors. One of the most renowned showmen from the Delta blues school was Charlie Patton from Bolton, Mississippi. In the late 1920s, people traveled great distances just to hear the performer make his guitar "talk" at regular Saturday shows on southern plantations. According to legend, Patton could attack the neck of his guitar like a dog shaking a stick, play it between his legs or behind his head, beat it like a drum, and ride it like a pony while still keeping the beat. Patton later taught Howlin' Wolf to play guitar and was said to be such a strict taskmaster that if you played the wrong note, he'd "smack you upside the head."

In the 1930s and 1940s, there was Aaron "T-Bone" Walker from Linden, Texas, one of the first electric blues guitar players to use his amplifier's volume control to sustain pitches and combine it with single string bending and finger vibrato. As part of his dance routine, T-Bone jumped straight up in the air with his guitar high above his head and landed in a split, with the guitar behind his head, still playing a fluid line.

Jimi's feel for electric blues was complimented by no less a figure than John Lee Hooker: "He was a man that was always in my heart from the first time I heard him. . . . He came out of nowhere and wrecked the world. 'Red House' was my favorite song of his. He really had his heart and soul in what he was doing. There was no end to what he could do."

Jimi underwent many changes while working in and around the Del Morocco. Free of the constraints of military service, Jimi and his guitar were so inseparable that his friends nicknamed him "Marbles," because they thought he was crazy and had lost all of his. Cox often found Jimi asleep in his room, sprawled out on the bed with the same clothes he had on the night before, the guitar lying on his stomach. It was obvious he'd been practicing all night.

Jimi also had something of a sexual awakening while working at the Del. He left far behind the world of young love and Betty Jean Morgan, with whom he had exchanged, as their letters revealed, so many "juicy kisses." His voracious sexual appetite, which at the apex of his career sometimes resulted in multiple simultaneous partners, quickly blossomed. One woman, a stripper named Margo, who had been in her prime in Chicago in the 1940s, often spent time in his room, and he also managed to juggle three regular lovers: Joyce Lucas, whom he had met in Clarksville; Florence Henderson; and one Verdell Barlow, a barmaid over at the Club Baron. However, after Mrs. Barlow's husband, who went by the nickname of "Treacherous," found out about Jimi's romantic involvement with Verdell, he threatened Jimi with a two-by-four. The brief affair quickly ended, but Jimi's sexual energy was not to be contained.

According to Larry Lee, Jimi, when playing backup for a singer at the Del, was sometimes overcome by a dancing girl, and he would drop his guitar and leave the bandstand. Lee was invited to take over Jimi's place on guitar while Jimi took the girl up to his room for an entirely different kind of performance.

In marked contrast to the joys of the flesh, Jimi became moved by the circumstances of the civil rights movement. The cruel degradations of racism were hard to miss in early 1960s Tennessee. In later years, he avoided public commentary on topics such as race and drugs, just as he did with the Vietnam War. He may have come from the ethnically mixed Seattle, but while living in Nashville, he now had an up-close view of outright racial hostility.

Even before Greensboro, North Carolina's, first official lunch counter demonstration, Nashville had test sit-ins at churches and small stores in 1959. In February 1960, black college students in Nashville launched formal, full-scale sit-ins to desegregate lunch counters at S. H. Kress, Woolworths, and McLellan stores. The battle was still ongoing when Jimi got out of the army. Almost three years later, most of Nashville's lunch counters were desegregated. Now, the blooming civil rights movement was working to take down the race-related signs at Nashville's restaurants, hotels, public pools, and movie theaters.

On December 3, 1962, the *Nashville Tennessean* reported that several organized sit-ins were taking place. One was outside of Herschel's Tic Toc restaurant on Church Street, which discriminated against black customers

"We don't serve niggers here and you ain't going to get inside," shouted an angry restaurant employee, identified as "Johnny Rebel," as he blocked the entrance. Moments later, he turned a fire extinguisher on black demonstrators, who were arrested on charges of disorderly conduct and had to post five dollars bail to be released.

For the next three weekends, often during a subzero degree cold snap that hit Nashville, crowds of up to sixty people marched and demonstrated, trying to desegregate downtown restaurants along the crossroads of Church Street and Fifth Avenue. Most were arrested for not following orders to disperse, fined fifty dollars, and, depending on their prior arrest records, served up to fifty-five days in jail.

Jimi mentioned his involvement with the beginning of the civil rights movement in the South with his typically dry and ironic wit: "We'd go down every Sunday for sort of demonstrations, take a little lunch with us and go to the riots. Well, we'd be on one side of the street, and they'd be on the other and we'd call each other names and all that."

The more the Negro community spoke up and poured out its communal anger, the more the police turned out en masse and turned up the heat. Disgusted with the situation, Jimi and Cox purposely ignored a "whites only" sign in a Nashville diner and were taken to jail for sitting in a section designated for whites.

"Back then, it was the cause. It was a serious thing," recalled Cox, noting the hypocrisy of southern blacks in the military having more rights than nonmilitary blacks. "When we first came into Nashville in the 101st Airborne, we sat where we wanted to and nobody gave a shit."

Uncle Teddy Acklen, who, ironically, was very light-skinned and often passed as white, had good relationships with Nashville city government. He bailed out Jimi and Cox and managed to get the charges against them dropped. But they did have the fines deducted from their paychecks.

Shortly after being incarcerated, Jimi wrote to his father, expressing both insecurity and love. In part, he penned, "Dad, I did just what I figured you'd do. I hope I didn't do anything wrong."

Al Hendrix had been an absentee father a good deal of Jimi's childhood. He had denied his son the opportunity to attend his mother's funeral and only reluctantly encouraged his musical talent. But on this issue, of Jimi taking a stand against bigotry, he showed an uncharacteristic warmth and support. In his letter of reply, Al assured Jimi he had done no wrong: "If that had been me, I'd be doing the same thing. As a matter of fact, I participate in a lot of activities in Seattle, even though it isn't as bad as the South. You stand up for your rights."

YEARS LATER, ONE OF JIMI'S LEAST KNOWN BUT MOST MEMORABLE shows would be related to the struggle for racial equality in America and the tragic assassination of Reverend Martin Luther King Jr.

The first time Jimi toured through Newark, New Jersey, it was ravaged, decimated by four days of rioting in July 1967. Newark and Detroit were among the worst epicenters during a summer that saw 125 American cities burn. More than half of Newark was black, and many citizens were subjected to what is now referred to as "racial profiling" from members of Newark's primarily white police force. Charges of police brutality in the arrest of a black cab driver touched off the mayhem. When Jimi and the Experience played there, tanks were still patrolling the shattered streets.

The second time Jimi headed to play Newark, less than a year later, Reverend Martin Luther King had been shot dead in Memphis. The Newark Police Department, expecting another disastrous reaction, informed manager Chas Chandler and the Jimi Hendrix Experience that they had to perform, that they could not cancel because in fury and anguish black citizens, Newark PD claimed, "would burn the city down."

The Experience decided the best thing was to perform, but the driver of the limo was so frightened to go downtown that he insisted Jimi ride with him in front or he would not drive. Jimi hopped in the front, and his white bandmates sat in the back.

Mark Boyle, who operated the light show for the opening act, Soft Machine, spoke in reverential tones about what happened that night. He and the crowd, which filled only a third of the hall, witnessed Jimi say at the end of the shortened show, in a soft, emotional voice, "This number is for a friend of mine."

Jimi then proceeded to improvise on the spot mournful, exquisite music that no one had ever heard. It embodied the anger and hurt and despair of a people. It was a purely instrumental ode to the life and death of King, to those who had fallen before him, such as Medgar Evers and Malcolm X.

Boyle was now an audience member, and, like the crowd, he was astonished and weeping at Jimi's performance. He saw the stagehands edge out onto the periphery, standing near the speakers, burly, rough and tumble men, openly crying at the emotional outpouring from Jimi's body and guitar.

Boyle heard gunfire outside and worried that Jimi or others might be shot in the maelstrom of tensions within the house: "Because we all thought there was some kind of conspiracy going on, to eliminate people who were seen as enemies of some kind of dream of America that had never been."

After inventing an instrumental that Boyle characterized as "haunt-ingly beautiful . . . appallingly beautiful," Jimi laid down his guitar. After one of his greatest performances, unrecorded but not forgotten, during one of the bleakest moments in American history, Jimi Hendrix left the stage, and the stunned audience was barely able to applaud.

3

I'd Rather Starve

(JANUARY–JUNE 1963)

JIMI WAS TRAPPED. ALTHOUGH UNCLE TEDDY OFTEN CALLED ON him to fill in as a replacement guitarist at the Del Morocco, Jimi did not make enough money to move out of his room above Joyce's House of Glamour. The King Kasuals did not earn enough to break the musical servitude that kept Jimi in place. Jimi's additional work at the Del, as viewed by Acklen, was compensation to pay back the club owner for meals and for the sound equipment that the Del had loaned to Jimi.

If Jimi had returned to Seattle, the ethnically mixed population might have provided more opportunities for him to back up integrated bands. And although Nashville was shifting somewhat from country and R&B toward rock and roll, so, too, would it take longer for southern audiences to accept groups that were not either all white or all black in composition.

There were approximately twenty black nightclubs at the time in Nashville. On the south side, the Top Hat was tops. John's Barbecue Stand and the Three Stooges were the most popular on the east side. And in addition to the Del Morocco and the Club Baron, where Jimi had gigs, there were the Viaduct, Wigwam, the Steal Away, and the Voters Club, all within a mile or so of each other on Jefferson Street.

As Cox explained, the clubs endured not only segregation of audiences but also problematic local liquor laws: "There was this place, the Voters Club, where this guy named 'Good Jelly' would help a lot of the students get their IDs and sometimes even pay their tuition for them. He was one of the few that was open on Sunday. Because in the sixties, liquor by the drink had not been passed here. It was illegal unless you had a private club. So he would sell you a membership to the Voters Club for one dollar. He was packed all the time."

Jimi's 1963 began with a potentially fortunate turn of events, a chance to leave behind the limitations of working the Nashville music scene. The Continentals, a very popular band, were looking for a replacement after the guitar player quit to join a jazz ensemble. Because the band was integrated, with three whites and three blacks, it had difficulty playing in Nashville's white clubs. Racist audience members often called the police to shut down its shows.

Larry Perigo, a white sax player with the Continentals, asked for Uncle Teddy's help to recruit a temporary guitar player, because the group was scheduled to play a four-week engagement at the Del Morocco.

Perigo recalled his conversation with Acklen: "The owner of the Del Morocco mentioned he had a guy staying in his apartments that did some cleaning up and played guitar. He said, 'I don't know if he'll work out, but you can use him until you find someone else, and I'll pay him on the side.'"

Jimi joined the Continentals as they headlined at the Del on Wednesdays and Thursdays and then served in the backup band when the big stars came through on Friday and Saturday. Jimi learned the songs easily during rehearsals, always having been a quick study, despite not being able to read music.

Despite his successes with a few different women, Jimi still projected an aura of insecurity.

"He was a little strange," Perigo claimed, echoing the nickname others had used in Nashville, "and we called him 'Marbles.' He didn't seem to mind. Any type of conversation he had with you, he'd cover his mouth and whisper, even if it was, 'I'm going to go have some lunch,' like it was some big secret. He didn't sing with us. We didn't even know he sang."

Nevertheless, Jimi repressed his impulse to cut loose with wild guitar lines and played a subservient role as rhythm guitarist. Despite his odd personality, he was part of the ensemble.

This time, finances proved his undoing. Jimi told members of the Continentals that he could not make a gig because he had pawned his guitar. Jimi told Perigo not to worry and offered up his buddy Larry Lee as a replacement. Lee, by his own admission, was one of the weaker players on the Nashville scene at the time.

Perigo complained about Lee's less than stellar skills: "After the first show, I told Jimi, 'You got to do something. This guy isn't that good.' Jimi took Larry's guitar, flipped it around so he could play it, but the strings were now upside down. He played it that way the rest of the night, and he was great. Jimi told me later he learned how to play guitar that way, but he eventually restrung it because he could watch and better see what right-handed guitar players were doing."

Left- or right-handed, Jimi had logistically turned the Continentals upside down, and band members did not appreciate it. Eventually, the group took a vote and decided to let Jimi go. According to Perigo, he was with the group between four to six weeks. "The last time I saw him, he was walking down Jefferson Street with his guitar in his hands, not in a case, and an amp cord was still plugged in. The other end was bouncing on the sidewalk."

SINGER JIMMY CHURCH OBSERVED THAT JIMI POSED NUMEROUS problems for himself and existing bands in Nashville. They included Jimi's resistance to R&B stage presentation and Jimi's use of stage tricks that excited some audiences but only annoyed the players on-stage with him.

Said Church of Jimi:

He played the guitar with his teeth. Larry Lee played with his teeth. He'd play behind his back. Larry Lee could do that too. It was nothing extraordinary. Jimi was okay but had trouble getting a steady gig anywhere by himself in Nashville. He needed another rhythm player to get it going. He wasn't a black act. . . . He was left-handed and had a little effeminate thing about him: soft-spoken, smiled a lot. And when he was on stage and flicked his tongue out, the girls really went for that. They didn't always like the macho guys.

The inescapable truth was that Jimi was in no position to break out as a major act with the King Kasuals. Irrespective of the members' development as musicians, they still were primarily doing cover songs. Billy Cox recalled the major tunes of the day done by the King Kasuals included "Blue Suede Shoes," "Green Onions," "Let the Good Times Roll," "Poison Ivy," "Hey Bo Diddley," "Tutti Frutti," "Stand by Me," "Twist and Shout," "I'm a Man," and "What'd I Say."

Already noted for his unorthodox personal behavior, Jimi worsened his situation with the King Kasuals by being irresponsible, an attitude likely fueled by his frustration with his surroundings. Cox remembered one of Jimi's most outrageous moments of forgetfulness: "We had a job at the Del Morocco. . . . Nine o'clock, no Jimi. Ten o'clock, no Jimi. We started to get a little worried, so I run up to the house where he lives. . . . I go in. He's lying there and I go, 'Hey Jimi, you're late for the gig.' He says, 'I dreamed the gig was canceled, so I went back to sleep.'"

Cox appreciated Jimi's unrecognized abilities better than anyone, and he shared Jimi's feelings of vocational entrapment. The Del Morocco was a steady gig with a free room thrown in, but the low pay and the lack of creative freedom kept the King Kasuals in their particular niche in Nashville. The band's resentment focused upon Teddy Acklen. Band members began to talk openly of leaving town.

Conniving club owners were not unheard of in Nashville. Larry Perigo recalled working for Joel Vradenburg, who owned both the Sandpiper and the Club Baron: "He was a very manipulative guy and was really taking advantage of his musicians. He'd transport bands back and forth from the Sandpiper to the Baron so each club would have two bands, and [he] didn't pay them anything extra." Eventually, Vradenburg would own virtually every club on Printer's Alley in

Nashville, with the exception of Skull's Rainbow Room, which had not only live music but also exotic dancers.

Jimi was no fan of Nashville's music venue owners. In addition to being shortchanged while playing onstage, he was put up in substandard housing, some of it still under construction.

"The promoters were the strangest and the most crooked there [in Nashville]," Jimi later stated. "We used to have to sleep in a big housing estate they were building around there. No roofs and sometimes they hadn't put floors in yet. That was wild. Nashville used to be a pretty funny scene with all those slick managers trying to sign up hillbilly singers who'd never been in a big town before."

Therefore, it is understandable that Jimi and Cox were willing to leave the Del after a year. "They didn't give us any raise," explained Cox. "They figured, 'We've got these son-of-a-guns here. They're at our mercy. Some of them owe us money.' Well, as a bandmate, I was determined. You don't kick me when I'm down. We decided we weren't going to take it any more."

Uncle Teddy, who served as Jimi and Cox's landlord and manager, caught wind that the boys had plans to leave, so he told them to start packing. Guitarist Johnny Jones visited them prior to their eviction from their rooms above Joyce's House of Glamour. Jones found Jimi lying on a mattress placed directly on the floor. All Jimi owned were a few scattered clothes.

Teddy Acklen Jr. saw his father's position at the Del in a different light. He claimed his father owned both their instruments and sound equipment: "Jimi and Billy told my old man they were going to quit and go somewhere else and play. I think they got a better offer or were propositioned. My father owned their instruments, but they always pawned them. He would get upset with them when they wanted to play outside of town and take these instruments. The last time Jimi left Nashville, my father kept his instruments."

IN OTHER METROPOLITAN AREAS DURING 1963, THE COLOR BARrier was no longer an issue for musical revues. For example, on March 2 the all-white group the Four Seasons was a guest on Chubby

Checker's "Limbo Party," staged at San Francisco's Cow Palace. Lou Christie ("Lightning Strikes") was another white entertainer, on the bill with Marvin Gaye and the black female group the Crystals.

What Jimi had in his favor was his location in Nashville, a musical hub that, despite the clear separation between black- and white-owned clubs, still had numerous acts come through town. In March, an R&B tour package passed through, with a variety of talented artists including a young Aretha Franklin, billed as "the New Queen of the Blues," and Hank Ballard and the Midnighters. The show's flamboyant MC-singer, "Gorgeous" George Odell, started inquiring at local clubs, explaining that he needed a guitar player for his backup band. In between selling pictures of performers and programs from tours he'd been on, George delivered his pitch at the New Era dinner club, a venerable establishment founded in 1939. It was from that inquiry that Jimi Hendrix met Gorgeous George.

His real name was Theophilus Odell George. (Theophilus originates from the bible, translated as "God's best friend.") Gorgeous George had been Hank Ballard's valet for years in the 1950s and designed his own clothes for a while, but now introduced top R&B acts on various touring revues for Henry Wynn's Supersonic Attractions. George was a self-promoter with a sharpened awareness of stagecraft. He wore a silver wig, and his motto was "Don't look back; if you do, it will hold you back."

George cultivated a reputation for showmanship and for his appearance. "I would change after each performance," remembered George, "and I usually had twelve acts to introduce. My outfits would kill because I dressed in European-cut pin-stripe suits. I didn't come up with the name Gorgeous George. My manager Henry Wynn did, because I was always sharp looking."

Gorgeous George came out of a tradition of traveling musical revues, when the person who introduced acts was seen as a "cleanup man," responsible for telling jokes or dancing during the transitions between performers.

George immediately took to Jimi and appreciated his eagerness to tour: "I told Jimi I couldn't pay him. The money I got from the concerts couldn't even fill my watch pocket. The main singers were getting about fifty dollars a night and their musicians only about half that. Jimi said, 'You don't have to pay me, just feed me, and let me play behind you when you go onstage.' So I figured out a way to get him on the tour, and I didn't have to go to the road manager. I was so tight with Henry Wynn. I told Jimi, 'I'm going to tell them you my cousin.'"

Jimi tolerated being the early 1960s equivalent of a "roadie" because it meant he could also be part of the nightly after-show gig. George ran a side hustle with the clubs that was tied in with the local concert's promotion.

After the concert ended, George grabbed the microphone and announced, "Hold on to your ticket stubs, ladies and gentleman, for reduced price admission to the after show." Most of the performers returned, and the club usually retained the majority of its audience. For his efforts, George received 50 percent of that show's profits from the club owner.

His first tour taught Jimi that being a player on the road required, more than anything else, stamina. One had to learn to tolerate the mood swings of bandleaders and other players, who were affected by cramped quarters, boredom, and repetition. The food was not the best, and there was little time for decent sleep. Jimi had a history of playing what he wanted or of being irresponsible, but touring with Hank Ballard, even with limited musical participation, clearly had an impact on him.

Larry Lee observed that the most important lesson Jimi might have gleaned on that first tour with Ballard and Gorgeous George was the importance of a complete performance, from beginning to end, of offering the audience a consistent level of entertainment. "He needed no rehearsal," Lee said of George. "The cat could put on a four-hour show in itself, and he knew about people and how to make them happy." Lee contended that Jimi acquired a general sense of showmanship, not just pyrotechnics on the guitar, by seeing Gorgeous George's energy, commitment, and flair. "Jimi got it from a cat that knew it as a second kind of nature . . . and it made him powerful, when he ran into George."

Jimi, however, did not value being a part-time valet, as George had been. Jimi's frustration about not performing more during the tour affected George, who told Jimi that R&B veteran Ballard might be able to use him as a guitarist.

Jimi was a big fan of Ballard's risqué hits, which were often pulled off radio station playlists. In 1954, Ballard's "Work with Me Annie," with suggestive lyrics such as "Annie, please don't cheat / Give me all my meat," caused an uproar with music critics and broadcasters. But it became Ballard's first number one R&B hit, selling more than 20 million copies.

But Ballard's biggest success came when he wrote and recorded "The Twist." Unfortunately, he didn't have the hit he deserved, because his record label slapped it on the B side, but Chubby Checker and other artists re-recorded it, making it the biggest dance-fad record ever. It helped revitalize Ballard's own career.

Ballard, like Gorgeous George, was every inch the showman. He was once hauled off the Eagles Auditorium stage in Seattle in the 1950s by police, midconcert, when he engaged in a playful bit during his 1954 follow-up to "Work with Me Annie," entitled "Annie Had a Baby." Ballard—in an act that the band had been doing without incident—wore a skirt over his onstage clothes and during the song pulled a baby doll out from under his skirt. The show was halted, and the previously enthusiastic audience was sent home.

Jimi was familiar with Ballard's sound and onstage antics. In 1959, Jimi attended a Hank Ballard and the Midnighters concert at Eagles Auditorium and was enthralled with guitarist Billy Davis's style of playing. Jimi watched intently as Davis swung the guitar behind his head and played it fiercely. At times, Davis stepped up close to his amp and used the feedback to sustain a note. During intermission, Jimi grabbed the attention of the Midnighters' trumpet player and told him he needed to speak to Davis about his techniques.

"Tell him I'm busy," Davis told his bandmate as he continued his conversation with one of the lovely young ladies backstage. A few minutes later, the trumpet player returned to say, "Billy, this guy won't leave me alone."

"I said I'm busy," Davis replied in a loud, firm tone.

On Jimi's third attempt, Davis gave in, and the anxious teenager was finally allowed backstage to meet him.

"I opened the dressing room door," said the guitarist, "and there was this kid with a big smile on his face. After we talked a while, he invited me back to his house so I could show him some of the things I did on the guitar, and for some reason I went twice. Hank was in town for a week. Jimi introduced me to his dad and showed me this little cheap guitar he was playing, and I showed him some licks on my Stratocaster."

Davis talked to Jimi about legendary guitarists such as T-Bone Walker and Eddie Kirkland, how they charted new territory for black guitarists, and how their styles influenced Davis's onstage performance.

Davis got his chance to play in Hank Ballard's band when he replaced former guitarist Cal Green in 1959 after Green had been arrested for possession of marijuana and given a two-year prison sentence in Texas. When Jimi again crossed paths with Davis the year after their Seattle meeting, Jimi explained his curious agreement with Gorgeous George and asked for some help.

"I used to spend my weekends in Atlanta, Georgia, where Gorgeous George had a place, and ran into Jimi," Davis said. "He still wanted me to show him a few things on the guitar. I pulled a few strings and got him in the Midnighters."

Playing with Hank Ballard's Midnighters was Jimi's first road tour experience with a major R&B act. The group had a Billboard Top 100 hit with "Finger Poppin' Time" and also hit the charts with "Let's Go, Let's Go, Let's Go" that same year. Jimi was clearly thrilled, and in a spare moment during a tour to South Carolina, he wrote a postcard home: "Dear Dad, Just a few words to let you know I made it to Columbia S.C. Tell everybody 'Hello,' with love, Jimmy."

But Jimi could not break out of his established pattern. He'd land a gig, learn the music, try to branch out, and get fired. Hank Ballard and the Midnighters were even less tolerant than a smaller act in Nashville. He was summarily fired from the group in the middle of the tour.

"He couldn't play the music right," explained Davis, although it might be more accurate to say Jimi refused to play the music the way he was expected. "So, they left him stranded with no money in Knoxville, Tennessee."

It was 160 miles back to Nashville. Remarkably, it would not be the last time the most revolutionary electric guitarist of all time was fired from a group and unceremoniously told to get off the tour bus.

BACK IN NASHVILLE, JIMI SETTLED BACK INTO FAMILIAR SUR-roundings. He patched things up with Acklen and found himself once again living upstairs at Joyce's House of Glamour. Soon, the King Kasuals were again playing gigs at the Del Morocco and backing up other groups coming through town.

In a letter home, Jimi refused to let a note of defeat or anger permeate his thoughts. His escape from the grinding poverty of Seattle and the regimentation of the Screaming Eagles may not have taught him discipline, but it gave him an amazing surplus of resilience and confidence. He wrote: "Dad, Here's a picture of our band named The King Kasuals. We're one of the two best Rhythm and Blues bands in Nashville."

Johnny Jones continued to be a fan of Jimi's playing. When Jimi came back to Nashville after his failure to work out with Hank Ballard, Jones occasionally caught Jimi at the Del. Jones witnessed Jimi and Larry Lee onstage, trading licks in a competitive style they called "yellin.'"

Jimi coped with his failure to break out of his smaller sphere by playing, when he could, in a wild style that would eventually gain him worldwide favor. In the meantime, it continued to garner him the adulation of Nashville area girls.

Raymond Valentine played organ in a group with Jimi for three months at Nashville's New Era Club. The band also included Cox, Lee, and alternately Harold Nesbit or Freeman Brown on drums. Most of their work was instrumental, and at times singers such as Jackie Shane, Frank Sheffield, and Joel Henderson sat in.

But significantly, the shouts from the crowd were never for the vocalists.

"When Jimi was really feeling good," Valentine contended, "he would do his tricks. Behind the back, the teeth, all that. The girls loved it. There was mostly girls in the club. He had a ball."

Within his circle, Jimi got female attention and enjoyed the freedom to find new sounds and styles of playing. Jones verified that Jimi did not seem to be a heavy drinker or an addictive type, given what musicians might lay their hands on in 1963: ""He used to smoke a little weed like some of us did, maybe a downer or some cough syrup."

Jones succinctly summed up Jimi's resistance to the opportunities that presented themselves: "I think Jimi couldn't stay in the R&B harness too long and got bored with them riffs. He had no chance to grow in Nashville. They were smothering him here in Nashville."

It was a certain kind of war that Jimi waged within himself, during his days in and around Nashville, in which his need to survive slammed up against his creative impulses. He likely explained it best himself in an interview he did in April 1968 with *Downbeat* magazine: "I get very bored on the road," he admitted, "and I get very bored with myself and my music, sometimes. I mean, I love the blues, but I wouldn't want to play it all night. It's just like although I like Howlin' Wolf and Otis Rush, there are some blues that just make me sick. I feel nothing from it."

His need for improvisation while he explored the burgeoning popularity of rock music in 1963 was irrefutably explained in that *Downbeat* article. "I love to listen to organized Top 40 R&B but I'd hate to play it. I'd hate to be in a limited bag. I'd rather starve."

4

Nothing But Someone's Coat on His Back

(JULY–DECEMBER 1963)

BILLY COX AND JIMI WERE JOINED AT THE HIP. THEY HAD GOT-ten through the 101st Airborne together and had formed a band to-gether, one so casual that they could not decide how to spell the band's name. The last incarnation, before they left the Del Morocco, was the Casuals.

Singer Frank Howard played with Jimi at the Del Morocco and noted that certain crowds were not ready to accept his radical per-formance style: "Back then, people were playing straight-up R&B and that kind of stuff he did, you wouldn't do to a favorite song. He'd hit one of them high notes, and I'd look over at him and say, 'You need to get in the groove.' People in the crowd used to throw ice and lemons at him.

More than once, Howard saw Jimi outrageously adapt standard tunes of the day: "He'd turn around and get some feedback on the guitar. We'd do routines with songs like 'Shout,' and he'd come up with some crazy things. It got so bad, one time I had to tell the owner of the club, Uncle Teddy, to tell Jimi he could play behind his back and pick the guitar with his teeth only during his own set, but not on ours."

Cox renamed the band Billy Cox and the Sandpipers, influenced by the fact that there was a club in Nashville called the Sandpiper, and he lined up a gig for them at the Jolly Roger as July turned into August.

Cox saw no problem with the group having a name similar to a local club. "I was trying to come up with something unique that would bring the people in, so we renamed the group the Sandpipers and added a horn player and a rhythm guitar player, and then, as an opening act, we backed Jimi doing all of his stage tricks. That was billed as 'Jimmy Hendrix and His Magic Guitar.' I felt kind of like a Barnum and Bailey type of guy, booking this whole thing."

It was the first time Jimi's name, in any form, was part of a band name. Cox again so believed in Jimi's abilities that he shared the spot-light. In fact, Cox was hired for a recording session in August and in-sisted on bringing Jimi along. Unfortunately, the producer in charge of the session was Hoss Allen, Jimi's old nemesis, who hadn't been able to understand his use of feedback the last time they were in the studio together.

Hoss Allen had returned to Nashville in August, after being on the road as a salesman pitching Chicago's Chess Records. Allen also nur-tured local talent who hoped to make the charts. He had produced guitarist Johnny Jones's first two singles as well as the work of other players who recorded for the Excello, Old Town, and Brunswick labels.

Cox's session was part of a flurry of recording dates Jimi had in August. Allen and Starday/King Studios were the only game in town for struggling musicians in Nashville.

Jones got Jimi back in the studio to assist with a blues tune Jones had written. It had the amusingly improbable title "Feels So Bad, Like a Ball Game on a Rainy Day."

"Allen tried the song on Frank Howard's Commanders, but it didn't work," Jones said, "so I did it with Jimi playing in the background. It took forever to get him to lock in on a rhythm part. We finally did. I know some sessions didn't turn out too well for Jimi."

"Feels So Bad" turned out to be a disappointing date for all involved. Although Jimi was not cut out of the recording and Allen had it pressed as a demo and played it on WLAC, Jimi's early studio session disap-peared into the annals of the unreleased.

Jimi's other recording session took place shortly after Cox had composed two songs. Because Cox and Jimi never considered themselves singers, Cox offered the songs to Frank Howard and the Commanders to record. In return, Billy and Jimi played on the session. Once again, the inescapable Hoss Allen was producing.

Howard reminisced: "Billy Cox wrote 'I'm So Glad,' and 'I'm Sorry for You' for me, and we went down to Starday/King Studios to cut them. All Hoss wanted Jimi to do was play a simple rhythm while Johnny Jones played lead, but Hoss didn't like what he was hearing from Jimi, so he turned his mike down and cut him in and out. Hoss didn't like it when musicians experimented on his session. He told me later that if he knew Jimi was going to be so successful, he'd let him get as wild as he wanted."

At the time of these early recording sessions, Jimi was getting a reputation among musicians as not just a wild man on stage but also a phenomenal talent.

Jimi later tutored Velvert Turner, an aspiring teenage guitarist, about the importance of learning chords when starting out: "'Forget about playing lead in the beginning,'" Turner recited Jimi's lecture. "'The main thing I want you to learn are chords. Everyone puts so much emphasis on lead guitar, but chords are more important. Because with those you can always paint colors and then put your lead on top. They're the most important part. I've been playing chords half of my life in all those rhythm and blues bands.'"

Besides his innate creativity, passion, and obsession with music, pure genetics aided Jimi's talent. His long fingers and a thumb could stretch over the fret board and allowed him to simultaneously play lead runs and low parts.

A major aspect of Jimi's musical development was the rapid succession of artists he met, saw, or played with during Nashville. Also in the summer of 1963, he gigged at the Club Baron with R&B singer Roscoe Shelton. Born in 1931, in Lynchburg, Tennessee, Shelton began singing gospel groups in 1947. He'd become friends with Sam Cooke when Cooke was lead singer of the gospel vocal group the Soul Stirrers.

Jimi also gained a further appreciation of gospel when he and Cox served as backup in singer Marion James's band for a while and did short road tours in cities surrounding Nashville. James, like Shelton, had a musical background firmly rooted in the church and later earned the title "Nashville's Queen of the Blues."

Jimi was also exposed to a wider variety of instrumentation during this time. Marion James's husband, Jimmy Stewart, was also her arranger and bandleader and an accomplished trumpeter. He'd played with B. B. King and recorded some solo sessions as a harmonica player under the name of Mr. Broussard. His fellow musicians jokingly nicknamed him "the Buzzard," but he and James were anything but scavengers. The couple's apartment served as a way station for struggling, hungry musicians coming and going between gigs.

Lattimore Brown, a singer on the Chitlin' Circuit, spent a good deal of time at the home of James and Stewart:

"At any given time, there'd be six to eight of us up there. . . . It was a two-bedroom apartment. I'd be in there cooking neck bones and pinto beans, corn bread. If a musician only had one piece of bread, he'd break it in half for his friend. . . . It was a bonding, like family. We had Billy Cox up there, Larry Lee and this kid that didn't have no name. He was just another guitar player . . . Jimi motherfucking Hendrix, man!"

One of the most important musicians Jimi met during the whirlwind of activity in Nashville was one of his blues guitar idols, Albert King. Both were left-handed players who'd become obsessed with the instrument at an early age. At six, after his stepfather told him he couldn't touch his guitar, King started fooling around with a homemade "one strand on the wall" he'd put together, a wire fastened to a wall at the top and to a brick at the bottom. He played the crude instrument with one hand and used a glass bottle as a slide.

King's first recording success came in 1958 with "I'm a Lonely Man," but it wasn't until 1961 that he had a major hit, with "Don't Throw Your Love on Me So Strong." King was Jimi's elder by twenty-two years. The six feet, four inches, ex–bulldozer driver developed a fondness for his young disciple and showed him some of his techniques.

Both King and Jimi faced the difficulties of learning to play a right-handed guitar at an early age. Jimi learned to flip a right-handed guitar over and play it "upside down." King had an additional challenge. Because his hands were so large, he had trouble holding and using a pick. When King first tried to negotiate the use of a pick, it often flew out of his fingers.

To compensate, King developed a technique that utilized the meaty part of his thumb and bent two strings at the same time, achieving several tones from a single note. King also showed Jimi how he tuned to an E minor chord, with a low C on the bottom, and mainly concentrated on the top three, higher strings.

"I knew him personally from when he was a boy in Nashville, Tennessee," recalled King of meeting Jimi. "Hendrix used to take pictures of my fingers to try and see what I was doing. He never quite figured it out."

Years later, Jimi took more than one opportunity to mention King's influence. In an interview for *Rolling Stone,* he told a reporter: "I like Albert King. He plays completely and strictly in one way, just straight funk blues. New blues guitar, very young, funky sound which is great. One of the funkiest I've heard. . . . That's his scene."

Inevitably, King endorsed Jimi's skills when he announced in an interview, "He's had it tough, but Jimi is a born blues man." King opened for the concerts Jimi did at the Fillmore West and Winterland Arena in San Francisco in 1968. In what must have been one of the blues master's proudest moments onstage, he won the huge audience over immediately. To make the Bay Area dates even more memorable, Janis Joplin joined Jimi and King onstage one night in an impromptu jam.

LARRY LEE PROGRESSED. NO ONE COULD ACCUSE HIM OF BEING the worst guitarist in Nashville any longer or the guy at the Del who took over Jimi's spot onstage when a good-looking girl caught Jimi's eye. Instead of eleven dollars a night for three sets at the Del, Lee was the featured guitarist with the Bonnevilles. The band had been around since 1961 and backed up well-known talent that passed through, including Chubby Checker, and emerging stars such as Rufus Thomas's daughter, Carla. The Bonnevilles' record "Cherokee Twist" bumped Elvis Presley's "Good Luck Charm" out of the number one spot on

Nashville radio in April 1962. Lee and Billy Cox, who had played bass occasionally for the Bonnevilles, suggested that the band's leader, Robert Fisher, needed to meet their friend Jimi.

Jimi was still living above Joyce's House of Glamour when Fisher was first introduced to him. "When I walked into the room that was more like a plain cubicle, with no windows," Fisher recalled,

> sitting on what looked like a very small twin bed was a tall stringbean of a young man. He was wearing a black do-rag on his head while plucking the guitar upside-down and left-handed. . . . I had gained a reputation of being a Good Samaritan towards underemployed musicians in Nashville, and now Billy and Larry wanted me to take on a left-handed, upside-down guitar player who I definitely didn't need. Still, judging from his skinny frame, I guessed that this Hendrix fellow had not been eating too regularly. So, that weekend I let him play with the Bonnevilles.

As part of the deal they worked out, Fisher bought him two guitar strings and got his suit out of the cleaners so that Jimi could play a gig in Huntsville, Alabama. There were no rehearsals, but the entire black audience was bowled over by Jimi, instantly and thoroughly. One female was said to have gotten so excited, she fell over backward when Jimi lasciviously flicked his tongue at her during a solo.

Jimi found a consistently welcoming audience for the first time and later looked back with affection on some of his southern gigs outside Nashville: "It's fun to play little funky clubs because that's like a workhouse. It's nice to sweat. . . . Even the amplifiers and guitars actually were sweating. Everything is sweating. It seemed like the more it got sweaty, the funkier it got and the groovier. Everybody melted together . . . and the sound was kicking them all in the chest. I dig that. Water and electricity."

Fisher—unlike certain audiences, owners, and Hoss Allen—was instantly impressed by Jimi's performance skills: "He could do more with a guitar than the Ringling Brothers could do with a red, white, and blue elephant. Whether it was playing the guitar behind his back or picking it with his teeth, his antics really fired the crowd up. Needless to say, after Huntsville, the Bonnevilles would boast two lead guitar players. Jimi's stage presence added confidence to the band. He took a group of musicians and made an even better band out of them."

Under Fisher's guidance, the new Bonnevilles included his own trumpet playing and that of a saxophonist. This incarnation predominantly played in white clubs, and it was especially a favorite with the fraternities and sororities at the University of Tennessee at Martin and Vanderbilt University. But white neighborhoods posed a problem for accommodations.

Fisher explained how the lack of accommodations for blacks forcibly split up the band members after shows: "The motel situation being what it was at the time, we were fortunate that my parents and my wife's parents had plenty of room and were always glad to accommodate the guys in the band. When we were on the road, the guys in the band were always happy to stay in Parsons and Decaturville, which are about five miles apart. There was always plenty of food and good hospitality. My parents, in-laws, relatives, and friends were always glad to put the guys up for a night or two."

When he toured with the Bonnevilles, Jimi spent as much time as possible around Dorothy Jean Scott, Fisher's attractive cousin in Decaturville. Jimi often stayed at Fisher's wife's parents, who lived just across the street from Scott.

"He saw her at one of our dances one night," Fisher remembered. "At that time, he was somewhat shy, but that first time he saw her, he seemed overwhelmed by her good looks. He asked me if I knew her and asked me to introduce them after the dance. He watched her all night, smiling and almost blushing each time Dot's eyes met his. . . . Under different circumstances, I think they could have enjoyed a lasting relationship. But Jimi had a mission to accomplish, and though he cared for Dorothy a lot, the mission had to come first."

As their mutual attraction grew, Jimi also became fond of Fisher's mentally challenged son, Edward. "One of the reasons why Jimi liked Ed so much," hypothesized Fisher, "may have been that, as a child himself, he had to take care of his younger brother, Leon. Jimi loved his brother, and I sometimes wonder if he saw Leon in my son, Ed."

It is also conceivable that Jimi was reminded of his baby brother Joe, born with physical disabilities, abandoned, according to Leon, and placed in foster care. Lucille never forgave Al for leaving the unfortunate child at a house in Seattle, with the promise of a neighbor picking him up. It was, at the very least, a significant factor in the dissolution of their marriage.

According to Fisher, Jimi revealed very little about his past, other than his overwhelming desire as a youngster to have a guitar. "Jimi said that, although his father had worked really hard, he could barely get enough money to cover the necessities. Jimi said very little about his mother, but I got the impression that she cared more for life in the fast lane than for being a housewife and mother."

Jimi's reputation grew while in the Bonnevilles, and he was offered a side gig in Bells, Tennessee, without the band's horn section. Jimi now enhanced Lee's rhythm guitar and then stepped forward for his solos. At some shows, Jimi called out to drummer Isaac McKay to toss him a drumstick so that he could use it to play slide-guitar style on blues numbers, a real crowd pleaser. Fisher, in appreciation of Jimi's growing talent, was soon distributing concert posters that featured Jimi as the main performer.

In that phenomenally eventful August, an opportunity arose for the Bonnevilles to back the Impressions, a vocal trio featuring Jerry Butler, Sam Gooden, and Curtis Mayfield, for an upcoming tour of the South. The group was originally formed as the Roosters in Chattanooga; in 1957 there were personnel changes, and first Butler and then Mayfield were recruited. Both sang in a local gospel ensemble.

The Impressions were promoting a new record, "It's All Right," written by Mayfield, when playing the Jolly Roger in July. Anticipating success from that release, the band was now ready to take the show on the road.

Isaac Washington, a Nashville promoter, agreed to put together the Impressions' tour of twenty-eight shows in thirty days, with the Bonnevilles as the opening act. It was a potential breakout chance for the Bonnevilles, and Washington pitched clubs about this musical package. But to his astonishment, many music industry people in Tennessee were more familiar with the Bonnevilles than they were with either Butler or Mayfield.

Fisher did all he could to help Washington fill the dates. On one occasion, they talked to a club owner and ran down the list of acts on the show: the Impressions, Nashville-based the Avons, Peggy Gains, and the Bonnevilles.

The club owner replied, "Oh, yes, Jimmy Hendrix's band."

Jimi later praised Mayfield by acknowledging his influence during the Nashville days: "The best gig was working with Curtis Mayfield and the Impressions. Curtis was a *really* good guitarist, but he was the star and he thought I was flighty. I learned quite a lot in that short time. He probably influenced me more than anyone I'd ever played with up to that time, that sweet sound of his, you know."

One reason Mayfield might have considered Jimi flighty was an incident during the tour. The Bonnevilles were using the amps supplied by the Impressions. Larry Lee claimed that Jimi hit a note at the end of a Bonnevilles set that blew out the amplifier.

"We went off stage. Curtis wouldn't let us play," Lee insisted. "I think he was scared of me and Jimi because he didn't play that kind of music." Mayfield demanded to know what had happened to his amp, and Jimi feigned ignorance. "He knew it all right, what did happen. He was just waiting to see Curtis come running back. . . . Man, that was funny."

Despite the lack of camaraderie between Jimi and Mayfield on the road, the latter's smooth style of playing and his political consciousness clearly moved Jimi. Mayfield's "Keep on Pushing" came out in June 1964. It delivered a message of hope, strength, and unity in the wake of the June 1963 murder of civil rights activist Medgar Evers in Mississippi and, three months later, the Birmingham bombing by Ku Klux Klan members of the Sixteenth Street Baptist Church, which took the lives of four young black girls. Jimi later covered Mayfield's 1961 song "Gypsy Woman" at a venue that officially announced worldwide his approval of Mayfield: the Woodstock music festival.

TOWARD THE END OF THE BONNEVILLES TOUR, FISHER CLAIMED he and Lee got into a heated argument over some back pay that Washington owed them. "Larry, being the elder statesman of the group," Fisher said, "took it upon himself to confront me over why they hadn't received their money, kind of insinuating that I was the culprit.... I warned Larry that he had better watch himself and reminded him that Nashville had more than its share of unemployed guitar pickers."

Jimi intervened and asked Fisher not to fire Larry. He reminded the head of the Bonnevilles that Larry was still in college, trying to work his way through school. It was typical of Jimi's psychology to be the mediator, his humility hammered into him during his impoverished Seattle childhood.

Later, significantly, after the formation of the Jimi Hendrix Experience, he would again avoid direct confrontation, this time with manager Michael Jeffery, who was skimming money from the band and putting it in his private offshore account in the Bahamas. At that time bassist Noel Redding complained, and Jeffery ordered Jimi to fire him. Jimi avoided the issue, but Redding left the group not long after the incident.

"Jimi persuaded me to keep Larry on," Fisher recalled. "Jimi also took the opportunity to tell me straightforwardly that he would probably be leaving the group, although I had already started to look at how I could strengthen the Bonnevilles by giving Jimi a role in the band. I even told him about some of my ideas, but I could see he had visions of his own."

Fisher asked Jimi what it would take for him to stay with the group. Jimi assured him that he appreciated all that Fisher had done for him but that he had composed some songs he wanted to record on his own, including the vocals. Fisher skeptically observed: "I thought to myself, yeah, sure, Jimi Hendrix on vocals. Give me a break."

Fisher calculated that a recording might bring in money and possibly convince Jimi to remain. Fisher took the band to Fidelity Recording, a small studio on Broadway Street in downtown Nashville, just around the corner from the world-famous Ryman Auditorium, home of the

Grand Ole Opry. The demo the Bonnevilles recorded consisted of four songs, including "Ouch," a tune that featured the playing of Jimi and Lee.

The songs sounded so good to Fisher on tape that he took them to, of all people, Hoss Allen. The scourge of Jimi's early career said he was impressed with the sound that the Bonnevilles had put together. But he still was not interested in producing the group.

This time, instead of being fired, Jimi decided to quit the band. On the surface, the decision seemed hard to comprehend, not only to Robert Fisher but also to Jimi's closest friends, Billy Cox, Alphonso Young, and Larry Lee. The Bonnevilles provided him a better income than his previous groups, and Jimi was allowed to play his solos in his own fashion.

But Jimi's sense of a greater destiny, which had sustained him during his time in the South, was now aided by the appearance of an unlikely advocate.

Carl Fisher, a concert promoter for Henry Wynn's Supersonic Attractions, was in town with a show he brought in from New York. Larry Lee recalled the dapper, sophisticated Fisher seeing Lee and Jimi perform at the Club Baron on Jefferson Street. Fisher approached Jimi, complimented him on his stage presence and musical ability, and offered to bring him to New York and make him the star he deserved to be.

Jimi looked out on eight inches of newly fallen snow in Nashville. He believed his time had come. He made the decision then and there to leave. Jimi told Lee he was going, though he did not even have a coat. Lee gave Jimi his own. Jimi thanked him and said he'd return to Nashville when he was rich and famous. According to Lee, Jimi always spoke in the affirmative. It was never said "if" he became famous. It was always "when."

Jimi was a gypsy, but he did try to stay in touch with Lee: "He did write me one letter from New York. He asked me to come up there. We were pretty good by the time he left, but I was in school and my parents wanted me to finish school. He said, 'New York is just a big country town' and 'We can take this town, man.' Jimi had no responsibility.

He was just foot-loose and fancy-free. I knew it couldn't be that easy in New York. It scared me."

WHEN JIMI GOT OFF THE GREYHOUND BUS THAT TOOK HIM and Carl Fisher to New York, all he had were his guitar and a few clothes stuffed into a small duffel bag. They went directly to the promoter's room, 406, at the historic Hotel Theresa. The elegant, white, thirteen-story building in Harlem, on the corner of Seventh Avenue (now Adam Clayton Powell Jr. Blvd.) and the main thoroughfare of 125th Street, was referred to as the Waldorf Astoria of Harlem.

Jimi learned that many famous black entertainers, such as Cab Calloway and Billie Holiday, had stayed at the Theresa. Activist Malcolm X maintained an office there when Jimi arrived. Even Cuba's Fidel Castro had famously chosen the Hotel Theresa in 1960 when attending the opening session of the United Nations. Amusingly, Castro and his eighty-person entourage left their first choice, the Shelburne Hotel, when management demanded $10,000 up front and accused them of bringing in live chickens and damaging property. Castro chose the Theresa in Harlem to show his solidarity with American blacks.

Almost immediately, Jimi became friends with R&B singers Dean Courtney and Johnny Star, who were also struggling. Both had worked with singer Jackie Wilson, who eventually found out Star was in his teens and sent him home on a bus. Star may also have affected Wilson's nerves, because of his high-pitched voice, stuttering, and tendency to nervously pace back and forth.

At the time Jimi met them, Courtney was living in a suite in the Theresa, paid for by Little Richard (Richard Penniman), with whom Courtney had worked. He shared it with Richard's valet, James Oscar Thomas, known as "Pushay," because that was the way he mispronounced the word "pussy."

Jimi was adapting to life in Manhattan, with its great, seething variety of personalities. His soft-spoken, kind demeanor made him appealing to the Hotel Theresa's effeminate beautician, Wilbur (or "Wilhelmina," as Jimi privately called him), who flirted when Jimi passed by his shop.

"I used to joke with Jimi," Courtney said, "and called him Top Cat and Snagglepuss, because of the way he talked, like those cartoon characters." Courtney referred to and imitated Jimi's vocalization of Snagglepuss, the pink, animated Hanna-Barbera mountain lion, patterned after Bert Lahr in *The Wizard of Oz*, voiced by Daws Butler. "He'd come up to me sometimes and say strange things like, 'Hey, Dino,' and I would say, 'Yeah.' He'd then cup his hand and very quietly say: 'Come here. I've got something to tell you.' I'd lean in and he'd say, 'How do you feel?'" Jimi reserved his Snagglepuss voice especially for Courtney.

It was no laughing matter for Jimi, however, when he learned that Carl Fisher, according to Courtney and Pushay, was a female impersonator and exotic dancer who occasionally performed at the Apollo's Jewel Box Revue. Upon hearing the news, Jimi understood why Fisher was scrutinizing him whenever he got out of the shower or was getting dressed. Jimi enticed a woman up to Room 406, just days after arriving. But Fisher walked in on them having sex and threw Jimi out, ending their extremely brief professional relationship. Jimi moved in with Courtney and Pushay.

Jimi's sexual voraciousness led him to another woman quickly, Big Sandy, the cousin of a girl Johnny Star was dating.

"We called her 'Big,'" explained Courtney, "because she looked liked Etta James back then." Ironically, Jimi would meet James shortly thereafter. But significantly, a dark side of Jimi developed while with Big Sandy: the ability to shatter his gentle, polite demeanor, to become violent.

Courtney was present when Jimi first snapped:

One time, Jimi, Big Sandy—the girl he was dating—Johnny Star and Pushay and I were up in the suite at the Theresa, and Big Sandy picked up Jimi's guitar and started fooling around with it. Jimi told her, 'If you drop my guitar, I will choke your neck.' And sure enough, she knocked it over. The next thing I knew, Jimi dragged her into the bathroom and proceeded to choke her with her head in the toilet. We could hear gurgling sounds coming from there. I walked in and began to pry loose Jimi's fingers from around her neck. Johnny Star didn't help. He just kept looking under Sandy's dress while she was bent over. He told me later, 'That S-S-Sandy's got a ba-ba-big hairy p-p-pussy.' I told him he shouldn't have looked, because she was still Jimi's girl.

When Jimi wound up in London, living with Kathy Etchingham, these violent tendencies reached an apex at a club known as the Bag O' Nails. It was two months after Jimi's arrival in 1966, at that same location where, in stark contrast, Jimi had previously performed in front of an amazing group of London's rock icons.

"I remember one night specifically, in the Bag O' Nails," said Etchingham.

Jimi and I were there, and I left the table to go upstairs to phone a girl friend, and I was gone a little longer than he thought I should be gone. And he came upstairs raging mad because he thought I was talking to some guy on the phone. He snatched the booth door open, snatched the phone out of my hand, and started beating me on the head with it. I thought he was going crazy, and I began to scream, and at the same time I was trying to have a go at him. . . . And then just in the nick of time, like as if it was in some James Bond movie, John Lennon and Paul McCartney were coming into the club, and they saw what was happening. And so they pulled Jimi off of me and took him over to the side and cooled him down. That may have been the first of our many fights.

WITHOUT WORK, JIMI'S SURVIVAL IN HARLEM DEPENDED UPON the support of the opposite sex. Courtney offered to introduce a female friend to Jimi, a woman who would both guide and protect Jimi in the roiling waters of New York City life.

Lithofayne Pridgon, known as "Apollo Faye" because she frequented the famous Harlem theater of that name, was born in the poor, black section of Moultrie, Georgia, known as "Dirty Spoon." She'd picked cotton growing up and arrived in New York at sixteen. Pridgon's sexual daring, according to her friend singer Etta James, resulted in many lovers who'd performed at the Apollo. James said Pridgon referred to them collectively as "my repertoire," and they included William Edward "Little Willie" John, David "Fathead" Newman, Jackie Wilson, Otis Redding, Johnny "Guitar" Watson, Brooke Benton, Wilson Pickett, and the one she liked to tout the most, Sam Cooke.

Courtney played matchmaker between Jimi and Pridgon for a good reason: "Faye had started going out with Pushay, and eventually they broke up. She was kind of down about it, so I told her, 'I got another friend you can meet right now,' and I introduced her to Jimi. He and Pushay looked a lot alike."

Lithofayne enjoyed her men on the younger side. She affectionately called them her "young tenders." "She was pretty and perky and full of so much sexy spunk, no man could resist her," said James. "She was thin-framed and big-breasted and wore spike heels and scandalously short skirts where you could see the cheeks of her ass."

Pridgon informed Peter Guralnick, for his biography of Sam Cooke, *Dream Boogie*, that she had met Jimi in one of her "sets," a slang term for orgies with musicians. After this liaison, the young guitarist explained to Pridgon that he was desperate to find work. As Sam Cooke's ex-lover, Pridgon introduced Jimi to Cooke's valet, Jerry Cuffee, who, with his troubled complexion and irregular hair process, seemed an unlikely gatekeeper for a possible steady gig with the smooth, handsome singer.

Cooke was playing an engagement at the Apollo, from November 22 through 27. On the 22nd, President John F. Kennedy was assassinated in Dallas, staggering the nation. With that pall over them, Pridgon and Jimi followed Cuffee up a flight of backstage stairs to Cooke's dressing room for what was to be a casual introduction and an informal interview. Jimi carried in his hand his guitar and in his head, an enormous list of R&B songs he had memorized, ready to play any one of them at a moment's notice. Just a few minutes passed before the frustrated guitarist came storming out of the dressing room, stomping down the theater's stairs.

Jimi grumbled about not getting the job, a job that wasn't really being offered, because Cooke already had a guitar player. Pridgon's connection to Cooke did not even produce a referral to anyone looking for a guitarist. As Jimi burst through the backstage door onto 126th Street, with Pridgon behind him, scores of Cooke's fans, huddled together, looked up suddenly and then, not recognizing the people in front of them, looked away, disappointed.

As Jimi and Pridgon walked downtown, they passed, among other Harlem residents, an assortment of prostitutes, hustlers, and desperate junkies. Jimi barely took any notice of them.

"I was impressed that Jimi was kind of naïve to what was going on around him," recalled Pridgon. "I explained there was a 'panic' going on and there weren't a lot drugs on the street." She pointed out a group of heroin addicts headed for a "shooting gallery" across 8th Avenue.

Pridgon, in her tight, pegged skirt and high heels, studied him. "He had processed hair and shiny black pants that showed where the knees bent. But he had something about him, a warmth, that none of the other fast-rapping dudes had. He thanked me for getting him backstage to see Sam Cooke. He referred to Sam as 'what's-his-face.'"

They walked to West 98th Street, and Pridgon invited him to drop in on her mother, who was always cooking, day or night. Jimi was delighted by the blues records that belonged to "Miss P.," as he affectionately called her.

"She had, you know, the low-down stuff," Pridgon said of her mother's collection. "Ruth Brown and, beyond that, she had Muddy Waters, Lightnin' Hopkins, Judy King, Junior Parker, and folks like that. And Jimi loved those people."

They ate and talked and ate some more, and Jimi endeared himself to the Pridgon women by playing along to the blues records as he laid the covers out on the floor. After many hours, Miss P. eased her daughter and the talented young man out of her small apartment.

"We went to the Hotel Cecil," Pridgon remembered, "where I was staying with a girlfriend. All the up-and-coming entertainers stay there. It's the next stop before downtown, for blacks. And we went there and found nobody home, so we hopped in the sack. That was about the size of it; that's how it started."

And there, in a small room on West 118th Street, Jimi and Pridgon spent their first night together. It was a departure for Pridgon. "I made the decision just to take care of him and sacrificed what I really wanted to do. My favorite pastime was to be on the scene, and I didn't want him to hear about it."

Jimi had been in New York City less than a month. The president was dead. Jimi had no money, no job, no leads. The heart of winter was coming. He had just turned twenty-one, and he'd found his way into the heart of a flamboyant, promiscuous woman who did not want to fall in love with him.

5

From One Family to the Next

(JANUARY–JUNE 1964)

LIFE TOGETHER WASN'T EASY FOR JIMI AND PRIDGON. MONEY was tight. They barely survived on sardines, crackers, and the occasional home-cooked meal from her mother. When they were thrown out of their hotel room for nonpayment, they stayed at Mrs. Pridgon's, but on the sly.

"We'd sneak into her place after she left work," Pridgon recalled of her mother's apartment. "We'd come in and go to sleep. We'd get up before she got back and straighten up or be gone or sit around like we just walked in."

At Mrs. Pridgon's apartment, Jimi discovered a Robert Johnson single, "Walkin' Blues," that had the label missing. He listened to certain riffs over and over and over, picking up and dropping the tone arm to the part he wanted to hear. One time he accidentally slipped, and the needle scratched the record. Pridgon and Jimi both looked over to the kitchen to see if her mother had heard the noise. They prepared themselves for a verbal berating, but there wasn't any. Miss P., impressed by Jimi's heartfelt affection for the blues, let it go.

"Jimi used to play a stomp-down, funky blues," Pridgon recalled of the time. "Elmore James was his favorite. He used to take one of those little hotel glasses and put it on the strings and get that sound Elmore got. He tried to make his voice sound like his, too. He used to wake me up all through the night: 'Hey, listen to this, I got it. I got it.' 'The Sky Is Crying' was his favorite. 'It Hurts Me Too' was also a favorite, but the 'The Sky Is Crying' was his main thing."

The song has been recorded by scores of notable recording artists. Jimi would perform it along with Buddy Miles, Eric Burdon, and others in an all-star jam at the 1969 Newport Pop Festival. The gifted Stevie Ray Vaughn, obviously influenced by Jimi in his own career, had a memorable and, to some, definitive version.

The elder Pridgon, not used to having a boyfriend of her daughter's around the house, initially was fond of Jimi. She bought him the odd shirt or tie. But the combination of his regular presence in her home and his lack of employment transformed Mrs. Pridgon's warmth into resentment. She doubted Lithofayne was going to have much of a future with him and began to get testy with Jimi.

Pridgon remembered the moment her mother warned Jimi to start looking for another girlfriend: "Then she'd get in his face and say: 'You just don't understand. Faye's just going through a thing. You shouldn't get yourself all involved.'"

ONE OPPORTUNITY THAT DID PRESENT ITSELF THAT WINTER WAS the Apollo Theater. Every week, Jimi saw the marquee change, emblazoned with the names of popular recording acts such as Martha and the Vandellas, Maxine Brown, master saxophonist King Curtis, or the new comedian everyone was talking about, Flip Wilson.

The Apollo also conducted a weekly, Wednesday night amateur competition. First prize was twenty-five dollars and the opportunity to come back the following week and play a song or two with the house band. Since 1934, the Apollo had offered its stage to aspiring performers. Musical stars who would soon enter Jimi's orbit—Sam Cooke, Little Richard, and the Isley Brothers—all launched their careers from there.

The Apollo's audience, however, was noted for its rowdiness. Especially during the amateur competition, performers were openly booed and jeered at if the audience did not approve. Bottles and even chairs were sometimes tossed from the balcony toward unfortunate performers. A lighter form of rejection was a throwback to the Apollo's origins as a burlesque house: At times, audience displeasure prompted a house siren to be sounded, followed by a regular Apollo character called Junkie Jones who ran onstage and shot the offending amateur with a gun that fired blanks.

Jimi showed up one Wednesday evening in January with several other anxious contestants. Billy Mitchell, now tour director at the Apollo, was thirteen years old and recalled that night when Jimi won the competition: "He came out and played a popular R&B hit with the Apollo Theater house band, led by Reuben Phillips. The audience loved him, and he really got into his groove."

But twenty-five dollars didn't last long in a fast-paced town like New York. And Pridgon and Jimi overstayed their welcome at her mother's home, thanks to a stray kitten that they found and Jimi adopted. He named it Foxy and grew concerned that the kitten might die, because it did not eat its food.

Jimi fed the finicky kitten a can of solid white meat tuna from Mrs. Pridgon's pantry, at forty-nine cents a can. When Mrs. Pridgon learned of this, she raged at her daughter and her unemployed musician boyfriend. Jimi carefully put the kitten in a large envelope, and they headed out the door to the subway.

"The cat scratched a hole in the envelope," said Pridgon. "We knew you weren't supposed to take animals on the subway. The conductor saw the kitty stick its black head out of the envelope and then jumped out. Jimi started laughing, acting like he was going to pee on himself. I tried to grab the cat. They threw us off the train at the next stop, and we had to walk all the way home."

But Pridgon explained why Jimi could not hold onto his foxy lady feline: "We were down to our last dollar and debating whether we should buy the cat some food or share a hot dog. The ASPCA made the decision for us. They charged us our last dollar to take the cat away because we couldn't feed it."

Inevitably, not only did Foxy have to go; so also did Jimi and Pridgon. Finding a new residence wasn't easy. Jimi and Pridgon slept on the floor of Etta James's hotel dressing room for a while.

"We used to have to get up and get out early before Etta returned," said Pridgon. "Etta didn't like Jimi, and she didn't want him staying in the dressing room. He was brokenhearted because the image he held of these entertainers was much different [than the] reality. Most of them didn't want him around unless they had ulterior motives."

Jimi started hanging out on 125th Street and frequenting clubs such as Small's Paradise and the Palm Café. Jimi found, once again, that region as well as culture dictated how much his stage tricks would be tolerated. Louder amplification, short bursts of feedback, and playing behind his head or with his teeth were all tricks that wowed a crowd in the Deep South but didn't impress the denizens of 1960s Harlem.

In the 1920s and 1930s, the Harlem Renaissance influx of creativity in literature, drama, music, visual art, and dance changed black American urban centers forever. But the outlandishness of elaborate floor shows and waiters who danced the Charleston while balancing trays of whiskey no longer presided. By 1964 Harlem's music audience was retrenched. Broadway musicals and 52nd Street jazz clubs reduced the amount of jazz found in Harlem. Eclipsing jazz, sophisticated rhythm and blues was the most popular music in the mid-1960s.

Pridgon was eyewitness to an early rejection at the Palm Café of Jimi's approach:

We used to go to the Palm Café and places like Small's, the Spotlight . . . places around 125th Street in the Harlem scene. And he'd tell them he wanted to sit in. These old fuddy-duddy, rough-dried never-beens, they weren't going to give him a break. They acted like they didn't even know that he was there. He'd sit there with this kind of look on his face for a few minutes, and he said, "I'm going to speak to them again."

I'd say, "Hey, don't say nothing to those cats because it's obvious they don't want you to play." Finally, they would let him come in and play, and they'd mess up so bad behind him, it was incredible. He'd be looking all disgusted on the stage, and he'd keep looking back at them, and some other guys would tell him he has to turn it down. It would take him through all kind of changes. He was a star and they knew it. That's why they didn't like him to plunk the guitar with his teeth and shake his long process . . . and come near the edge of the stage and flick his tongue at the girls because they would all scream. They should have treated him like he was the star and they were the fucking sidemen.

Guitarist Horace "Ace" Hall, who would soon meet and work with Jimi via Curtis Knight and the Squires, also saw firsthand that Jimi's style of playing, onstage behavior, and appearance did not fit in with the clubs in Harlem:

"Jimi turned his amplifier up and wanted to be heard at those clubs. But when he wanted to sit in again, those cats would tell him, 'Well, we're just going to intermission' or 'You can catch us on the next set.' These were supposed to be jam sessions. Anybody could come up, but they'd always give him some excuse. . . . Most of the guys then had their conked and Marcels [hairstyles] and not in a do-rag like Jimi would wear. He was just different."

HARLEM, OF COURSE, HAD RADICALLY CHANGED FROM THE DAYS of its Renaissance. Jimi was living in a community that, since the end of World War II, had developed into the focal point for the distribution of heroin to the East Coast of the United States.

On January 17, the Apollo held a midnight-to-dawn show in an effort to raise $100,000 to assist a halfway house campaign to help rehabilitate Harlem's drug addicts. The campaign's mission was all too evident: Of the 30,000 heroin addicts estimated to live in New York City in 1964, 15,000 to 20,000 lived in Harlem.

Another character Jimi came across in his effort to find work in New York was "Fat Man" Jack Taylor, also known as "Fat Jack" or, simply, "Fats." Harlem has seen many legendary dope kingpins, but "Fat Man" Jack Taylor was, if not the most powerful or ruthless, truly the most unusual drug boss of them all. A number of people in Jimi's Harlem circle of contacts knew him personally.

Taylor, who ruled Harlem's 116th Street, was, according to Dean Courtney, just under six feet, soft-spoken, with a dazzling, winning smile. Taylor was homosexual, and some claimed he had never learned to read. And he had an uncanny ability to charm and manipulate people.

"I remember the Muslims wanted him out of that area," Courtney said of Taylor, "not knowing that he owned a lot of property there. It was hard to get him out of Harlem because he took care of a lot of the people in the area. During Thanksgiving, Christmas, and all of the holidays, he'd pull up in a big truck and made sure all of the kids got toys, or at Thanksgiving, everyone got turkeys."

Taylor reputedly had extraordinary understandings with the police, dealers, and gangsters in the area that enabled him to freely conduct his drug business. As a lover of music, Taylor started Ro-Jac Records to help blues singer Big Maybelle (Mabel Louise Smith). She hit the apex of her career in 1955 with the Quincy Jones–produced "Whole Lotta Shakin' Goin' On," two years before Jerry Lee Lewis's version. Her use of heroin and her failing health prevented her from getting a new record deal, and Taylor created the label just to record her.

Eventually, from 1979 to 1985, Taylor ran the posh, three-story Harlem World complex, which housed a disco, his offices for his music labels, and a haven, social network, and place to sleep for musicians, producers, and street hustlers of all kinds. Charlie Rock, DJ for the Harlem World Crew, stated that Taylor could barely read or write but had politicians and street people alike invest in Harlem World. It boasted chandeliers, wall-to-wall gold shag carpeting, a one-hundred-foot bar in the shape of a lightning bolt, and a full-wall mural of figures dancing under a hovering flying saucer.

Eventually, Temple Number 7 under the Nation of Islam (now Masjid Malcolm Shabazz), down the block on 116th Street, after years of picketing and legal wrangling, brought Harlem World and Taylor's drug empire down. Ironically, the mosque had formerly been the Lenox Casino and later, the site of the murder of Malcolm X.

Etta James knew Taylor. When a pimp she dated beat her savagely and sent her to the hospital and then, in her hospital room, blamed James for his mother's sudden death upon hearing this news, she was terrified. James abruptly left the hospital, put on a wig, and immediately went to Taylor, who loaned her his feared brother, Willy Jack, as a bodyguard. Thus, it was no surprise that Jimi, through Etta James's friend Lithofayne Pridgon, would meet the drug baron of 116th Street.

Taylor, according to author Charles Cross in *Room Full of Mirrors*, suggested the starving and unemployed Jimi run drugs for him and Jimi politely refused, determined to succeed with his music. According to Pridgon, "Taylor turned out to be just another homosexual that had designs on Jimi."

In her autobiography, James expressed her lack of respect for Jimi. "About this time, I met Jimi Hendrix, except we were calling him 'Egg Foo Yung' because all he did was eat Chinese food at a chop suey joint on 125th Street. Ate egg foo yung every night of the week. It was Faye who said the boy was talented, but to me he looked like a roadie working the R&B circuit. Someone said he could play the blues—the John Lee Hooker blues—but back then, we were looking at country blues like sharecropper's music. I mean, we were more into the Isley Brothers."

The three-man Isley Brothers formed their vocal group in 1954 and sang strictly gospel music. Three years later, they added doo-wop and rock and roll to their repertoire. The trio had, at first, a modest success with "Shout" in 1959, but this call-and-response, gospel-tinged classic eventually became the Isleys' first gold single.

Ronald Isley, three years later, was wailing "Twist and Shout," a cover that shot up to number two on the R&B charts. A new rock band from England called the Beatles covered it on *Please Please Me*, its first album, and one-upped the Isleys. The Beatles' cover of the song went to number two in America in April 1964, during a week when the top five spots were all held down by Beatles songs. The Isleys entered the UK charts with "Shout," which established a series of successful, high-energy hits that followed.

In early February, the Isley Brothers had a guitarist quit, despite the fact that a spring tour and recording dates had been booked. Once again, Dean Courtney, along with Pushay, stepped forward to help Jimi, mentioning him to Tony Rice, a local singer and friend of the Isleys.

"We had a friend named Tony Rice," Courtney said. "Jimi had done a few sessions around town, so Pushay said, 'Why don't we tell Tony about Jimi?' . . . Tony, in his high-pitched voice, said, 'You mean the guy who plays the guitar upside down?' A few weeks passed and Tony said to us, 'Where's the guy who plays the guitar upside down?'"

Ronnie Isley described Rice's enthusiasm for Jimi: "Tony said this kid—he was about fifteen or sixteen—was the best and that he played right-handed guitar with his left hand. I said to Tony, 'Aw, come on, man, he can't be that good. Is he better than . . . ' and then I started naming all the guitar players we knew we'd like to have in our band, and Tony said, 'He's better than any of them.'"

Jimi met Ronnie Isley and Rice at the Palm Café for an audition. "The night we met," recalled Isley, "Tony went up to the bandstand and asked if Jimi could sit in, but the guys in the band didn't want to let him on. So I went up and asked them, and they said, 'No, he plays too loud' and so forth, and I knew it was jealousy. . . . So I said to Jimi, 'Look, come out to my house this weekend. I've got amplifiers and the band will come over and we'll have some fun.'"

The Isley brothers were living in a rented a house on Liberty Road in Englewood, New Jersey. Isley brothers Ronald, O'Kelly, and Rudolph shared the rented house with their two younger siblings, Ernie and Marvin, and their mother, Sallye.

Jimi did not even have enough strings on his guitar when he arrived, so Ronnie bought him two and then brought him back to the house. Jimi was the picture of an itinerant musician. All of his worldly possessions were packed in his guitar case. Jimi never wore underwear and had only Larry Lee's old jacket to wear against the cold of winter. In the event he failed the audition, it was a six-mile bus ride back to Harlem, to no job and no place of his own to live.

The Isleys assembled a backup band in their basement, with Al Lucas on bass and Bobby Gregg on drums. Jimi leaped into "Twist and Shout," followed by "Respectable" and "Shout." Jimi knew and fluidly played them all and was hired as a member of the backup group, the I. B. Specials, that afternoon.

That night, Sunday, February 9, Jimi and the Isley family, along with 73 million other Americans, tuned in to the *Ed Sullivan Show* and watched "Beatlemania" being born. The Beatles' sex appeal, harmonies, and style of amplified rock music, whether during the sultry "Till

There Was You" or the screaming, head-bobbing "I Saw Her Standing There," prompted shrieking, even crying from the girls in the studio audience. It buoyed Jimi's hopes of being allowed to perform with more panache.

The freshly hired guitarist was given a spare room and quickly adapted to his surroundings and newfound family, often watching Saturday-morning cartoons with the younger Isley brothers, Ernie and Marvin. The brothers nicknamed him "the Creeper" because he moved so softly throughout the house.

"He was quiet, well behaved, and minded his own business," remembered Ernie Isley, who was only eleven at the time. Ernie often watched Jimi quietly sit and play his guitar while looking out the Isleys' front window: "Jimi would practice phrases over and over again, turn them inside out, break them in half, break them in quarters, play them slow, play them fast. . . . Jimi would even use the guitar to do his talking for him: 'How are you doing, Jimi?' 'Bading dada dooo' on the guitar. 'Is it cold outside?' 'Wheeooooow.'"

JIMI BRIEFLY STOPPED BACK IN HARLEM TO TELL PRIDGON THE good news about joining the Isley Brothers band. They spent time together before Jimi left, and the tour began in early March. The first stop was in Canada.

After their first show at the Grand National in Montreal, the Isley Brothers and band stopped in at a local club. Jimi was fascinated by a talented, seventeen-year-old drummer, Buddy Miles.

"One night, this band came in," remembered Miles.

They all had yellow and black on, like Tom Jones' [frilly] shirts. They were just coming over to get a drink because there were a lot of beautiful French Canadian girls in there. This one guy came through that was a little bit different from everybody else. He had the same garb on, but he had chains and stuff, and his hair was like down to his shoulders. And so he was sitting there checking me out, because I was getting into this solo. We was doing one of Wilson Pickett's songs, and I was singing, too.

After we got done, he came backstage and says: "Hey, man. I must say, you about the funkiest drummer I ever heard, man."

Jimi gave Miles his New York contact information. The two crossed paths several times over the years. Most notably, Jimi, Miles, and Billy Cox became the first all-black power rock trio in 1969, known as the Band of Gypsys.

As an I. B. Special, Jimi earned thirty dollars per night while on tour, which was good money for an unknown. Still, he wasn't shy when it came to asking for an extra ten dollars to buy guitar strings or flamboyant stage clothes.

His individuality was definitely starting to show. He'd wear brightly colored scarves, earrings, shiny bracelets, and at one concert, he used a gold chain for a belt. The brothers, who neither smoked nor drank alcohol, prided themselves on a clean-cut, well-tailored look. Eventually, they enforced a dress code, and when they noticed Jimi's shoelaces didn't match, he was fined five dollars for the violation.

The Isleys' tour bounced them from a club in Canada down to a baseball stadium in Bermuda, where they headlined.

"We'd been advertised for months, so the place was filled," remarked Ronnie Isley, "and those who couldn't get seats were standing on hills overlooking the stadium."

The I. B. Specials also backed the local acts opening in Bermuda. While the Brothers got ready in their dressing rooms, they heard a loud roar coming from the stadium. When they took a peek, they saw the commotion was for Jimi, who happened to be down on his knees, biting the guitar strings.

The tour took them to the West Coast, where they played a college circuit. By this time, Jimi was starting to feel more comfortable on stage with the Isleys, and they developed a call-and-response routine. The brothers sang a phrase, and Jimi mimicked their voices on his guitar.

In Seattle, Jimi ran into his old girlfriend, Betty Jean Morgan, and they mused over old times, and Jimi informed her of his new whirlwind of a life.

Recalled Ronnie Isley: "He wanted to stay over and meet us the next day in the next town. We said okay because we thought he knew where the next gig was. He didn't show up, and we didn't see him until a week later in New York. His guitar had been stolen."

The Isleys traveled to Atlanta and performed on May 16 at a street dance in Peters Park set up by the Georgia Institute of Technology to celebrate its Greek Week festival. But they did so without Jimi's now-proven stage persona.

Missing the Atlanta concert was a blessing in disguise for Jimi. Arriving in New York prior to the Isleys, Jimi ran into his friend George Clemons, a nightclub singer. Clemons told Jimi soul singer Don Covay needed a guitarist for his latest single.

"Jimi used my house to sleep, and his guitar was always in the pawnshop," said Clemons. "Don Covay came around shopping for a record deal. He'd come down to the Harlem clubs looking for somebody to use on the songs he was looking to sell to Atlantic."

Covay had Little Richard as producer on his 1957 single "Bip Bop Bip," under the name of Pretty Boy, which Richard dubbed Covay because he had a similar pompadour hairstyle. Chubby Checker took "Pony Time," which Covay cowrote, all the way to number one in 1961, introducing a new dance that mimicked horseback riding.

Jimi arrived at A-1 Studio on Broadway, which was owned and operated by Herb Abramson, one of the founders of Atlantic Records. Jimi joined the Goodtimers, Covay's band. He was told to play a simple Curtis Mayfield—like R&B riff and not overstep his boundaries at the song's dramatic pause. WWRL disc jockey (Nathaniel) Magnificent Montague financially backed the session, and the record came out on his Rosemart label. Jimi was paid under the table and was not asked to join Covay's band. Jimi had no idea that "Mercy, Mercy" would eventually hit number thirty-five on *Billboard*'s pop chart six months later or that it would be covered by England's newest hitmakers, the Rolling Stones.

A few days after Jimi's session with Covay, the Isleys returned to New York and reunited with Jimi. Kelly Isley took Jimi down to Manny's Music Shop in Manhattan and purchased him a white Fender

Duo-Sonic. Jimi customized it with an Epiphone "Temtone" vibrato unit that changed pitch and volume on demand. It was a quantum leap in equipment, after the guitar that had recently been stolen. Jimi's lack of focus and childlike wandering in life had resulted in a previous theft while he was a teen in Seattle, when his Supro Ozark was lifted from the stage when the Rocking Kings played Birdland. Kelly Isley teased Jimi about keeping his new guitar under lock and key.

The Isley Brothers made a deal in 1964 with Atlantic Records to distribute their independent label T-Neck, named after Teaneck, New Jersey, where the family settled in 1962 after "Shout" became a hit. Few black artists had their own label in 1962.

According to Ronald Isley, after the session Jimi remarked, "Oh, is this how you make records?" Hoss Allen was a thing of the distant past. Because the song they recorded, "Testify," ran just over six minutes, the engineer made it radio friendly by editing it into two parts and splitting them on sides A and B of the single. The studio used a four-track deck. Rudolph and O'Kelly's background vocals were mixed on one track and Ronald's lead vocal on another.

"Testify," an upbeat song, emulates parishioners expressing the Holy Spirit in the black church, as each Isley brother individually "testifies" about R&B acts such as James Brown, Jackie Wilson, and Little Stevie Wonder, paying tribute to their unique singing style and stage performance. Unfortunately, "Testify" was trampled on the charts by the new soul sounds emerging from Motown.

Jimi settled back in Harlem with Lithofayne and a few dollars lining his pocket, before hitting the road again. On June 19, the Isley Brothers called Jimi up for a gig at the Rockland Palace in the Bronx.

The event was billed as a farewell dance and show for Magnificent Montague, who was leaving to work in Chicago radio. Montague was not only a savvy businessman; he was also a trailblazing DJ who championed integrated radio playlists. Montague told National Public Radio that when he got his big break in Texas, "you were not allowed to put a record on. You were not allowed to choose a record. You were not allowed to comment whether it was good or bad." Montague popularized the phrase "Burn, baby, burn" for records that he loved. But when the catchphrase was echoed after the 1965 civil rights riots in Watts, a

Los Angeles suburb, management asked Montague to stop saying it. He refused and lost his job.

The Brothers joined thirty other performers for the Montague tribute. Each group got to play its big hit and say a few kinds words to the jock before leading into the next act. The six-hour lineup, from 9 p.m. to 3 a.m., included Solomon Burke, King Curtis, Don Covay, and Wilson Pickett.

After the show at the Rockland Palace, the Isley Brothers headlined for a week at the Apollo Theater on a bill with Dionne Warwick. Jimi had come full circle in Harlem, winning the amateur contest and then coming back to play the Apollo with a major group in just a few months.

Yet Jimi's brilliance as an artist was offset by naïve and sometimes immature behavior, laced with a tendency toward despondence. Twice, his performance behind the wheel of a car nearly foreshortened what would inevitably be a tragically truncated career.

The first accident took place on the Isley Brothers tour. On short-distance gigs, the group traveled by station wagon. Jimi liked to verbally fantasize about amps so big, the sound would signal the world's end. His imagination led him to talk of a special dragonlike guitar that breathed fire. The alto sax player, who was driving, finally had it.

He pulled the car over, turned around, and said: "Man, this cat is too weird for me. He's spooking me out."

Jimi didn't speak a word and took over driving duties, even though his poor eyesight prevented him from legally doing so. After about twenty minutes, when the lead vehicle lost sight of Jimi and the second station wagon, it turned around to see what had happened.

There had been a terrible accident. With his weak vision and doing eighty-five miles per hour, Jimi hit an eight-point buck deer. The hood peeled back upon impact, and the two-hundred-pound animal went right through the windshield. The car was completely demolished. As the other car pulled up, the passengers could see that everyone in the other car was okay and laughing at this absurd brush with mortality.

Jimi nearly met his end again in Los Angeles in 1968. Buddy Miles bought an extremely flashy Corvette Stingray, with mag wheels, lowered. Jimi, renting the house in Benedict Canyon that the Beatles had stayed in when first in LA, surprised Miles early the next morning. To one-up Miles, he had bought a brand new, blue, convertible Corvette Stingray 427.

"Jimi says, 'Come on, man,'" Miles recalled. "He says, 'I want to take you for a ride.' I said, 'No, I'll drive my own,' because mine was looking tough, man. So we went up U.S. 1. Then we went to North Hollywood, dragging each other, right?"

Jimi's impetuousness later led to another near-fatal incident.

"Jimi was crazy," Miles stated flatly.

First of all, he needed some glasses, because the dude had astigmatism or something. I used to remind him of that. Later on, I got a call about four or five in the morning, saying that Jimi drove his 'Vette off the side of a cliff. I said, "What?" So I got on my clothes, and I took the fast route. LAPD stopped me and said, "How come you're going so fast?" I said: "A friend of mine just got hurt. Jimi Hendrix." So the cop escorted me down, and when I got there, Jimi was dazed. He had like a little scar on his right eye. And I said, "What the hell happened?" "Man, I was just stoned out," he said, "I just wasn't watching, you know, one of those type of things."

His unique mixture of talent, single-mindedness, self-confidence, naïve relentlessness, and fatalistic inflexibility had both served him and proved his undoing, time after time. But halfway through 1964, Jimi was unhappy with his position in the Isley Brothers, who treated him with more respect than any group with whom he had ever played.

The Isleys had given him the closest thing he had experienced to a family structure since Seattle. And once again, despite its advantages, and without an alternative, he was about to reject the comfort he had been given.

6

An All-Consuming Fire

(JULY–DECEMBER 1964)

"IF I'M FREE," JIMI ONCE SAID, "IT'S BECAUSE I'M ALWAYS RUNNING." And 1964 was the busiest year yet in his young career. But in his travels, Jimi came to realize there were few, if any, well-known black R&B guitar players noted for their hot licks and wild stage antics.

The Isleys' summer tour brought them to Georgia, where they played a show with Carla Thomas, Joe Tex, Esther Phillips, and the Drifters. Each group was given roughly thirty minutes of stage time in these R&B revues, but Jimi was lucky if his solo lasted thirty seconds. Occasionally, the tour intersected with a British Invasion band, and the Isleys put their guitar star in the spotlight.

"In the middle of a show," Ernie Isley recalled, "Kelly might say, 'Come on out here, Jimi, and show them how it's done.' . . . And he'd do something like play the guitar behind his back, and everyone would go, 'My God, how did he do that?'"

The Isleys had recently signed a deal with Atlantic and hoped to have Jimi play on a September session in New York, but shortly after an August gig in Macon, Georgia, Jimi was told, once again, to leave a group.

Jimi's good friend Dean Courtney remembered, "One day, Jimi called me and said the Isley Brothers fired him. I said, 'Why did they fire you, Snagglepuss?' Jimi said [in his Snagglepuss voice], 'Kelly and Rudolph get jealous of the attention I get when I play with my teeth, with my ass, and upside down. They were a good group, but not great performers. They weren't like the Temptations and didn't dance a lot.' I think Rudolph Isley felt they were coming to see Hendrix more than the group."

But in a later interview, Jimi confessed that his attitude may have been the dominant factor: "I got tired of playing in the key of F all the time and turned in my white, mohair silk suit and patent leather shoes."

Jimi later amplified his pent-up feelings about playing backup in an interview with filmmaker Tony Palmer. In talking with Palmer—noted for his music documentaries—Jimi in essence said he could not help himself, despite trying to fit in with other groups: "When I traveled all over the country, I got a chance to sit in and express my-self. . . . I was a backing musician [but] it was really getting to be a hang up because I might have an idea for song—because I got tired of playing the same song over and over—and they would say, 'No, man, you have to do it exactly right. You have to do the steps.' . . . You can get very bored."

Lithofayne Pridgon recalled that Jimi developed an ulcer due to the stress he felt while resisting the requirements of the Isleys. Many of the same symptoms that had allegedly bothered him in the army, in-cluding weight loss and chest pains, returned with him as he went back to Harlem. She also observed he was generally nervous, he chain-smoked, he hardly ate, and he had trouble sleeping. But there was an even more troubling physical condition.

"Jimi would like to play the guitar on the bed," observed Pridgon, "and he'd often fall asleep on his back with his guitar lying on his chest. He had trouble sleeping on his back, and he'd make these chok-ing sounds, followed with muscle spasms in the middle of the night that woke me up. Many times I'd have to roll him over on his side to make him stop. He'd never want to see a doctor about it." Pridgon, when informed of Jimi's demise, said she wasn't surprised he died from choking-related circumstances.

ON SEPTEMBER 18, 1970, JIMI WAS FOUND DEAD IN THE WEST London hotel room of girlfriend Monika Dannemann. Forensic evidence suggested the nine German Vesparax sedatives and an excessive amount of red wine had not been willingly ingested. Doctor John Bannister, the attending physician, found red wine soaking Jimi's hair and oozing out of his lungs.

No stories mentioned what scores of Jimi's friends knew: He feared his manager, Michael Jeffery, a former member of British intelligence, and wanted to end his contract as soon as possible.

In his book *Rock Roadie*, James "Tappy" Wright, who worked for Jimi, claimed Jeffery emotionally admitted to him, one year after Jimi's death, in Wright's apartment: "I was in London the night of Jimi's death and together with some old friends. . . . We went round to Monika's hotel room, got a handful of pills and stuffed them into his mouth . . . then poured a few bottles of red wine deep into his windpipe." Wright also insisted Jeffery told him he had taken out a life insurance policy on Jimi worth £1.2 million, with Jeffery as beneficiary.

AT THE SAME TIME THAT JIMI WAS FIRED FROM THE ISLEY BROTH-ers, however much he was to blame, a fairly unknown white English guitarist by the name of Pete Townshend was itching to put his own stamp on the style of music his band was playing. By August 1964, the High Numbers (previously and soon again called the Who) played popular R&B dance hits at small clubs in London. The band had recently signed with the management team of Kit Lambert and Chris Stamp (brother of actor Terence), two men who would be instrumental in the production of Jimi's first LP when he arrived in London.

The Who's lead guitarist, like Jimi, discovered the marvels of melodic feedback when he aimed his guitar at his stack of high-powered amps. But one thing Townshend experienced that Jimi hadn't was the thrill of smashing a guitar to bits during a performance.

As Townshend later recalled, "The guitar, when it became electrified, in my case, was an instrument of control, aggression and latent violence." Austrian pop artist Gustav Metzke lectured at Ealing Art College, which Townshend attended in England. Metzke was known for pouring acid on paintings to transform them. Townshend was particularly affected by an experimental short film Metzke showed in which two college-age kids mutilated a piano on a sidewalk with hatchets. It was "auto-destructive art," as Townshend later explained it to the members of the Who.

But interestingly, Townshend's first impulse to smash a guitar during his performance came out of an accident, not premeditation. During one of the Who's summer of 1964 shows at the Railway Tavern, Townshend broke the neck of his guitar against the club's low ceiling.

Townshend contended: "I had no recourse but to completely look as though I meant to do it, so I smashed the guitar and jumped all over the bits. It gave me a fantastic buzz. Luckily, I'd brought a spare guitar, the twelve-string. I picked it up and carried on as though nothing had happened." The audience responded with joyous abandon.

In the documentary *The Who: In Their Own Words*, bassist John Entwhistle added an explanatory note to the quirky development of rock guitar auto-destruction: "That was the first gig," Entwhistle said of the Railway, "that our manager Kit Lambert had been to. And he thought that was part of the act, and when he found out it wasn't, he said, 'Keep it in.'"

AFTER BEING TERMINATED BY THE ISLEYS, JIMI JOURNEYED TO Atlanta, where Gorgeous George was based. The eccentric though sartorially impressive MC once again helped the struggling guitarist find work. With George's aid, Jimi joined a tour that featured Solomon Burke, Jerry Butler, the Drifters, Patti LaBelle & the Bluebelles, and others. Jimi was slated to play only during Gorgeous George's brief musical introductions and with the opening act, the Tams.

The Tams were an Atlanta vocal group that took its name from the Scottish tam o'shanter bonnets band members wore on stage. Jimi replaced their former guitarist, Clyde Stroger, who hadn't always shown up for gigs. One wonders if, like Jimi, he objected to the costumes he was obliged to wear. At the time the group agreed to employ Jimi, it was enjoying the success of a song that inadvertently commented on the mercurial relationship between Jimi and Gorgeous George. It was called "What Kind of Fool (Do You Think I Am)."

Tams founding member Charles Pope recalled: "We always had to buy food for Jimi. He never had any money. And when we were on tour, Jimi and Gorgeous George would sometimes fight on the bus. We really didn't care too much for his playing. He played more of a rock style."

On September 28, while on tour with the Tams, Jimi wrote a postcard from Columbus, Ohio, to his father, Al: "I'm on a tour which lasts about 35 days. We're about half way through it now. We've been to all the cities in the mid-west, east and south."

Shortly after a Cincinnati gig, the tour arrived in Missouri, where Jimi went missing. Reflecting later, Jimi blamed himself, admitting, "I got stranded in Kansas City because I missed the bus, you know." Another one of Henry Wynn's Supersonic Attractions tours came along and dropped Jimi back in Atlanta, where he stayed in an apartment in the same building where Gorgeous George lived.

George explained to Jimi that Wynn was organizing a brief fall tour with Jackie Wilson and Sam Cooke that was billed as "the Greatest Show of the Year." Other acts included Hank Ballard and the Midnighters and the Upsetters, Little Richard's old band. Gorgeous George hired Jimi and picked up the house band drummer from Atlanta's Royal Peacock Club to complete his group.

Cooke and Wilson hadn't toured together since the spring of 1959, and a clause in their contract stated that Cooke would close the shows, as he had back then.

"Every night was a packed house," recalled Upsetters' bandleader Gene Burks. "That was the baddest show that ever hit the road. Sam Cooke and Jackie Wilson would switch it up, but the crowd loved us too, and we didn't even have a record on the charts."

Cooke was moved by Bob Dylan's "Blowin' in the Wind," interpreting it as a plea for racial tolerance, and shortly after speaking to a group of civil rights sit-in demonstrators in Durham, North Carolina, in May 1963, he wrote the first draft of the stirring "A Change Is Gonna Come." It was a departure from Cooke's uptempo hits, such as "Twistin' the Night Away," and its concluding lyrics made it a rallying cry among those battling for equal rights, saying that it had been a long time coming but societal change was going to arrive.

THE CHANGE WAS FAR TOO SLOW IN COMING, BUT IT WAS ON ITS way. In October 1958, Cooke was scheduled to perform in front of an integrated crowd of 6000 for Dick Clark's Saturday Night Beechnut Show in Atlanta. The Ku Klux Klan threatened to disrupt the live telecast. Host-producer Clark asked Cooke if he wanted to back out. Cooke's answer was "I'm going on."

And six years later, on October 15, 1964, while hospitalized in Atlanta, Dr. Martin Luther King Jr. was informed he had won the Nobel Peace Prize. The thirty-five-year-old King told the press of his plans to donate the entire $54,123 award to the civil rights movement.

The Cooke/Wilson tour left Atlanta on the next day, October 16, and headed three hundred miles south to Mobile, Alabama. While Cooke and Wilson traveled in style, sometimes in limousines, band members and artists who had one or two records had to ride the bus, where fellow left-handed guitarist Bobby Womack routinely sat behind Jimi. The Rolling Stones were currently having their first number one hit with Womack's song "It's All Over Now."

British groups opened a new market for American R&B music. The Animals, on their 1964 debut LP, covered John Lee Hooker and Chuck Berry and educated their mostly white European audience with a song called "Story of Bo Diddley." Eric Burdon even wrote an article for the American magazine *Ebony*, contending that if it weren't for British rock's interest, many of America's black performers would have disappeared into obscurity. Bobby Womack might have agreed. The best that he and his brothers, who performed as the Valentinos, could do with "It's All Over Now" in America was two weeks at number ninety-four.

Womack, like Gorgeous George and others, was both fond of and annoyed by Jimi. He observed that the only time Jimi put his guitar down was when he went to the bathroom. Jimi habitually practiced on the bus, to the detriment of his fellow musicians, who barely slept through it.

"Ting, ting, chink, ting. That's all I heard, all night, every night," remembered the sleep-deprived Womack. "I'd get mad and scream, 'Just put that fucking guitar down for an hour, half an hour? Fifteen minutes. . . . Please?'"

The Upsetters always opened the show, and then Gorgeous George came out and entertained the crowd before he brought on the other artists.

"He'd tell the crowd he was prettier than Jackie Wilson," said Upsetters' guitarist Melvin Sparks. "George would say, 'How could someone be prettier than me?' Many people still don't realize it, but that's where Muhammad Ali got that line."

The Valentinos were the next act to perform. Cooke had spotted the band on the gospel circuit and offered a record deal on his SAR label. The tour helped promote the new single "Everyone Wants to Fall in Love," and the group managed to work in "It's All Over Now," released just months before, in June.

Jimi could not tone down his stage persona even for Gorgeous George, who twice falsely claimed Jimi was his relative to gain him employment. While George clowned around, pulling off his shirt and preening, the girls would scream for Jimi.

Womack noticed Jimi's unintentional but repetitive upstaging of George from his own position onstage: "Jimi would take the guitar and be playing it with his teeth while George be singing a ballad. Then George would turn around and say, 'I'm going to tell you one more time, Jimi, I'm going to make you eat that guitar the next time I see it in your mouth. This is my show and you're embarrassing me.' Jimi would say, 'I'm only trying to help you.' George would say, 'Don't do nothing to help me!'"

Womack contended Jimi played so loud it dominated the other instruments. He played in a style that moved away from the genre of the group into a hard rock sound. But Womack also credited Jimi with a technique that far outstripped anything his fellow musicians could do. He played solos and rhythm seemingly simultaneously. The complexity of his musical mind and the exponential growth of his abilities meant he could sound like two guitarists at once.

Oscar Wright of the Upsetters, not unlike other Jimi naysayers, felt the loud rock overtones in Jimi's work on the tour were a sign of lack of technique: "In places like Houston and in the Deep South, you could find a dozen players as good if not better than him. What set him apart was that he was loud and could play that rock thing."

According to Bobby Womack, Jimi's unkempt image also alienated him from the other artists on the tour. "If you didn't have a process, a trim haircut, and suit and a tie, you wasn't in it," remembered Womack. "He wore raggedy old clothes and looked like a beatnik."

Still, the Cooke/Wilson tour was exceptionally successful. The Richmond, Virginia, date was at the 3,200-seat Mosque Theater, selling out two shows on the same night.

"The concert stops were spread out about two to three hundred miles apart," remembered guitarist Melvin Sparks. "Most of the time we slept on the bus instead of checking into a hotel."

Memories from previous package tours still haunted Bobby Womack. "You always kept a good watch and a good ring. You never knew when you'd have to hock it to get out of town. You had to deal with being stopped on the highway; everybody would get out the car. They'd say, 'Let's see what you got. Don't be in the town past two o'clock.'"

Womack had been present during earlier Cooke shows when racial tension had permeated the air: "The whites would come in and be seated. Then the blacks would come in and be seated, and you had a stage in the middle. The K9 [police] dogs would be going up and down the aisles. Black people reacted more than whites, so when they heard a song that they'd been hearing on the radio, man, you thought they were going to heaven. [When] they jumped up and screamed, them dogs would come up and attack."

The Cooke/Wilson tour of 1964 was stricken with problems and not only because of race. After one gig, when everyone was packing up the gear, Bobby Womack's brother Harry noticed that a couple of hundred dollars he had earned from the tour were missing. Instead of putting the money in the bank or buying a ring or watch as Bobby had, Harry had kept it stashed in his shoe. He immediately accused Jimi, who firmly denied taking it. The next night, while it appeared everyone was asleep, Harry grabbed Jimi's guitar from the overhead luggage rack. Bobby awoke to see his brother toss it out an open window. The roar of the noisy diesel engine muffled the sound of it splintering on the highway.

Jimi slept through the whole ordeal but had a fit the next morning when he couldn't find his guitar. Other members of the tour chuckled cruelly as Jimi climbed on top of the bus and searched through the luggage, unsuccessfully. Gorgeous George replaced Jimi's guitar with a pathetic substitute: Its previously broken neck had nails driven into it to hold it together. After learning what had happened, Jimi suspiciously eyed Harry Womack for the rest of the tour.

Another unfortunate incident happened in St. Louis when Jackie Wilson narrowly escaped the police by jumping out of a second-floor window. The police were after him for a $2,200 judgment dating back to 1959, when Wilson had failed to appear for a club date. Wilson rejoined the tour in Nashville, where he was arrested. Henry Wynn posted his $3,000 bond, and the tour resumed.

Guitarist B. B. King briefly joined the Cooke/Wilson tour for a few shows. Although they didn't get a chance to meet, Jimi watched King, one of his guitar heroes, every night from backstage.

In his autobiography, King recalled his performances on that tour. "I knew I didn't have Sam's good looks or Jackie's dance moves, but I was going to give them a taste of the in-your-face blues and give it to them good. I'd do a short set. I wouldn't overstay my welcome and I'd sing 'Rock Me Baby,' which is after all, about rocking your baby all night long. It was my sexiest song."

Mentally, Jimi took notes of King's signature riffs and approach. Through King, he eventually saw a way to break out of the R&B mold and be recognized as an accomplished electric guitar player, but whereas King's repertoire was strictly blues, Jimi felt there had to be a way to add a hard-driving rock element to the sound as well. Jimi keenly watched King play. In fact, years later, he updated King's "Rock Me Baby" into a fast tempo song he titled "Lover Man."

After a show in Nashville, the R&B revue stopped in Memphis, and Jimi dropped by Stax Records studios, hoping to find a sympathetic ear. It was not an uncommon practice. Singer Otis Redding did it in October 1962 when he was just a valet and driver for Johnny Jenkins and the Pinetoppers. Jenkins's session at Stax flopped, and there were thirty minutes of studio time remaining. Redding, who'd been singing in Macon, Georgia, for years, pestered the band to start playing a ballad in triplets. After the session's producer heard him sing just a few bars, a call went out to locate the engineer so that a demo could be captured. Redding's song was "These Arms of Mine," and he went on to become the label's biggest star.

Arriving at Stax on a Tuesday, Jimi was disappointed to learn that Steve Cropper, whom he had come to audition for, was in the studio and could not come out.

In 1962, Cropper, along with Booker T. Jones, Al Jackson, and Donald "Duck" Dunn, formed Booker T. & the MGs. The half-white, half-black band's funky instrumental "Green Onions" sold 1 million copies, establishing the band on a national level. By 1964, the group served as Stax's house rhythm section, and Cropper was promoted to session producer and songwriter.

With Cropper tied up in production, Jimi killed time looking at all the records for sale. Stax was housed in an old movie theater on East McLemore Avenue. The company had taken out the concession stand and replaced it with a small record store and added a few chairs. After milling about, Jimi left word that he was going across the street to get a bite to eat.

When Cropper came out to get a sandwich at the Satellite Snack Bar, Jimi introduced himself, and in talking about his work, he mentioned having played on Don Covay's "Mercy Mercy."

"That about knocked me to my knees," admitted Cropper, "because that was one of my favorite records at the time. I hadn't worked with Don yet, but I asked Jimi to show me that great lick he played. So after we finished eating, I took him over to Stax.

"We didn't have any tape running, but Jimi took my guitar and started playing that sucker upside down. I laughed and told him, 'I can't learn that lick by looking at it that way.'"

The final night of the tour came on November 9. Jimi returned to Atlanta with Gorgeous George. The Tams, who were appearing at the Soul City nightclub, offered Jimi a temporary gig until he got back on his feet financially.

While in Atlanta, Jimi always had a place to stay. Guitarist Herman Hitson, introduced to Jimi by George, described their digs: "Gorgeous George had about three rooms at the Bellevue Hotel, and Jimi was staying in room seventeen. Drummer William Powell and I would go visit him, and he'd always be sitting in there playing his guitar. He was broke and would ask us, 'You got a Pepsi Cola? Some crackers? Anything?' Henry Wynn's restaurant down the street [Henry's Grill] would feed us. I noticed Jimi started wearing some of Gorgeous George's fancy clothes. We'd all go up to the Royal Peacock and sit in."

Sam Cooke traveled to Atlanta for a five-day engagement at the Wynn-owned Royal Peacock that lasted from November 26 to 30. On December 11, less than two weeks later, in the Los Angeles suburb of Watts, Cooke was shot and killed by Hacienda Motel manager Bertha Lee Franklin. A drunken liaison with a woman had gone wrong, and his assumption that his clothes and money had been stolen and that she had fled into the motel office led Cooke to confront Franklin, who kept a .22 handgun sequestered in her unit, a precaution taken after a series of robberies. The case was ruled "justifiable homicide."

Jimi was devastated by the tragic news. Without getting to know Cooke well, Jimi was still moved by the singer's style, smoothness, and soul during their time on the road together.

"I'd have learned more," Jimi was quoted as saying later, "if they'd let Sam finish his act, but they were always on their feet and cheering at the end, and I never heard him do his last bit."

Gorgeous George knew that Jimi was barely surviving. While playing with the Tams in Atlanta, Jimi had pawned his guitar and amp and relied on the largesse of the women who were attracted to him.

Little Richard was staying at the Royal Hotel when he heard that Gorgeous George was in town. He wanted to meet the legendary performer who, like him, dressed and performed so flamboyantly. George met with Richard; his road manager, Henry Nash; and Bill Murray, who handled the tour bus.

To help Jimi, George laid out a proposal similar to one he had suggested before: "I want you to meet my 'cousin,' Maurice James. He plays guitar. Can you let him come on the bus?" Richard's band already had one guitar player, but he couldn't resist George's persuasive pitch about the talented and handsome young man.

"I told them it'd take about $150 to get Jimi's guitar and amp out of the pawnshop," George recalled, "so he gave me $175, and I put it in my sock, went back, and got Jimi. He really didn't want to tour with Little Richard at first because the Sam Cooke tour was getting ready to go back on the road in a few weeks, but I took him down to meet Little Richard, and he hired him."

Jimi came on board in mid-December 1964, just a few days after the sudden death of Cooke. Jimi had been given many nicknames already in his chaotic life, and now he decided on the stage name Maurice James. He had seen Little Richard preach in his neighborhood in Seattle. He had heard his music for years, had been aided by Richard's friends and associates when he first arrived in Harlem. And now Jimi was about to play in Little Richard's band.

"I will never forget [Jimi] loading his belongings on the bus," Henry Nash mused. "His guitar was wrapped in a potato sack. It only had five strings on it. He made a good impression on the band, though, and they welcomed having him on stage with them." On New Year's Eve, at an after-hours club in Greenville, South Carolina, "Maurice" sat in for the first time with the Crown Jewels, Little Richard's tight backup band.

But by 1964, Little Richard, the self-proclaimed King of Rock and Rhythm, was a tough act to sell to a new audience of rebellious youth. He was big in the 1950s, screaming and shouting during rock and roll's infancy. In his heyday, Richard Penniman outraged conservative America, wailing, "Tutti Frutti" and "Good Golly Miss Molly," pounding the piano on his tiptoes, sporting a turquoise suit and mascara, singing about a girl who "sure likes to ball." In the South, radio stations that included Fats Domino in regular rotation wouldn't play the more suggestive music in Little Richard's catalog.

In the early 1960s, Little Richard began a comeback in Europe as the headliner for upcoming British act Gerry & the Pacemakers, whose hits included "Don't Let the Sun Catch You Crying" and "Ferry Cross the Mersey." The other acts that opened for Richard looked very promising as well. They were the Rolling Stones and the Beatles.

"The Beatles were with me, opening my show," Richard recalled. "I didn't know that they would get to be famous. If I'd have known that, I'd have had a contract as long as from here to my toenails."

Little Richard hit the road in 1964, promoting his frenetically energetic comeback single, "Bama Lama Bama Loo." To capitalize on the British Invasion sweeping the States, Richard hired a six-piece band called the Crown Jewels, three guardsmen known as His Royal Company (dressed in traditional Buckingham Palace uniforms, red tunics, and tall, black, furry headgear the Brits dubbed "bearskins"), several dancers, and a throne carrier.

During Jimi's two years of touring the rhythm and blues circuit in the South, he saw and emulated many flashy stage tricks. But according to Bobby Womack and Gorgeous George, Jimi invented one of the most iconic images of rock showmanship: setting his guitar on fire.

"Blacks thought he was crazy," said Womack, "especially when he took out the lighter fluid and set his guitar on fire. He only had one guitar, so he'd run backstage, get a big old blanket, and put it out. . . . I used to laugh at him because I thought his guitar looked like a piece of barbecue." But significantly, in the same year Pete Townshend was whipping up London crowds, breaking his guitar purposely, Jimi set his own ablaze.

Many have cited Jimi's quite literally incendiary performance of the Troggs' "Wild Thing" at the 1967 Monterey Pop Festival. Others will be familiar, prior to that historic set at that landmark event, with Jimi burning his guitar at the London Astoria Club, at the suggestion of British rock journalist Keith Altham. That March 31, 1967 gig was presumed to be the first time Jimi utilized that particular bit of stage flash. But its origins, according to Womack, were the tour of 1964, although no known photographic evidence exists.

Jimi's philosophy about touring led him to travel most of his life. "The road was so much a part of my soul that I can't imagine life without riding the highway . . . the rhythm of the road rocking me to sleep, making me feel like I'm moving on and going where I need to go. . . . It's monotonous but steady. In a strange way, it's secure. Moving on means I'm never where I am; I'm always leaving the past behind and heading into the future."

His future with Little Richard, a legendary icon of rock and roll, should have been bright. But it turned out to be more contentious and troubled than his time with any other group.

7

Life and Near Death
on the Road

(JANUARY–JUNE 1965)

THE 1965 TOUR PROMOTED A NEW RELEASE, *LITTLE RICHARD: HIS Greatest Hits*, featuring twelve re-recordings of his most successful songs from the 1950s. Little Richard's sextet, known as the Crown Jewels, featured Wade Jackson (drums), Johnny Franklin (bass), Frank McCray and Boogie Daniels (saxophones), and Glen Willings and Jimmy Hendrix, aka "Maurice James" (guitar).

The first stop returned Jimi and the entourage to Atlanta for two gigs, one at the local branch of the Whisky a Go-Go and the other at the Royal Peacock. Fans who saw Jimi perform in Atlanta claimed that when he suddenly launched into one of his wild solos, Richard beat on the piano, yelling: 'Stop the music! Stop the music!' The band started the song over. The audience, used to Richard's outlandish theatrics, did not fully realize that this was not part of Little Richard's act.

The tour then headed west, where it played the Harlem Duke Social Club in Pritchard, Alabama. It was at this gig that Jimi finally worked up the courage to speak with one of his blues inspirations, B. B. King, backstage during an intermission. They sat on stools, and Jimi introduced himself and told King how long he had loved his music. King responded by asking Jimi, as so many had, about the difficulty of playing right-handed guitars upside down without changing the strings.

King later noted that even in the Deep South, rock was making an incursion on audiences who listened primarily to blues: "They didn't care too much about blues because Little Richard was so electrifying that when he got through, everyone was ready to leave."

Although Richard's show was full of high energy R&B, the next few stops were decidedly blues territory: Louisiana and Texas. Those states, along with Mississippi, were the spawning ground of most of America's blues singers from 1943 to 1966.

On January 27, Texas bluesman Albert Collins jammed with Jimi. A cousin of the legendary Lightnin' Hopkins, Collins developed his signature full, fat tone by using his fingers instead of a pick and obtained a stinging vibrato by quivering a string with his wrist. Collins's guitar of choice was a Fender Telecaster, with an amp fully cranked. Some referred to him as "Master of the Telecaster."

Texas-born Collins, also known as the "Ice Man," recorded a number of singles whose titles reflected that nickname. "The Freeze" was a regional hit in Houston and sold more than 100,000 copies. "Frosty," a million-seller in 1962, was still popular with his fans.

The 1965 LP *The Cool Sound of Albert Collins* also featured "Thaw Out," a Collins original that impressed Jimi so much, he later recorded his own version, renamed "Driving South." Jimi always stretched the tune past Collins's original 2:41 duration, and in a live recording of the song later that year bandleader Curtis Knight can be heard yelling, "Eat that guitar, Jimi," while Jimi played the solo with his teeth. The purely instrumental version of "Driving South" on Jimi's *BBC Sessions* album features a definitive, propulsive blending of R&B and rock guitar, of feedback and fluidity.

Remembering Little Richard's invitation to jam with his new guitar player, Collins said: "I was in this little club called the Club 500 in Houston. The Third Ward. That's where I was raised up. So Little Richard say, 'Weee-oooh, I got a guy with me. I want you to hear him play. He can play so gooood.'"

Collins agreed to meet Jimi and gave him permission to sit in at the Club 500. "Man, he came rolling out to the end of the stage, and one of Little Richard's roadies say, 'Man, you don't get him off of there, he's going to end up on the tables!' Oh, he was rough. Ooh, man, he was powerful even then. He could play some blues."

Jimi incorporated bits of what he learned from the many musicians he admired, regardless of their genre or style of playing. In the case of Collins, the sustained note that opened "Collins Shuffle" was cited on Jimi's 1968 track "Voodoo Chile."

Little Richard's tour continued through the South, playing two more Texas dates, Dallas and Fort Worth, and then headed north to Oklahoma for shows in Tulsa and Oklahoma City.

In addition to writing postcards and letters home, Jimi made the occasional phone call from the road. His brother Leon recalled: "Jimi loved to go on the road. He used to call me up and go, 'Will you listen to this song?' And I'd go, 'Oh God, not again.' I'd put the phone down for about ten minutes, and he'd still be playing on the guitar over the phone."

The closest Jimi got to his Seattle stamping grounds on the tour was California. Los Angeles, by then an epicenter of the music industry, had a subgenre of music, folk-rock, beginning to take hold in a big way on the Sunset Strip. The Byrds recorded Dylan's then-unreleased "Mr. Tambourine Man" in January. When it finally was available as a single in June, it went to number one in America.

On February 5 and 6, Little Richard and his band played Hollywood's Red Velvet at 6507 Sunset Boulevard, an after-show hangout for celebrity rock 'n' rollers such as Elvis Presley and the Righteous Brothers. Shortly thereafter, Richard commuted between his home in LA's Larchmont Village and the studio, where he cut five new tracks, all without Jimi.

Richard appeared without the Crown Jewels on the March 9 telecast of Dick Clark's weekly music show, *American Bandstand*. Biographer Paul MacPhail described the visuals: "Richard was dressed in a white shirt and white trousers with a big medallion around his neck, covered by a huge white cape and hair high and waving with the music. He sat at a baby grand piano, surrounded by three guys dressed like Buckingham Palace guards, as he faked [playing] piano, lip-syncing his hit, 'Lucille.'" But despite the national broadcast, Richard was under great stress. He had difficulty getting bookings with the shifting tastes of popular music audiences.

Author Charles White bluntly observed: "Richards' recording career became very erratic. His stage act was rapidly becoming a form of self-parody. The undiscriminating audiences, who seemed to love his camp fooling more than his music, encouraged his displays of narcissistic nonsense and he became even more eccentric."

During some of his 1965 performances, Richard compared himself to another flamboyant dresser and eccentric pianist of the time: Liberace. The effeminate manner and dazzling costumes may have worked well in some clubs for the self-proclaimed "bronze Liberace," but privately some of Richard's band members and road crew were derisive.

It had been a little over two weeks since the Crown Jewels had performed, when Richard informed the band there was a gig for everybody up at San Francisco's Fillmore Auditorium. Charles Sullivan, the prominent black businessman who owned the Fillmore, did little promotion, save for a few handbills scattered throughout the neighborhood and a short commercial that ran on low-watt black radio station KSOL. Nevertheless, there was a sizable audience, including one white teen from the North Bay who was in the front row to take pictures of his idol, Little Richard, not the showy lead guitarist.

John Goddard recalled, "I remembered him because he was playing guitar with his teeth and behind his neck, but to me that night, he was just a guitar player who kept getting in the way of me taking pictures of Little Richard."

Like Gorgeous George, Little Richard wore a gaudy, shiny silver wig when he was at the Fillmore, and he sported a matching sequin jacket, silver lamé pants, and silver shoes for the concert. Jimi and the rest of the band, as usual, were relegated to wearing their obligatory uniform: white shirt, black suit, tie.

Because Richard offered no gigs for several weeks thereafter, Jimi auditioned for the Ike and Tina Turner Revue as second guitarist for the revue's backup group, the Kings of Rhythm. In his autobiography, Ike Turner admitted he was constantly firing and hiring his band members at the time. Either the female background singers looked great on stage but couldn't sing, or his musicians fell in love with them and then split.

The mid-1960s were a difficult time for the Turners. Before "River Deep, Mountain High," a number three hit in the UK in 1966, they had no successful records in the States and earned what they could on the road. In 1964, Ike changed record companies and recorded a pair of live LPs for the R&B Loma label, produced by Robert "Bumps" Blackwell, Little Richard's manager.

Ike Turner was predisposed to hire Jimi because of Ike's profound respect for Little Richard: "I'd be writing songs with Little Richard in mind," Turner admitted, "but I didn't have no Little Richard to sing them, so Tina was my Little Richard. Listen closely to Tina and who do you hear? Little Richard singing in a female voice." Jimi was hired.

Jimi performed with the Turners at a newly opened rock club called Ciro's Le Disc on Sunset Boulevard. Author and former *Rolling Stone* editor Ben Fong-Torres described in his book *Not Fade Away* how a typical Ike and Tina show kicked off during the period: "The Ikettes came storming out of the wings in a train formation, in mini-skirted sequins, haughty foxes thrusting their butts at you and then waving you off with a toss of their long, whippy hair. Tina came out, eyes flashing, until she became a fire on stage."

Ike's 1951 tune "Rocket 88" is often considered the first rock-and-roll record and features an early example of guitar distortion emanating from an amp's slightly damaged speaker. It was not unlike Jimi's fascination with a broken amp when he was playing with the King Kasuals in Clarksville.

By 1965, Ike was the band's road manager, stage manager, songwriter, booking agent, and bandleader. He was a temperamental taskmaster and not about to tolerate any of Jimi's tendencies toward showmanship. It is well known that Ike had been physically abusive toward Tina. She wrote of it in her own best-selling memoir, *I, Tina*, and in his 1999 autobiography, *Takin' Back My Name*, he admitted: "Sure, I've slapped Tina. . . . There have been times when I punched her to the ground without thinking. But I have never beat her." It was no surprise that Ike Turner quickly and methodically fired Jimi.

"He was a real good guitar player," Ike later stated, "but his problem was that he liked gimmicks. He would fuck up the whole solo to the song, trying to stop the feedback or bring up the volume." Regardless of Ike's temper, his complaints about Jimi were not unlike those of previous bandleaders. "I'd give him a guitar solo, and he didn't have balanced lines. I told him about it three times. It was a case of three strikes and out."

During his period of newfound unemployment in Los Angeles, Jimi saw several local shows, including the legendary "King of the Surf Guitar," Dick Dale. Surfing and surf music were a popular trend in early 1960s Southern California, spearheaded by the Beach Boys. Dale's 1961 hit "Let's Go Trippin'" is acknowledged to be the first recorded surf instrumental.

Dale, a surfer himself, wanted to re-create the thunderous crash of the surf on his guitar, but he was limited by the volume capacity and sound quality that Fender's ten-inch amp speakers offered at the time. He and Leo Fender tested several prototype amps on large audiences, but nothing seemed sufficiently powerful.

"That's how I blew up over forty-eight speakers and amplifiers," bragged Dale.

> They would catch on fire. The speakers would freeze or tear from the coils. I wanted to get a fat, thick, deep sound, like a big floor tom-tom. We never had mics in front of amplifiers, so the amps had to be thick and pure on their own merit. ... Leo Fender finally went back to the drawing board and invented the Dick Dale Dual Showman amplifier with [two] fifteen-inch [J. B.] Lansing speakers. . . . That, along with the creations we did to the Stratocaster, making it a real thick body. . . . The thicker the wood, the purer the sound.

Like Jimi, Dale was yet another left-handed player and offered the curious guitarist some helpful advice: "I went to see Little Richard in a Pasadena bar with about thirty people in there. Jimi was the bass player. I showed him the 'Dick Dale slides' and how I got the power sounds."

According to Dale, when Jimi later learned that Dale had been diagnosed with colon cancer, he paid tribute to the pioneering guitarist with spoken words in his spacy instrumental "3rd Stone from the Sun."

"That's where the quote 'You'll never hear surf music again' came from," Dale proudly proclaimed.

JIMI WAS HANGING OUT AT THE CALIFORNIA CLUB IN LA WHEN he met a go-go dancer and aspiring R&B singer named Rosa Lee Brooks. Taken by her attractive face, his first words to her were that she looked like his mother. As a romantic relationship developed, Brooks also nurtured long-term musical ambitions.

"I felt we had an Ike and Tina, Mickey and Sylvia thing happening," Brooks fondly reminisced. "We were Jimmy and Rose."

Brooks knew Jimi was hungry and needed a place to stay, so they moved into a room at her mother's house in the Crenshaw district. Conveniently, Brooks and her mother were partners in Dixie's Café, a soul food restaurant in front of their house. In exchange for helping Brooks and her mother clear tables, sweep up, and fill empty sugar jars at Dixie's, Jimi feasted on beef short ribs, rice, gravy, collard greens, cornbread, and candied yams. When they weren't working together, Brooks drove around Los Angeles in her 1959 frost blue Chevy Impala convertible, while Jimi strummed his guitar in the backseat, stretched out, trying to create songs for them to perform together.

Eager to start a joint career with Jimi, Brooks got the idea to record a song called "My Diary," written by her musician friend Arthur Lee, who later founded the band Love. Rosa had known Lee for about four months, and she and her singing partner, Pat Patricks, often hung out with him and Johnny Echols, future Love guitarist. At the time, Lee, Echols, John Fleckenstein, and Don Conka, known as the American Four, were the house band at the California Club.

Brooks and Jimi auditioned the song for Billy Revis, a local R&B producer and owner of his own label. Realizing the song's potential, he asked them to pull a band together for a recording session. "My

Diary" was a heartfelt ballad about Lee's first love, Anita "Pretty" Billings, and her mother's unfortunate discovery of a tell-all diary.

"I had to break up with my girlfriend because of this whole deal," Lee revealed. "We were born on the same day. I was born on the seventh, and she was born on the seventh. . . . [My band] Love had a hit with 'Seven and Seven Is.' . . . Same chick . . . same thing."

Brooks and Jimi recruited a bassist and drummer from Major Lance's band, which was performing at Ciro's.

"Jimi was the kind of guy who would walk backstage and introduce himself," said Brooks. "We wound up partying with them that night, and they agreed to come do the recording."

On the day of the session, Brooks and Jimi picked up Lee at his mother's house on 29th and Arlington. Lee jumped in the backseat of her convertible, but according to Brooks, there was a little tension when the guys first met: "Jimi thought Arthur to be his rival. All was quiet the whole trip to the studio, except when Jimi spoke to me."

In an effort to save money, Revis often invited emerging R&B acts to his house on Hass Street, where he had converted his garage into a recording studio. "My Diary," according to Brooks, was nailed in two takes.

"If you listen carefully, you can hear that the horns and the backing voices are very loose," said Brooks, "because they weren't really familiar with the song. Jimi and I were the only ones who had much of a chance to rehearse it."

Revis needed another track to complete the single, but it seemed no one at the session had any material to offer. It was mentioned there was a new dance in which the steps formed the letters U and T. Composers Brooks and Revis simply lifted the familiar hook from "The In Crowd," Dobie Gray's R&B hit from earlier in the year. "They know the In Crowd is out of sight" was replaced with "You know the Utee is out of sight." Unlike his shaky sessions with Hoss Allen in Nashville, Jimi was encouraged to be daring with his solo. Jimi and Brooks's session wrapped up in two hours, and the tapes were taken over to Hollywood's Gold Star Studios for mastering.

Brooks could see that Jimi was pleased with the new recording, but he let her know he was extremely uncomfortable with Little Richard's controlling behavior and sexual advances.

"When I first met Jimi, he was under so much stress from being chased by Little Richard," recalled Brooks. "He was ready to get away from him."

Jimi and guitarist Glen Willings often made jokes about Richard's homosexuality. "They'd imitate his high-pitched voice and say, 'I'm Little Bitchard, and I'm the Queen of Rock-and-Roll,'" said Brooks.

But joking aside, Jimi had to rebuff Richard's physical urges while not offending his boss. When Jimi gently made clear that he was not sexually interested, Richard asked if he could simply watch Jimi and Brooks have sex together. The answer was still no.

"Jimi told me that Richard wanted to see us make out and stuff, but I was never into any of that," Brooks delicately explained.

In his autobiography, Richard bragged about his bisexuality with shocking bravado, including a wild backstage encounter during the 1950s in New York with Buddy Holly and a female companion named Angel: "One time, we were playing at the Paramount Theater and Buddy came in my dressing room while I was jacking off with Angel sucking my titty. . . . Buddy took out his thing. . . . He was having sex with Angel, I was jacking off, and Angel was sucking me, when they introduced him on stage!"

When onstage, Little Richard did not allow anyone to upstage him in behavior or in dress. Rosa Lee Brooks witnessed Jimi's challenge to Richard's dress code rules during an April concert:

It was at the Golden Bear Club, in Huntington Beach. My partner, Pat, went with me, and I did Jimi's hair before the show. I gave Jimi a white, puffy, Errol Flynn type of blouse to wear, with the big sleeves and pointed collar. I also gave him a bolero, like a vest. Before the gig, Jimi said to me, 'I'm going to show you something special tonight.' I wasn't sure what he meant, but I went along with it. He played the guitar behind his head, between his legs, and with his cuff links. After the gig, we were all supposed to leave together, but Little Richard called for a meeting with his two guitar players.

Glen Willings had worn a shirt that was apparently too colorful.

Jimi later imitated Little Richard's lambasting of his and Willings's unacceptable fashion statements:

> "Hendrix, you be deaf? You get rid of that shirt, boy! Brothers, we've got to have a meeting. I am Little Richard, and I am the King of Rock and Rhythm, and I am the one who's going to look pretty on stage. . . . Will you please turn in those shirts or else you will have to suffer the consequences of a fine." He had another meeting over my hairstyle. I said I wasn't going to cut my hair for anybody. Little Richard said, "Uh, what is this loud outburst? That will be a five dollar fine for you." Everybody on the whole tour was brainwashed.

Jimi later elaborated upon the dressing down he received when he wore another frilly shirt at a rehearsal. Little Richard reportedly took one look at Jimi's sartorial splendor and announced, "Shit . . . you fired!" Jimi was rehired the next day, after selling the shirt.

Richard's last LA gigs took place on April 9 and 10 at Ciro's. The nightclub at 8433 Sunset, now the Comedy Store, was where the Byrds debuted in March 1965. Bob Dylan joined them on stage shortly thereafter, and many contend that their popular versions of his songs, along with the success of the Beatles, gave Dylan the inspiration to go electric, despite the infamous and still unexplained mixed reaction he received for doing so at the Newport Folk Festival three months later in July.

Ciro's was started by William Wilkerson, founder of the trade paper the *Hollywood Reporter*, and in the 1940s and 1950s many stars enjoyed congregating there. When it became a music venue, the chandeliers and red flocked wallpaper were still there, but the multilevel dining floor plan had given way to a forty by sixty foot dance floor.

Morgan Cavett, a friend to the Byrds' David Crosby, described the scene at Ciro's in John Einarson's book *Mr. Tambourine Man*. Ciro's, in the spring of 1965, was in an undefined but exciting transitional phase: "There was all these kind of leftovers from the Beatnik generation, but not yet hippies. Rock-and-roll wasn't respectable yet, so it was kind of a weird, eclectic combination of berets, beads and bellbottoms. The Byrds played and there was a groove happening . . . which ranged from little kids to teenagers to older women, old people, gay people, black, white, all dancing and just flailing away with wild abandon."

The Byrds, now Ciro's house band, were present when Little Richard—and Maurice James, aka Jimmy Hendrix—performed. "It was early days for us then. We were unknowns and he [Jimi] was an unknown," said Byrds' front man, Roger McGuinn. "I noted him as a flamboyant guitar player in a conservative setting. He was obviously a good musician and a great band player at that time, in an Ike Turner style, touches of Motown, to suit the band he was in."

The Byrds' bassist, Chris Hillman, also remembered seeing Little Richard at Ciro's. "[Drummer] Michael Clarke and I watched them on the nights they played. The 'palace guards' escorted Richard onto the stage, and he wore a huge red cape. One couldn't help but notice Hendrix on the other end of the stage as a 'sideman,' but playing so well. Not moving much, just playing guitar, but what a guitar player, even back then in a diminished role.'"

Jimi didn't hang around Los Angeles long enough to see if "My Diary" or his relationship with Rosa Lee Brooks had a future. He was back on the road, headed east with the Crown Jewels.

"Little Richard came through with an offer Jimi couldn't pass up," Brooks recalled. "I remember the day he left. They were all staying at a motel on Sunset. It was raining, and I remember Jimi telling me, 'I wish I didn't have to go.'"

RICHARD'S MANAGEMENT SET UP SEVERAL NEW TOUR DATES FOR the rest of 1965, and Richard decided to add a new opening act to his show. Buddy Travis and Leroy "Stacy" Johnson Jr. were one of the hottest song-and-dance duos on the club circuit, and Richard used their energy and syncopated moves to get the crowd warmed up. Richard found the singers, billed as Soul Deuce, at the California Club and made them not only change their name to Buddy and Stacy but also cut their opening act to one song.

"Jimi was my best friend and my seatmate on the tour bus," said Travis. "Every time we'd stop for gas, Jimi would be out talking to some pretty girl, and after we took off, we'd say, 'Where's Jimi? Hold up, driver. He's not on the bus,' And we'd turn around and go back and get him. Jimi was the bandleader, and he often stayed with Stacy and I in our hotel room. The problem was, he'd be up all night playing his guitar, making noise, and waking us up. We'd have to pour water on him and tell him, 'Shut up and go to sleep.' All he cared about was his guitar."

Jimi had his moments of full musical expression and sonic revenge upon Richard, using his Fender Jazzmaster guitar. The Jazzmaster was popular with rock players because it had a long tremolo arm to facilitate controlled note bending, and it tended to produce feedback, especially if the body cavity was left without magnetic shielding. There were moments when Jimi whipped Richard's head around with frenzied bursts of sound.

"I found it difficult to contain myself," Jimi later reflected on his time with Richard. "It was okay at first, but then you get to a point when you can't stand anymore."

Jimi was not the only one who resented Little Richard's artistic totalitarianism.

"Little Richard would fine us fifty dollars if we didn't call him 'King,'" said Buddy Travis. "He even fined Thomas, the captain of the Royal Company, for smiling once during a performance. They were just supposed to stand there without any expression."

When the tour arrived in New York City, Little Richard and his revue were part of the weeklong Soupy Sales Easter Show at the 3,660-seat Paramount Theater in Times Square. The lineup featured, among others, the Hollies, Shirley Ellis, the Vibrations, the Exciters, the Detergents, the Hullabaloos and the Hullabaloo Dancers, and a sixteen-piece orchestra led by a sax player Jimi was shortly to play with, King Curtis.

The *New York Times* reported that about 3,000 kids had waited in line since midnight, and when the doors opened after 8 a.m., pandemonium broke loose. Fans broke box office windows and rushed through police barricades; many were knocked or fell to the ground. Two hundred city policemen were stationed inside and outside the theater, while the Paramount hired forty additional private police to control the wild crowd.

The last comparable Paramount show had happened in October 1944. Then, approximately 35,000 fans caused a near riot outside the Paramount because they could not get in to see Frank Sinatra.

The Soupy Sales run, which broke the attendance record at the Paramount, had multiple daily performances, like the Sinatra engagement. To add even more chaos, Roulette Records allocated 30,000 albums to be given away during the ten-day run, and singles and LPs were sold in the lobby, along with Soupy sweatshirts, tote bags, and other gear.

Headliner Sales (born Milton Supman) attracted the large, youthful crowds based on the popularity of his children's show on WNEW-TV, Channel Five. Sales's skits often ended with his trademark pie-in-the-face gag. He created a sensation with his goofy record and dance "The Mouse," which featured Sales wiggling fingers near his ears and jutting out his upper row of teeth.

On New Year's Day 1965, Sales asked his young viewers, jokingly, to go through their hungover parents' clothing and purses and send him little green pieces of paper with pictures of men with beards.

"Put them in an envelope and mail them to me," Sales said to his naïve audience, "and I'll send you a postcard from Puerto Rico!"

The dollars that arrived that were not from the Monopoly board game were donated to charity. One parent's complaint to the Federal Communications Commission managed to remove Sales's show from the air, but only for two weeks.

In contrast to the hilarity of Sales's act and demeanor, the Paramount run was significant because after misunderstandings, threats, and a physical confrontation, both Little Richard and Jimi came extremely close to injury or death.

Richard's first show began grandly, as a belly dancer cavorted while Jimi and Glen Willings played. Richard then entered to a burst of drumbeats. Cascading down a red carpet, wearing a long, magnificent black cape, he began pounding out "Lucille" on the piano.

Furthermore, on the first day of the Paramount shows, Richard removed his shoes and tossed them out to his screaming admirers. When they begged for more, he began removing more items of clothing under the privacy of his cape and flung them to young girls who fought madly to grab a piece of them.

In his autobiography, *Soupy Sez!* comedian Sales explained how the trouble began:

> The show lasted more than three hours and we were doing five shows a day, which was insane. So, the promoter of the show called us in after the first show and he said to us, " . . . Cut down your act to ten minutes, because we've got so many acts in the show." And then he turned to me and said, "Soupy, you can do fifteen, eighteen minutes, whatever you like." . . . What I didn't know was Little Richard got very upset, because he thought I said I didn't want him to do more than ten minutes.

As the self-titled King of Rock and Rhythm, Richard didn't take well to promoter Morris Levy's decision to shorten the act of everyone except Soupy Sales, even though Sales was the biggest draw. Richard felt he was the top performer on the bill and made his feelings clear, with the moral support of Jimi. Richard did not take into account, however, whom he was dealing with in Levy.

Morris Levy (Moishe Levy) was the owner of Roulette Records and had booked the Paramount Theatre for the next year. He was also Mob connected and not about to have any performer make demands of him. He forced his name onto songwriting credits of his recording artists to unjustly gain additional publishing monies. (The character of Herman "Hesh" Rabkin, the corrupt Jewish music industry power-broker on the HBO Mafia TV series *The Sopranos*, was partially based on Levy.)

Little Richard's section of the Paramount show had run long, which prompted warnings from Levy. Furthermore, Richard, who had recorded on Roulette Records, suggested he was under the impression that he was the headliner, not Sales. Whether or not Levy deceived

Richard in order to get him to sign on for the show, one thing is clear: Richard felt insulted by Levy's decision to give Sales more time on stage.

"So I was very, very mad. He wanted Soupy to close the show. Me and Morris Levy got into a fight. He got mad with me and Jimi Hendrix and he told me, 'You'll find yourself floating in a lake.' I never heard that before, so I called him a black dog. And when I said 'black dog,' he leaped up from behind that desk. I didn't know Morris could jump that high." It is possible that Richard added other words to prompt Levy's furious reaction.

Theater manager Bob Levine described the action during a later performance that sealed Richard's fate at the Paramount: "Little Richard did about ten minutes or so, but then turned to the audience and said, 'Management doesn't want me to play any more music. How do you feel about that?' The crowd of course went wild and he continued to perform, running over his scheduled time. We immediately closed the curtains and had the house band play over him. Richard stormed off the stage in a fit of rage. Things got out of hand, and one of the stagehands called the cops."

The Animals, in New York shooting an episode of NBC's teen pop show *Hullabaloo*, ventured down to the Paramount to catch Little Richard's appearance. Lead singer Eric Burdon recalled: "I was riding up the elevator with Richard, having watched him from the wings while he performed. Richard had gone ten minutes overtime. The stage manager warned him if he did that again, he'd be fired. Richard exploded. . . . With his high-pitched voice, he sounded like an old woman gone berserk. The young black kid trying to hold him back was Hendrix."

Bobby Taylor, drummer of the Hollies, witnessed "my hero, Little Richard, restrained in an arm lock, screaming inside the open elevator. 'Those little white girls out there love me!' It was quite a tantrum. Richard seemed oblivious to the fact that the burly cop had a gun pressed into his neck while he carried on with his loud protestations. Fortunately, the trigger wasn't pulled."

British journalist Keith Altham, who developed an ongoing friendship later with Jimi, continued the story: "The security officer who was in the lift drew his gun, stuck it under Little Richard's chin, as if to say, 'If you don't shut up, I'm going to blow your head off.'"

Animals bassist Chas Chandler was at the Paramount to see the show and greet his friend Tony Hicks, the Hollies' guitarist. Altham described the aftermath of the confrontation: "The lift stopped a few levels below where they were supposed to get out, and Chas Chandler got out with Jimi, only he didn't know who he was, right? And they got out together, just to avoid the furor that was going on in the lift. Chas and Jimi, on their own, just sat on a window seat together having a cigarette and talked about what just happened. Just before Richard was tossed out of the theater, he said, 'I'll get even with Soupy.'"

As Sales prepared to go on stage, Levine told him what had transpired and explained that extra police were there because of a report that a person with a gun was now lurking in the balcony. Sales nervously sang his first number, "Your Brains Will Fall Out," while standing extremely close to King Curtis, who led the band. Curtis had heard the rumor about the gunman and told Soupy to back off. In fact, the police did catch a young man with a gun who had been hanging around the balcony, although no shots were fired.

"Years later," Sales wrote, "it came out that Jimi Hendrix had told everyone that I was jealous of Little Richard and wanted him off the bill, which is bullshit. . . . I've always encouraged good talent. Nice talent. Talent that doesn't hire a hit man."

The maelstrom of suspicions and accusations at the Paramount show thankfully did not result in anyone being harmed. But Little Richard's operation was bleeding cash.

Back in September 1964, Richard had invested $16,000 to organize the tour, purchase elaborate costumes, and employ the band, background vocalists, comedians, and dancers, seventeen members altogether. Richard's plan was to come on loud and gaudy, to come back as what he called "the Living Flame."

However, by May 1965, Richard's accountant calculated it was costing $12,000 per week to maintain the extravagant production. As a result, many venues couldn't afford his show and bookings declined.

Producer Art Rupe tried to revive Richard's career: "He came back and did a few sides for us, one of which was 'Bama Lama Bama Loo.' I really was hoping we could do something better than that, but Richard was still hesitant about doing rock records." When Richard did make the effort to change musical genres with a May release of a fast rocker, "Dance What You Wanna," his reward was not even making the charts.

Richard's next engagement, later in May, was at the Long Pond Inn, Greenwood Lake, New York. For a few shows, Richard added standup comedian Jackie "Moms" Mabley and the duo of Don "Sugarcane" Harris and Dewey Terry. Both Don and Dewey played guitar, and Don doubled on electric violin. In addition to his duties with the Crown Jewels, Jimi was utilized in this lineup. But the ongoing tension between Richard and Jimi did not dissipate.

"Little Richard's style of playing was much different than Jimi's," admitted Terry. "Jimi would let the guitar feed back some nights, and that would piss Richard off, because his music was straight ahead, and it covered up Richard's vocals. They would do 'Lucille,' 'Tutti Frutti,' and others at most of the shows. Little Richard put him with us because he wanted that rock-and-roll sound. Hendrix looked like a hippie. He talked about 'playing in space.' We would say: 'Okay, man. Cool.'"

While in New York, Richard set up a June session at Bell Sound Studios. This yielded his next single, "I Don't Know What You've Got (But It's Got Me)," a slow blues ballad that opened with Jimi's developing use of tremolo for special effect. It had been written by Don Covay, who sang backup, and included the young Billy Preston on organ.

Because the complete version of the song ran over four minutes, it was split into two parts, making it more compatible for mid-1960s radio play. The song peaked at ninety-two on *Billboard*'s Hot 100, although it fared better on *Billboard*'s R&B chart at number twelve.

But it was clear that Little Richard was on the downward side of his career. And it was unlikely that Jimi would continually hold back his resentment at playing Richard's music and playing by Richard's rules.

The Paramount scuffle between Richard and the armed officer could have resulted in Richard or Jimi being shot. Instead, Jimi shared a brief conversation with a musician he had never met, Chas Chandler. Both men smoked and remarked about the strange circumstances of the conflict. And neither Jimi nor Chandler, as they went their separate ways, knew that together they would join forces in just over a year, which would lead to recognition of Jimi as the greatest electric guitarist in rock music.

8

How Would You Feel?

(JULY–DECEMBER 1965)

SHORTLY AFTER LITTLE RICHARD'S SOLD-OUT JULY 4 WEEKEND concert in Wildwood, New Jersey, Johnny Franklin, the Crown Jewels' bassist, quit the tour. Jimi immediately had a suggestion for a replacement: his old friend and army bandmate, Billy Cox.

Cox had to turn down Jimi twice, once on the phone and once in person: "I said, 'Well, Jimi, right now, I'm working.' I took the Kasuals' name and had another guitar player. In fact, I did most of the booking. Jimi wasn't taking no for an answer, though. So I looked up one Sunday morning, and this bus had pulled up in front of my house. Out come Little Richard and Jimi to try to get me on the road, but I had other obligations, so I couldn't go."

Richard's tour stopped in Nashville to do a show at the New Era Club, as well as to tape a segment for WLAC-TV's *Night Train*. This was an all-black, R&B, syndicated program that debuted in October 1964, hosted by WVOL radio executive Noble Blackwell. It featured Nashville's best talent, and top stars such as Otis Redding and Percy Sledge dropped by on occasion.

The Crown Jewels played "Shotgun" at the taping, a Junior Walker & the All Stars tune that had hit number one a few months before at the end of April. While the camera mainly focused on Buddy and Stacy's singing and exuberant dance moves, Jimi, directly behind them, fanned the neck of his guitar with an open hand and even appeared to play it with his elbow. Although he never made eye contact with the camera, Jimi let a sly grin show as the song progressed. After the taping, the Crown Jewels joined Little Richard for a performance at the New Era.

To cap off the evening, everyone went over to the Del Morocco, so much a part of Jimi's recent history. Guitarist Johnny Jones, who had showed up Jimi not long before in a guitar duel, now joined Jimi, Glen Willings, and others in a jam.

The tour boomeranged back to New York for a week at the Apollo Theater, familiar territory to Jimi, who'd won the amateur talent contest there in 1964.

Richard demanded royal treatment for all of his Apollo shows, regardless of the expense and his accountant's warnings. "The great soul stars that the theater first projected to the world became so successful, Harlem couldn't afford them," said Apollo MC Ralph Cooper. "Economically, the Apollo put itself out of business. We could seat fewer than fifteen hundred people, which meant we couldn't pay an act $40,000 or $30,000 or even $25,000, which by the late sixties was cheap for a big name group."

Little Richard's shows weren't profitable, and bandmates eventually found themselves locked out of their rooms at Harlem's Hotel Theresa during their weeklong performance at the Apollo.

According to Robert Penniman, Little Richard's brother and tour manager, Jimi was fired after playing the Apollo Theater. "He was a damn good guitar player," recalled Penniman, "but the guy was never on time. He was always late and flirting with the girls. . . . It came to a head in New York, where we had been playing at the Apollo, and Hendrix missed the bus for Washington, DC. I finally got Richard to cut him loose. . . . So when Hendrix called us in Washington, DC, I gave him the word that his services were no longer required. We had some words."

Jimi's version of his final termination from Little Richard's band was different. He claimed he wasn't paid for five and one-half weeks, so he quit in the middle of July. He was clearing approximately $165 a month after taxes, according to his paycheck from May 27, which may well have been his last.

Glen Willings agreed that Jimi's departure was predictable: "We did have a problem getting paid sometimes, and I think Jimi just quit before they fired him. He might have missed the bus one time, maybe, but it was not a continuous thing happening. Richard felt upset after he found out Jimi had gone from the band. I don't think Richard thought he was going to quit that quick."

Jimi and Willings weren't alone in being paid late. Other members on the 1965 tour felt cheated, too. "Little Richard didn't pay us either," said Buddy Travis. "He was supposed to pay us $40 a night, but that soon grew to $1,500 that he owed us. After we played Newport, Kentucky, I grabbed a wire coat hanger, and I was going to stab Richard if he didn't pay us our money. Robert Penniman stepped in and stopped the scuffle, and Richard ended up giving us $400, but he didn't let us back on the tour bus."

For all the disagreements, the sexual tension, and the false firings, Little Richard eventually paid Jimi, if not all his salary, then an unreserved compliment. "He was the greatest guitar player I ever had," said Richard. "Not one of my men has ever come close to him. He would wander off stage playing his guitar. He was into his guitar, really wrapped up in it, and that's the way it should be. He put his heart into it. He never sounded like just one man. He put so much under me, I just had to sing hard."

Despite how tumultuous their time together had been, Jimi repaid the compliment, as he once told a reporter he wanted to make his guitar sound as wild as Little Richard's voice.

WITH BARELY ANY MONEY LEFT OVER FROM THE TOUR, THE FUture seemed grim. Jimi wrote to his former lover Rosa Lee Brooks, requesting sixty dollars to get a guitar out of a New York pawnshop. Jimi claimed his hard times in New York became so bad that he even tried eating orange peels and tomato paste to survive. Brooks, who had become a popular go-go dancer at the Club LaRouge in Los Angeles, sent the money without question.

"I was often in a situation where I didn't know where my next meal was coming from," Jimi recalled of this difficult period. "People would say if you don't get a job, you'll just starve to death. But I didn't want to take a job outside of music. I tried a few jobs, including car delivery, but I always quit after a week or so. I'd worry a bit about not having any money, but not enough to go out and rob a bank."

With few places to turn, Jimi called upon one of his first and most loyal friends in Manhattan: Dean Courtney. "When Jimi came back to New York from being on the road with Little Richard, he had no place to stay," said Courtney, "but he always had a place to stay with me. But soon that became a problem. At the time, Johnny Star was staying at my place at the America Hotel, so the three of us shared it together. Jimi and Johnny would sit in their room and play guitar most of the time while I'd be trying to write some music."

Jimi's fortunes turned once again when he bumped into a singer with the peculiar professional name of Mr. Wiggles. Born in 1937 in Richmond, Virginia, Alexander Randolph began singing in the late 1950s. He started touring with various R&B revues and had a knack for merchandising, often selling hats at concerts that had photos of B. B. King or Bobby "Blue" Bland glued on them. Rudolph used his merchandising money to finance his recording sessions when he became Mr. Wiggles.

Mr. Wiggles, like many in Jimi's circle, was a friend of Little Richard's. And despite the finality of Jimi's departure, Richard didn't mind Mr. Wiggles using Jimi for his recordings or using Richard's old band the Upsetters, for that matter.

Mr. Wiggles understood Jimi's frustration with Little Richard's tight control of his band's image and encouraged the newly liberated Jimi to explore a more flamboyant style of dress: "Jimi had a misunderstanding over Little Richard's rules. He'd like to wear a do-rag around his head, drink a little, and keep a cigarette lit on stage, and Richard didn't go for that. You couldn't tell Jimi nothing. He always wanted to be a star, and he'd use anybody to get there. I used to take him down to Stone the Crow and help him shop for clothes. All those crushed velvet shirts and those funny-looking hats—I started him wearing that."

Jimi was brought into a series of recording sessions in mid-July. Starting at Cameo Parkway in Philadelphia and then moving to A-1 Sound Studios in New York City, Jimi played rhythm and lead on Mr. Wiggles's "Fat Back" and "Wash My Back," but more notably on a session with sax player Grady Gaines and the World Famous Upsetters.

Jimi knew Gaines from the previous year's high-profile tour with Sam Cooke and Jackie Wilson, and their session yielded the single "K. P." b/w "Cabbage Greens" on the Sound of Soul label. Both tracks were upbeat instrumentals that featured Jimi's solos, complete with enough distortion to rival any rock record for 1965. The only large station that played "Wash My Back" was, ironically, WLAC in Nashville.

Mr. Wiggles also used Jimi on sessions for emerging R&B artists in his stable, such as Little Tommy, Lulu Howard, Sebastian Williams, and a group called the Wigglin' Men. Jimi parted ways with Mr. Wiggles in late July.

But now, while still struggling, Jimi had major tours and recording sessions under his belt and a wider circle of contacts in both Nashville and New York. And on July 27, just about the time he left the employ of Mr. Wiggles, Jimi signed his first exclusive recording contract with Henry "Juggy" Murray, head of Sue Records and Copa Management in New York. Murray saw Jimi perform with the Isley Brothers in 1964 and was so impressed with the young guitar player's talent, he could scarcely believe it when Jimi walked through the doors of Juggy Sound Studios looking for work with demo in hand.

Bored with a job in real estate, Murray formed Sue Records in 1957, naming it after his mother and daughter. Ike and Tina Turner brought him five straight top ten R&B singles from 1960 through 1962. But by 1965, Murray's label was beginning to suffer financially. Stax, Atlantic, and, especially, Motown were churning out hits on a regular basis, and Sue was being left behind. Murray's solution was to start making R&B crossover hits that could be played on white as well as black pop stations.

Jimi returned several times to Murray's studio on West 54th Street to rehearse with other session players and to witness the speed with which Murray produced sessions, often completing two albums' worth of music in three hours.

Within a week of their initial meeting, a recording contract was prepared for Jimi to sign. Jimi was unfamiliar with the contract's language, so Murray went over it line by line. Jimi later recalled the extent of the management contract: "I think it was two years option with options of one year apiece. In other words, it came to September, 1970." (Eerily, this turned out to be the last month of Jimi's life.) Jimi never kept a copy of the contract, fearing he'd surely lose it.

Jimi's need to form his own band conflicted with his insecurity about his singing voice: "I tried to write my songs so I could present them to him, you know, sing them to him. . . . But I didn't feel like my songs were together enough to bring on, especially to sing these songs in front of him, standing there without any instrument." When Murray offered Jimi unfinished songs by others to record, Jimi turned him down.

Jimi conveniently forgot about his contract with Murray when the Isley Brothers came calling with another studio session. On August 5, Jimi recorded "Move Over and Let Me Dance" and "Have You Ever Been Disappointed" with the Isleys at Atlantic Studios in New York.

A letter Jimi wrote his father in early August explained that his sideman apprenticeship was all part of the learning process: "There's a few record company's [sic] I visited that I can probably record for. I think I'll start working toward that line because actually when you're playing behind other people you're still not making a name for yourself as you would if you were working for yourself."

The Isley Brothers dates were mostly small clubs up and down the East Coast, which kept them busy for most of August and part of September. Realizing he would soon be back in New York with nowhere to stay, on September 1 Jimi wrote a letter to Lithofayne Pridgon with unabashed romanticism. In part, it read:

> *Dearest Faye—*
> *. . . Darling, even though I know what I'm talking about when I say no one can love you as much as I do, ever . . . and even though you don't really understand real true love when it's there, it's alright. . . . I have been hurt before but not nearly the way you*

*could hurt me—Faye I'll never let you go as far as my feelings in-
side are concerned.*

"I often referred to him as 'the Baby,'" Pridgon admitted. "He didn't
like that term of endearment. The irony was I really did feel like his
mother at times."

But Pridgon and Jimi made a go of it again. In early October, they
moved into the America Hotel, a low-rent dive on West 47th Street.
But he found no work. His guitar was back in the pawnshop, and the
rent was overdue. The hotel's management was ready to lock them
out and keep what little possessions they owned.

It was at this desperate moment that Jimi met a fellow musician in
the America Hotel: Curtis Knight.

Soul singer Knight (Mont Curtis McNair) had already recorded a few
singles in the 1950s with an R&B band out of Los Angeles called the Ti-
tans. His 1961 solo effort "Voodoo Woman" made a little noise on WABC
New York's pop survey, but subsequent recordings failed to chart.

Jimi's Chitlin' Circuit road stories and list of famous entertainers
he had played with impressed Knight. Jimi returned to his hotel room
and told Pridgon of his promising encounter with Knight.

"I was in bed when Jimi came back," said Pridgon. "I was always
hearing this stuff that he was going to get a guitar and get this and
that, and someone was going to come for him one day. 'Yeah, well, is
this guy going to pay the rent? Because tomorrow, we're out of here.'"

Because she didn't lend an understanding ear, Jimi contacted Dean
Courtney, who happened to know Knight and later described him in
unvarnished terms: "Curtis was a full-time pimp when he didn't have
a music gig. But he was playing at a place called the Lighthouse up on
Broadway. I took Jimi up there, and he brought Jimi up to sit in and
gave him a solo, and Jimi rocked the whole place, unbelievably so.
Curtis really liked Jimi, and Jimi needed a gig bad. Curtis hired him."

The following day, Knight met Jimi at his hotel, and they walked
four blocks so that Knight could introduce Jimi to his manager, Ed
Chalpin. Knight was eager to find music for the civil rights–themed
lyrics he had recently penned, "How Would You Feel."

On August 11 race riots broke out in the Los Angeles suburb of Watts over tensions with the police, and after six days 34 people had been killed and approximately 4,000 arrested. Knight's timely new song touched on discrimination and the ongoing struggle for equal rights in America. Jimi arranged a melody heavily influenced by his new musical hero, Bob Dylan, and his 1965 hit "Like a Rolling Stone." Chalpin saw its commercial potential and set up a session to record it.

Ed Chalpin, an independent New York record producer, formed PPX Enterprises in 1961. He found his niche in the overseas record market by making cover versions of British and American hit songs in the languages of other countries. Chalpin dealt only with major labels, such as EMI, RCA Victor, and CBS, which had an international market for their product and distribution throughout the world.

Chalpin recorded at Studio 76, located on the seventh floor at 1650 Broadway, in the heart of New York's music district. He produced roughly seventy cover versions per year in this fashion. Before meeting Jimi, he had seen success with Bernd Spier's version of "Memphis," a big hit in Germany in 1964, and later with Clare Lapage's cover of Cher's "Bang Bang," which went to number one in Canada.

Knight was not a great singer, but he was supported on this new single with background vocals by Johnny Star and Jimi. "How Would You Feel" had a strong hook, aided by Jimi's fuzz guitar effect. Nevertheless, the single failed to see any chart action when it was released the following year. According to Knight, radio station managers considered it "too controversial" for airplay. Jimi, however, did receive credit for the arrangement on the single's label.

Because there was no upfront money for the Chalpin-Knight session, Jimi left town with the Isley Brothers for a weekend show at DePauw University, in Greencastle, Indiana. It was a quick thirty bucks, and then he headed back to New York.

On October 15, eight days after Jimi's recording session with Knight, Ed Chalpin signed him to an exclusive, long-term recording deal. The single-page agreement contracted Jimi to produce and play exclusively for PPX for three years (1965–1968), with a minimum of three sessions per year.

According to the terms of the contract, Jimi would receive only minimum scale for any arrangements he offered, would have no control over the release of the recordings, would not be compensated for equipment costs, and would receive a 1 percent royalty on the retail price of all records sold, but only after PPX had recouped its studio expenses. Jimi was paid a one-dollar advance. His brother Leon reported that Jimi derived benefit by arriving numerous times late at night, unannounced, at Chalpin's studio, with friends, to cut tracks into the wee hours.

During a 1968 pretrial deposition over the 1965 contract, Jimi described, under oath, the moment when Chalpin asked him if he could legally sign the PPX contract:

"He asked, did I have any contracts with anybody? So I said, 'Yes, I have a recording contract with Sue [Records]. . . . It came down to, how would you like to sign a contract as backing musician or producing things, maybe songs, or arranging them? And the way he explained it to me was that it had nothing at all to do with, I wouldn't . . . interfere with the Sue contract whatsoever."

Jimi also testified that he hadn't read or completely understood the PPX contract before signing it. Jimi's carelessness eventually led to legal proceedings that haunted him for the rest of his life. Since Jimi's death in 1970, Chalpin has gone to court several times regarding this financially rewarding 1965 agreement. In March 2007, he was ordered by the U.S. District Court, Southern District of New York to pay Experience Hendrix, LLC, which owns and licenses music rights for Jimi, almost $900,000 in monies generated from thirty-three master recordings done in 1965 with Curtis Knight at Chalpin's studio.

Knight, like Chalpin, also foresaw a long-term partnership with Jimi and talked about forming a band with him. However, in late October guitarist Gene Cornish of Joey Dee and the Starliters quit and moved to California. In need of a replacement for Cornish, Dee asked his drummer, Jimmy Mayes, to recruit a new guitarist. Born Joseph DiNicola, Dee and his Starliters became the house band at the Peppermint Lounge in New York City in 1960 and scored a number one hit with "Peppermint Twist" a year later.

Dee was unlike other white bandleaders of the time because he purposely integrated his group: three whites, three blacks. In certain parts of the country, some white audiences and club owners refused to accept racially mixed bands. Jimi himself hadn't performed in an integrated group since his Seattle days with the Rocking Kings.

To keep the racial balance in the group, the guitarist whom Mayes picked had to be black. Mayes got a lead from Johnny Star that the guitarist formerly with the Isley Brothers was staying at midtown's Alvin Hotel.

"When I got to Jimi's room, I saw this big, old, lazy, goofy-looking guy, laying on the bed with his big boots on the floor," said Mayes. "I had to wake him up. After talking to him for a while, he didn't show much interest in joining our band. But then I told him that Joey never treats anybody like a sideman and once you're in the group, you're a Starliter. He pulled out his guitar and played me a few things. I then called Joey and said, 'I think we got the guy. He's a nice looking guy, got a few rough edges, but we can fix him up. We then went over to Joey's house in Lodi, New Jersey, and plugged him in."

Dee had transformed his two-car garage into a makeshift rehearsal studio. Halfway through Jimi's second audition number, Dee told him to stop. He'd heard enough. Jimi was a member of the Starliters. Dee then explained how the show was structured. The set list included Dee's hits and top ten songs from the early 1960s. Jimi rapidly learned the rock-and-roll tunes and a few sanitized R&B numbers, many of which Jimi had played for the Isleys only a few months before.

"Hendrix told me how frustrated he was with Little Richard," recalled Dee. "He was such a taskmaster, and you could never steal any of his thunder. It was just the opposite in my group. If you had the talent, I'd share the spotlight. I gave him a few solos and even had him sing the *bop-a-shu-bop* parts in 'Peppermint Twist.' That's when I found out he couldn't sing too well, but he more than made up for it on the guitar."

The group now consisted of Joey Dee (lead vocals), Tommy Davis and David Brigati (background vocals), Jimmy Mayes (drums), Calvin Duke (keyboards), and "Jimmy James" Hendrix (guitar).

Joey Dee's fall tour mainly concentrated on the tristate area of Connecticut, New York, and New Jersey. Their first show was at the chic Manhattan discotheque Ondine. But Jimi was missing.

"I had to get a cab and go to 110th Street, to this apartment up in Harlem," recalled Mayes. "There was a party going on there, with many entertainers like Otis Redding. I kept knocking on the windows, but they wouldn't let me in. My reputation was now at stake because the guy I recommended was completely wiped out. I finally got him up and in the cab and made it back to the gig. Thankfully, he pulled through, and we did the show."

Mayes recalled another performance when Jimi suddenly appeared mere minutes before showtime. He casually explained to his fellow Starliters that he'd been getting his hair pressed and curled up in Harlem.

To keep better tabs on Jimi, Dee assigned Mayes as Jimi's roommate and caretaker for the rest of the tour. They became fast friends.

"He was going by Jimmy James," remembered Mayes. "I never knew his last name was Hendrix until later. He used to call me his 'little funk brother' because I could play that New Orleans funk on the drums."

In fact, Jimi and Mayes not only shared a room; they also had sex partners in the same room, one part of the open-minded world of Joey Dee and the Starliters. In addition to his band, Dee's entourage included several attractive female go-go dancers, and some nights the two Jimmys would have themselves a private party.

"Before our shows, all the go-go dancers would be lined up in the hallway backstage," Mayes fondly recalled. "We'd be stepping over chicks just to get to the stage. Sometimes, I'd get upset with Jimi because it seemed the girls always wanted the guitar player and not the drummer. We had two separate beds, and we'd bring the go-go dancers back to the room. There were no partitions. One night, the two of them made so much noise, my date and I had to use another part of the room."

On November 2, a severe snowstorm snarled traffic as Joey Dee and the Starliters struggled to make their way to the next gig in Buffalo, New York. Dee was scheduled to perform a six-night run at McVans, an Italian restaurant that doubled as a nightclub. The cold weather did not dampen the after-show extracurricular activities of the band at the Hotel Buffalo.

On one evening, singer Tommy Davis brought his date back to Brigati's hotel room, and soon thereafter Davis and his female partner were under the blankets. As the Starliters were a truly integrated band, Brigati was invited to join them.

"I'm not that type of person," admitted Brigati, "so I called up to the third floor where Jimmy Mayes, Jimi Hendrix, and Calvin Duke were staying and told them that things were getting pretty exciting down here." Duke didn't believe Brigati, but Jimi and Mayes were almost at the door before Brigati could hang up the phone.

Bashful at first, Brigati soon changed his mind about getting involved. "I was in the middle, but started to wiggle my way out, after Jimi took his cowboy boots off and joined in. I remember thinking at the time, looking at what was going on, 'Two minutes ago, nothing, and now, it's a circus.'"

According to Brigati, Jimi wasn't orally satisfying the lady, and Mayes showed him what to do. "I guess he had more experience," Brigati surmised. "Hendrix took over having regular sex with her, but he was still not exciting her, so Mayes took over again. That's when I decided to take a shower and get a bite to eat. By the time I came back, they were just winding up. Later on that evening, that girl told me it was the best night of her life. Hendrix thanked me the next day, too."

Gusty winds blew and eighteen inches of snow fell in some areas of Buffalo during the engagement at McVans, but it didn't stop Dee's loyal fans from coming out. Jimi came up with a rather imaginative idea for a special performance to thank the fans for their loyalty.

"We got snowed in," said Mayes.

Buffalo was like a snowbelt, so we rehearsed in our motel rooms. That's when Jimi said to me, "For our last set, let's bury the show." In other words, "Let's pull out all the stops." Jimi said, "Why don't we change clothes with the go-go dancers?" So we put on their dresses, and they put on our suits and bowties. Their dresses had those little fringes on the hem, above the knee, that shimmied when you moved. We even wore their go-go boots. We all danced on stage while playing "Shout." The crowd went wild. Jimi loved to joke and pull pranks all the time.

The tour with Joey Dee never seemed to lack for unpredictability. The next gig was at the Beach Ball Club, located on the beach in Revere, Massachusetts. The British group the Undertakers opened the show.

"They even had a casket on top of their van," Mayes claimed. "I remember they ran down the beach, jumped in the ocean, and came back and played their set, still wet. It was very strange."

Dee's tour turned around and headed south to Syracuse, New York, where the group played Mario's Club Au Go-Go in early December. The band was billed in the local press as "The Fabulous Joey Dee and his Starliters, The Kings of Go-Go." Mario's was known for its Italian cuisine, sexy strippers, and popular slogan "It's Good for Your Health." However, it wasn't so conducive to Jimi's well-being.

Prior to the engagement, singer Dave Brigati heard a loud noise coming from the club's basement and went down to investigate. To his surprise, he found a tough-looking guy angrily shooting his .22 caliber gun at a picture of his ex-girlfriend nailed to a wall. After the man fired a few more shots, Brigati excused himself and immediately ran upstairs.

Startled, the furious gunman followed Brigati, only to find his new white girlfriend was sitting at the bar talking to a black guitar player by the name of Jimmy James. "Before I knew it, the guy was running back to the basement to get his weapon," said Brigati. "With gun in hand, he was ready to take action." If not for Isadore "Cy" Mitchell, Dee's road manager, interceding, Jimi's career might have been over before it took off.

Brigati remembered Mitchell calming down the weapon-wielding man, saying: "'Hey, wait a minute. This guy owes us a lot of money, and we have to wait until we get back to New York before he can pay us back. Then you can take care of him.'"

The jealous man backed off and went downstairs. Jimi and the others breathed a sigh of relief.

Unfortunately, the Joey Dee tour was also eventful for another reason: racism. Prior to Jimi's arrival, Brigati recalled playing Baltimore, where a net was set up to keep the black members of the Starliters safe from thrown beer bottles. And even in 1965, in the midst of the civil rights movement, the integrated band still experienced hostility. Band members sometimes had to stay in black-owned motels, up to fifty miles away from gigs.

"It became quite common for the white guys in the band to run into a grocery store and buy food while the brothers waited in the van," said Brigati. "There were many incidents where we'd all walk into a restaurant or a bar and get stared down, and we decided it was just easier to leave."

Joey Dee was so busy with club dates, there was never an opportunity to get Jimi into the recording studio. His tenure lasted about two months and concluded by mid-December. Jimi returned to New York City the way he had left it: broke.

"Jimi was like a jewel," said Mayes. "We didn't realize we had this genius in our midst. Many entertainers he'd work with didn't respect him or his talent. When he left us, he pawned one of his guitars with Joey, but never came back to get it. Joey ended up selling it for $150."

DESPITE THE WILD ROAD STORIES HE AMASSED, JIMI WAS BITTER about the paltry "Peppermint Twist salary" he received and the lack of originality in the group. He later told a reporter, "I had all these ideas and sounds in my brain and playing this 'other people's music' all the time was hurting me. I jumped from the frying pan into the fire when I joined up with Joey Dee and the Starliters. Mind you, this is an out-of-sight group, but . . . " Jimi would never be satisfied until he discovered his own artistic voice in his own band.

While Jimi was on the Joey Dee tour, Curtis Knight assembled his new backup group, called the Squires. Jimi reconnected with Knight and joined the band for an afternoon audition at the Club Allegro in Garfield, New Jersey. Only a couple of hours and a missed connection might have prevented Jimi from being discovered earlier and finally achieving the acclaim he sought.

Legendary guitar player and pioneer of multitrack recording Les Paul, now beset with arthritis, entered the Club Allegro by chance, on the same day Jimi played. Paul had transitioned into artist management. By 1965, he had accumulated a stellar group of acts, including Simon and Garfunkel, country singer Willie Nelson, and guitarist José Feliciano.

Paul and his son Gene were taking master tapes from their home in Mahwah, New Jersey, to Columbia Records in New York. "I came up playing with the best of the best jazz and pop musicians in the 30s and 40s," said Paul, "and I believe if you want to stay at the top of anything, you've got to remain curious. That's why I dropped by places like the Allegro. There was a guy on the stage, left-handed, playing the hell out of his guitar. Real raunchy."

Paul asked the bartender for Jimi's name, but he didn't know. Realizing his son was still outside in the car, Paul decided to come back after his visit to Columbia Records.

"When we got back to the Allegro, Jimi was gone. I said to the bartender, 'Where is that guy?' 'Are you kidding?' the bartender said. 'He was too loud. We threw him out.'"

Paul searched for Jimi in local musician unions and clubs in north and central New Jersey and Harlem. No one could match a name to his description.

Still obsessed, Les Paul told his manager to hunt him down. The following year, Paul's manager told him that the left-handed guitar player that had amazed Paul in New Jersey had died in a fire, started accidentally with a cigarette.

In 1967, London Records asked Paul to come out of retirement and produce one more album. He agreed but wanted to hear what the current crop of guitar players sounded like.

"Walt McGuire with London [Records] brought over ten albums and threw them on the carpet and said, 'Here are some of the best guitarists,'" remembered Paul. "One of them, the picture, as soon as I saw it, I said, 'There's my guitar player!' He didn't die in a fire."

He was looking at the cover *of Are You Experienced*. Les Paul missed by about two hours his chance to be forever known—in addition to all his other accomplishments—as the man who discovered Jimi Hendrix.

DURING THE TIME JIMI WAS WITH CURTIS KNIGHT AND THE Squires, members came and went, but things really clicked when the lineup included Marion Booker (drums), Hank "Napoleon" Anderson (bass), and Nate Edmonds (keyboards). Knight handled lead vocals and filled in with rhythm guitar. "How Would You Feel," the single Jimi had cut with Knight back in October, was still unreleased. Knight knew he was going to lose Jimi if he didn't land steady club gigs and some studio work.

Jimi considered Knight's ensemble nothing more than, in his words, "a juke box band" because it rarely played originals and the sets consisted of mostly top ten R&B and pop tunes. The group started playing in small clubs such as George's Club 20 in Hackensack, New Jersey, the site of one of Jimi's earliest live recordings.

Lithofayne Pridgon remembered an incident that took place on December 26 at that location. "Curtis wanted the set list mixed up with some slow and fast songs," recalled Pridgon. "Jimi told me he didn't care if I danced with somebody, just as long as it was on a fast one. No touching. But it seemed like all they were playing were slow ones that night."

Jimi grew extremely jealous when he noticed Pridgon's dance partner leaning over to plant a kiss on her cheek. The situation turned ugly, according to Pridgon: "Jimi jumped off the stage and came over to confront the guy I was dancing with. Still plugged in and playing, he nudged the guy's back with the guitar's tuning pegs and told him to back off his girl. The guy turned around in disbelief and said, 'You don't tell me who to dance with,' and then went and got his gang and came back. Jimi saw what was going on and said to me, 'Well, I guess it's okay if you talk to him.'"

Despite Jimi's own flourishing sexuality and numerous liaisons, he was still jealous of Pridgon and tried to control her behavior and movements. One of the most extreme examples of Jimi exerting control over Pridgon occurred when he physically restrained her for hours in one of their many New York hotel rooms.

"One time, Jimi tied me up," Pridgon remembered.

I woke up from a dream, ankle tied, one arm. He was working on another ankle with a dirty, stiff, nasty, stinking sock. It felt like somebody had put a heavy tire on my feet. "Be quiet," he said. He was jealous and didn't want me running around while he going off to rehearse with Curtis. When he came back, he wanted me there. I then started screaming, so he put one of his shirts around my mouth. He was gone three or four hours. I fell back asleep. When stuff like that happened, I'd try to get away. Eventually, I'd go back.

According to Pridgon, Jimi's temper was often uncontrollable:

Jimi fought a lot and whipped Johnny Star's ass on occasion. Once at a club, he had me pinned down under a booth, with his knee on my chest. Billy Hamburg, an albino dancer, tried to talk to him and told him to get off me. He turned around and lunged at him and "Big Jimmy" the bouncer. Little Richard came to my rescue a couple times. But he pounced at him, too. One time, someone told me to get over to the Hotel Theresa. Jimi had gone mad, all crazy. He tore up the room and pulled the phone out of the wall, but when I got there, things had got back to normal.

Most casual observers saw Jimi offstage as quiet, contemplative, polite, absentminded, even ethereal. But what Pridgon experienced was likely the repressed anger Jimi harbored from an upbringing in an alcoholic household full of infidelity and domestic violence. "He used to always talk about some devil or something that was in him that he didn't have any control over," Pridgon sadly recalled.

He didn't know what made him act the way he acted, and what made him say the things he said, and songs and different things that came out of him. First I'd think it was a copout, when he'd really done me in, right? And he would say: "I don't know what came over me. I really can't understand." He would grab his hair or cry. Oh, Lord, it was sad when he would cry. Maybe he was the first man or maybe the only man that I'd ever seen crying. It just killed me when he cried. It seemed to me that he was so tormented and just torn apart, like he really was obsessed with something really evil.

9

Next Planet, Please

(JANUARY–JUNE 1966)

IN THE WINTER OF 1966, JIMI HENDRIX WAS A DIVIDED MAN, CON-
flicted in numerous ways.

He was a musical gypsy, and yet he could not suppress the Seattle
childhood that haunted and shaped him. Despite his youthful energy
and love of the road, the constant travel and lack of a permanent address wore him out. His infrequent calls to Leon were a radical departure from the surrogate parent he used to be for his little brother. He
sent a series of postcards to his father, and he could not alleviate his
need to impress Al, to assure his father that he had indeed followed
the right path in life. But it was clear in his mail to Al that he deeply
missed his relatives, who had helped protect and raise him.

Jimi was divided about which musical genre was his. He had an innate love of all kinds of music and the ability to play any style the gig
required. But his relentless pursuit of a then-experimental rock sound
consistently led to him being fired by rhythm and blues bands. And
rock and roll as a genre was in a state of change itself.

Jimi knew there was a schism in his own racial identity. Uptown in
Harlem, R&B clubs did not support his sonic experimentations on
guitar and, frankly, did not care for his style of dress either. He had

been given great freedom in Joey Dee's Starliters, but he was still playing other people's music, and he was subject to racial prejudice in the South. That an integrated rock band was still unacceptable in certain parts of the country indicated how far America still needed to evolve.

And finally, the part of Jimi that wanted to have his own group was at war with the part of him that simply was not ready. The harsh fact was that in the beginning of 1966, Jimi did not have the confidence or defined artistic direction to create his own band, despite how much he resented playing other musicians' music. He still did not have enough songs to create an album, and his hesitancy about his own singing voice held him back from achieving what he wanted most.

All of these factors might well have contributed to a troubled soul. The desperately poor little boy who had had to politely accept the generosity of neighbors and friends in Seattle was now the stunningly gifted young man with a persistent belief in his own eventual success. He devoted his waking life to playing his guitar and trying to find opportunities for work. The man who spoke shyly and sometimes barely looked at those he was introduced to was also not immune to rages that turned violent toward those closest to him.

When Jimi finally found his way in the music world, some of his most emotionally powerful work opened a window into how low he sank within himself. "I Don't Live Today," dedicated to the genocide of the American Indian, contains one of the most despondent utterances in all of rock, when Jimi, amid his wailing guitar, murmurs, "There ain't no life nowhere." In "Manic Depression," his lyrics open with the insistence that he knows what he wants but "I just don't know how to go about getting it."

AND THOUGH HE MOVED WITH LITHOFAYNE PRIDGON FROM Harlem to an apartment to its south, in Park West Village, he still was not about to commit himself to one woman. There would soon be three other women who were important to his life in New York, and, amazingly, he managed to spend significant time with all of them.

Pridgon recalled, "People had to survive and the music industry wasn't paying that well, so most people ended up as hustlers, pimps, or were involved in other ways to make money, like dealing drugs. . . . I knew musicians that were also janitors because that was the only legitimate source of income they could find."

Jimi had turned down "Fat Man" Jack Taylor about dealing in Harlem, and he refused to look for menial service jobs. Pridgon and her mother helped him out financially, but if he made twenty dollars at a gig, "that was a banner night," as Pridgon put it.

When he was not performing, Jimi gave Pridgon guitar lessons. The two cowrote songs together with unorthodox titles such as "House of Confusion," "Alligator Sun," and, suggesting Jimi's love of science fiction, mysticism, and yearning to transcend his status in life, "Next Planet, Please."

On January 6, they went down to the Apollo to catch the last night of a big blues show that included Sonny Terry and Brownie McGhee, T-Bone Walker, John Lee Hooker, Muddy Waters, and headliner Bo Diddley. It was in the middle of a twelve-day transit strike, when all buses and subways were shut down. Within the Apollo, sheltered from the exceedingly bitter cold of that year, Jimi reveled in the performances, despite the fact that he had already edged away from rhythm and blues as a career choice.

Shortly after the Apollo show, Jimi sat down and wrote his father a postcard, alluding to the difficulties of becoming a working musician and assuring Al and his other relatives he had not abandoned the blues music they had all grown up appreciating: "I'm just dropping in a few words to let you know everything's so-so here in this big raggedy city of New York—I hope everyone is alright—tell Leon I said hello—I'll write you a letter—And will try to send you a decent picture—So until then I hope you're doing alright, Tell Ben & Ernie I play the blues like they NEVER heard—"

Still under contract to producer Ed Chalpin, Jimi was summoned for some session work with actress and *Playboy* centerfold model Jayne Mansfield (Vera Jayne Palmer). The busty pinup yearned to be accepted as a talented film actress after winning a Golden Globe award for Most Promising Newcomer in 1957 and performing in successful Hollywood films *The Girl Can't Help It* and *Will Success Spoil Rock*

Hunter? She was in a revue at the Latin Quarter called *French Dressing* that featured dozens of sexy showgirls. Her performances there lasted from January 18 through February 28.

Capitalizing on her nightclub popularity, Chalpin coaxed Mansfield into his studio to cut a pop single with his new session player, Jimmy Hendrix. The session yielded two tracks, titled "As the Clouds Drift By" and, on the B side, "Suey."

"Suey," a silly bump-and-grind tune, was ideally suited to Mansfield's persona. It featured Jimi on bass and lead guitar. Philadelphia DJ Douglas "Jocko" Henderson, on drums, had cowritten the song with Chalpin. Henderson was an East Coast radio icon on WHAT-AM and known for his opening line: "Hello, Daddy-o and Mommy-o. This is Jocko." His famous "rocket ship" shows at the Apollo featured his entrance from a rocket suspended on wires, complete with sound effects and smoke pouring out of his spacecraft.

Mansfield's spoken words on "Suey" were replete with sexual innuendo. When the song came to a break, Jimi slid his fingers down the neck of the bass as Mansfield stage-whispered sultry lines such as "It makes my liver quiver." The A side, "As the Clouds Drift By," was a somewhat more serious musical effort for the sex symbol, but her limited vocal range trivialized the song. In her *New York Times* obituary, after a tragic automobile accident in 1967, Mansfield's singing style was defined as "a soft-voiced coo punctuated with squeals."

Shortly after the session, *Billboard* reported that Chalpin and Henderson planned to launch a new label, Chalco Records, and that the first release was going to be "Suey." The song had commercial potential as a novelty record but wasn't released until after Mansfield's sudden death.

Jimi put further commitments to Knight and Chalpin on hold when a vacancy opened in King Curtis's band, the Kingpins, in mid-January. From the mid-1950s through the 1960s, tenor saxophonist King Curtis was featured on hit records such as Ben E. King's "Spanish Harlem," Bobby Darin's "Splish Splash," and the Coasters' "Yakety Yak." In 1965, he opened for the Beatles on their American tour.

Despite the Little Richard fiasco at the Paramount in April 1965, Curtis and his band were impressed with how Jimi traded riffs with

Glen Willings. "We were a well-traveled band at the time Jimi joined us," said Curtis bassist Chuck Rainey.

> We were doing six sets a night in club gigs, traveling around the Eastern Seaboard. We played a little bit of everything: big band, R&B, jazz, and pop. A typical one-hour show started with all of us playing, and then about halfway through the set, Curtis featured someone special. He used a variation of male and female singers, dancers, James Brown impersonators, and people like that. When we had Jimi, he fit in real well during that spot. Curtis let him go wild, playing the guitar behind his neck or with his tongue. Jimi usually did an Elmore James tune. In fact, Jimi back then reminded me of a young Elmore, doing the same riffs and style of playing.

The first King Curtis recording session that utilized Jimi took place on January 21. The song was called "Help Me (Get the Feeling)," and Curtis included fellow Fort Worth, Texan, Ray Sharpe on vocals.

Sharpe needed no aid in recalling the "Help Me" recording: "The session ran about two days, and it was phenomenal to watch Jimi work. I could tell he came from a blues background, but that wasn't the only way he played. He could interject just about any style he wanted in whatever he was playing."

As February approached, Curtis organized a tour covering parts of the East Coast, but before the Kingpins hit the road, Jimi had to learn their set list. A regular at Small's Paradise in Harlem, Curtis conducted pretour rehearsals there.

Drummer Ray Lucas observed: "On a lot of the songs that Jimi didn't know, the bass player had to whisper the chords to him. But I never, in all my fucking life, saw anybody pick up songs as fast as Jimi did that night."

"On that tour," said rhythm guitarist Cornell Dupree, "we mostly did frat parties and concerts in the little college towns of upstate New York and some in Virginia and Kentucky. We'd leave to play and be gone for the whole weekend, but all Jimi brought with him was two shirts, a tube of toothpaste, and a toothbrush. That's it. He traveled light."

When the tour concluded, Jimi resumed working with the other Curtis in his life, Curtis Knight and the Squires, in clubs and in the studio. During a mid-March session at Studio 76, the group recorded one of Jimi's originals, with the painfully accurate title "I Ain't Taking Care of No Business." After securing a licensing deal with RSVP Records, Ed Chalpin made plans to release Knight's "How Would You Feel" single. And for the first time in his life, Jimi's name appeared on a record label, a credit for his musical arrangement.

IN EARLY APRIL, AROUND 1:00 A.M., JIMI SAT ALONE IN A RESTAU-rant on 52nd and Broadway. He was so poor, all he had in front of him was a glass of water. He noticed a young, attractive, light-skinned black girl sitting nearby and smiled at her. She was a runaway, new to Manhattan. Her real name was Diana Carpenter, but to avoid her parents finding her, she used the street name Regina Jackson. She was only sixteen years old, and to survive, she had become a prostitute.

"I saw this real skinny guy," Carpenter remembered, "but he had the biggest, prettiest eyes I have ever seen."

Carpenter's self-published autobiography gives some clues as to the nature of her relationship with Jimi. She wrote that she was molested by an uncle when she was five, in Minneapolis. Harboring her secret, she ran away at twelve and again at thirteen, eventually arriving in New York.

Jimi used a line on Carpenter that he had employed before, but it genuinely came from his idealization of and abandonment by his mother, Lucille.

"I was told," said Carpenter, "I resembled his mother and maybe that was the connection between us. When I first met Jimi, I knew there was a void in his life: the mother's love he so much needed."

Jimi stayed at the California Hotel, where Carpenter soon joined him, but the couple eventually moved to the Lexington Hotel.

Carpenter claimed that when she revealed her terrifying childhood molestation memories to Jimi, he, too, had a similar situation he wanted to share: "I don't recall if it was a police officer or a youth counselor, but it was somebody Jimi had confidence in that sexually molested him as a teenager. He said he was afraid to tell anybody and lived with this secret until now." If so, it was a story Jimi never shared with anyone else.

Carpenter recalled that their part-time relationship lasted through August. Jimi's paltry pay from random gigs with Curtis Knight and others hardly covered their $120 per week rent at the California Hotel. At times, they resorted to shoplifting food. Once, they were caught by a shop owner who chased them down the street. According to Carpenter, she laughed as Jimi dropped fruit as they ran, but Jimi was furious and disgusted with the way he was living.

"We didn't always know if we were going to have a place to stay," Carpenter said. "I told Jimi, 'You have a daddy. Why don't you call him and let him know what's going on?' Jimi said 'no,' and didn't want to let his father know what was really going on in New York. He wanted his father to be proud of him."

Even though Jimi pleaded with her to give up prostitution, Carpenter did not. Once, she was kidnapped and eventually returned to their room wearing stolen shoes and a pair of overalls, allegedly prompting a belt beating by Jimi.

What brought about the end of her prostitution, as well as their brief affair, was Carpenter's pregnancy in May. There is evidence that she was arrested three times during her relationship with Jimi, and in her third court appearance the judge threatened to send her to Westville Correctional Facility in Indiana for three years if arrested again. Whether this legal admonition or an additional arrest prompted Carpenter to pack her bags and return home to Minneapolis, one thing is certain: She left without telling Jimi of her decision to leave or her whereabouts.

Carpenter gave birth to her daughter Tamika on February 11, 1967. By then, Jimi had exploded as a major act in Europe. She reminded him several times through letters from her attorney that he was the father, and she showed up at concerts at the Oakland Coliseum in 1969 and in Berkeley in 1970. After the Oakland show, Jimi asked her to follow his limousine to San Francisco International Airport, where she gave him a photograph of Tamika, two years old, in a pink dress, lacy white socks, and black leather shoes. Carpenter claimed that his reaction on looking at the photo was, "She has my eyes, doesn't she?" When Jimi died in September 1970, he hadn't given the court a requested blood test to determine if he was Tamika's biological father.

ON MAY 5, THERE WAS A RECORD INDUSTRY RELEASE PARTY FOR vocalist Percy Sledge, who, after being signed to Atlantic Records, delivered the hit "When a Man Loves a Woman." Sledge, a former Sheffield, Alabama, hospital orderly, recorded what would become his signature ballad back in February on a twenty-five-dollar Sears and Roebuck record maker. A local disc jockey eventually got it in the hands of Atlantic's Jerry Wexler and Ahmet Ertegun, and it went to the very top of *Billboard*'s Top 100 and R&B charts.

The evening show at New York's Prelude Club featured Sledge, Esther Phillips, and Wilson Pickett. King Curtis and the Kingpins were the house band.

Sledge stated that Pickett, in the audience, was invited up to sing his hit "In the Midnight Hour." When he declined, Curtis and Sledge began to sing it, and that got "Wicked" Wilson Pickett flying onto the stage to put on a fiery performance.

"After the show," Sledge said, "I approached Curtis. I told him, 'I'd really like to steal your guitar player.' Curtis said he really hoped to hang onto Jimi for at least another year or so, but after that, nobody would be able to hold him down. He's sure to be a superstar."

Just when things seemed to be going well for him, Jimi had another case of "admired, hired, fired." "Jimi left us shortly after that show," said Chuck Rainey, "but it wasn't over money. Curtis always paid on time, right after a gig. Like me, he must have got tired of playing the same songs over and over again, like 'Misty' and 'When a Man Loves a Woman.' I still get sick to my stomach every time I hear those songs."

Jimi's roommate Dean Courtney remembered the situation differently. Shortly after leaving Courtney for a gig with King Curtis at the Park Sheraton on Seventh Avenue, Jimi returned, asking to borrow his tuxedo. Shortly thereafter, Jimi was back, angry and demoralized.

"Jimi," Courtney recalled, "in his Snagglepuss voice, said, 'He pissed me off. I told King Curtis to kiss my ass.' . . . He said King was talking down to him about coming back late and not having a tux. He reprimanded him on stage, right in front of the crowd, so Jimi just walked out."

Jimi's string of firings was counterbalanced by the fact that he kept getting hired by some of the greatest acts in 1960s R&B. Shortly after his parting with Curtis, Jimi briefly became sideman for the legendary soul duo Sam & Dave. Sam Moore (Samuel Hicks) and David Prater were technically Atlantic Records artists, but the label "leased" them to Stax. They were in *Billboard*'s R&B charts for five months with "Hold On, I'm Comin" in 1966, hitting the top in June.

But Jimi set a new personal speed record for getting thrown out of a group. Sam Moore remembered Jimi's first gig with them at a midtown New York club. "He plugged in," said Moore. "We start doing, 'Hold On, I'm Comin,' and he starts doin' this *nawaaaaahhh*. You know how Jimi played. I cut my eyes over at him. Next time, I go over to him and said, 'There is no solo in that, Jimi. Stop.'" When Jimi did it a second time, Moore fired him on the spot.

For a brief period in May, Jimi jumped back in with Curtis Knight and the Squires. Knight finally came through and got his band an exciting, well-paying gig at a brand new hot spot. Cheetah, formerly the dance halls the Riviera Terrace and, before that, the Arcadia Ballroom, was an elaborate, three-floor Manhattan discotheque at 1686 Broadway at 53rd Street that opened on April 28, 1966. It was co-owned by Olivier Coquelin—who had created Le Club in 1960, one of Manhattan's first discos—and financed by Borden Stevenson, the middle son of 1956 presidential candidate Adlai Stevenson.

It was the most stylish club in Manhattan. Cheetah had an 8,000-square-foot dance floor and a wheel in the ceiling that bounced colored light off strips of reflective mylar in response to musical tones. The 1,800-person-capacity venue had other rooms devoted to Scopitones (jukeboxes that showed short, sixteen-millimeter color music films), a reading area, and a "Space Age Boutique," which sold sexy, hip clothing. It included hanging, cylindrical dressing booths for men and women. Inside each one was a photo of a member of the opposite sex leering lasciviously at the customer as he or she changed clothes.

Cheetah's opening night entertainers included singer Monti Rock III, the Chambers Brothers, and Joe & Roy & Company. Rock (Joseph Montanez Jr.) made a rapid transition to the pop scene, from a gay Puerto Rican hairdresser to club performer who, in 1966, presaged the next decade's disco era.

"Olivier Coquelin put me in white satin with white pancake makeup," Rock recounted, "fashion designer Roy Halston made me this big silver hat to wear, and I came riding down in an elevator when the Chambers Brothers started my set. They sang 'Ain't That Peculiar,' and they made me look like a star."

Time magazine described the scene at Cheetah's opening: "Men in flowered shirts and wide ties squired girls wearing everything from Pucci prints and Paco Rabanne disks to weirdies from London's Carnaby Street and vinyl suits from Manhattan's Third Avenue boutiques."

Two weeks later, Curtis Knight and the Squires did a two-week run at Cheetah, May 12 to 25. To stand out from the other bands on the bill, Knight decided they needed to wear attire that fit the name of the club.

"Jimi and I thought we'd better get some of those way-out clothes ourselves," said Knight. "We went down to the Village and found some material that was almost the same decor at the club, and we designed ourselves shirts and jackets out of it. We added white bell bottoms, and we looked like we were coming out of the walls."

Marion Booker, the Squires' drummer, took proud notice of the reaction of their toughest possible audience: other musicians. "Bands would come from all over with their mouths and eyes wide open, just watching us. Jimi played the guitar with his elbow, tongue, teeth, and everything else he could use to get a new sound. I'd do all these tricks with my drumsticks, where I'd throw them up and catch them behind my back . . . bouncing them off the drums. They would look at us like, 'What planet are you guys from?'"

One of those who watched in delighted awe at Cheetah was Salvador Dali, the surrealist painter, who told his table guests how "psychedelic" he thought Jimi's music was. Jimi had not yet had his first hallucinogen, but it was to follow in the weeks to come, and the experience would profoundly change him.

Charles Neville of the Neville Brothers claimed that Cheetah, unlike other clubs, could rightfully claim that it had "nonstop music." "I remember seeing Jimi play the Cheetah Club with Curtis Knight," recalled Neville. "There were three bands each night, and each band would get several forty-five-minute sets. So when one band's time was up, the singers in the band would start leaving the stage. Their rhythm section kept playing while the new band took over. One drummer kept the cymbals going as the new drummer sat down and kept the same rhythm going. You went out of one song right into another. No talking in between songs, no pauses."

Jimi returned the following week, May 26, to Cheetah, but this time as a guest player with the Philadelphia-based Carl Holmes and the Commanders. The Commanders' gig at Cheetah lasted only a week, but Brooklyn-born folksinger Richie Havens was there one night and was so nonplussed by Jimi's performance that he actually walked up to the stage during the show, knelt down, and looked under it to see if Jimi was using some special equipment to get his sounds.

"The band went on and I turned around from the bar," Havens said, "and there was a guy standing there biting his guitar. I thought, 'Nooo, he's not playing the notes like that.' It turned out to be Jimi Hendrix. He had gotten the gig with Holmes through this guy from the union [Musicians Local 802]. I didn't even think that the union got rock guitarists jobs. So when the band was finished, I went backstage and said, 'Where in the hell have you been all of my life?'"

Another amazed fan walked up and asked Jimi how he created such sounds with his guitar. Havens heard Jimi, in his low-key, dryly humorous manner, reply: "I don't play guitar. I play amplifier."

Havens became a good friend to Jimi, encouraging him to sing and lead his own band in the burgeoning coffeehouse scene. He suggested Jimi check out Manny Roth, owner of a small, basement club, Cafe Wha?. It was Havens who later showed Jimi the chord changes on Dylan's "All Along the Watchtower," prior to Jimi recording the definitive version. And sadly, it was Havens who saw an exhausted, unhealthy, frustrated, and paranoid Jimi at the Isle of Wight concert years later in 1970 and gave him the name of an attorney to help him escape from a manager who was leading him to ruin. It was a lifeline that Jimi never took.

CHEETAH PROVIDED AN OPPORTUNITY FOR JIMI TO MEET MANY people who played major roles in his life as he neared the turning point of his career. It was there Jimi crossed paths with Carol Shiroky, a beautiful blonde everyone called Kim. Their romantic relationship started with one of Jimi's most surprising pickup lines, and three days later they moved in together at the Lennox Hotel.

"I was Curtis' girlfriend," admitted Shiroky.

> Jimi and I started making eyes through a whole performance at the Cheetah club, and Curtis noticed it. He pulled me aside and told me, "Don't you think I see the looks passing between you and Jimi?" . . . Next thing, Curtis walked out and Jimi came over and sat down at the table. He then leaned over to me and said, "I want to tell you something, but I know you'll laugh." I said: "I won't. I promise I won't. What is it?" He said, "The one thing I want to do more than anything in the world is kiss you on your knee." That's the one place I don't think he ever did.

But Shiroky, like the other women Jimi temporarily lived with, was subject to his frustrations and mood swings. "Jimi used to come home really pissed off, four nights out of six," said Shiroky, "for whatever reason: angry at Curtis, fighting with the band, fighting with the material. He came in one night . . . came to bed. He got up. He wrote something down. He threw it at me. He said, 'Read this,' and went back to bed. He sounded very hostile in this poem."

In it, Jimi bitterly referred to "my friends of fashion" being "my enemies of thought." He condemned what he felt was the false friendship and questionable acceptance of those he knew in his sphere.

JIMI WAS FED UP WITH CURTIS KNIGHT'S ATTEMPTS TO BE *THE* guitar player on stage, despite limited skills. Jimi was jealous he was

Jimi at four years old, Leschi
Park, Seattle, Washington.
DOLORES L. HAMM

Ninth grade yearbook photo of James Hendrix
(far right), Washington Middle School, Seattle.
JOE GRAY'S FAMILY COLLECTION

Private James Marshall Hendrix,
U.S. Army Infantry Training Center,
11th Battle Group, 3rd Brigade, Fort
Ord, California, 1961.

"Open House" at Fort Ord, 1961. Jimi with unknown drummer, during army basic training.

Jimi performing with the King Kasuals at the Club Del Morocco, Nashville, Tennessee, December 23, 1962. COURTESY OF EXPERIENCE MUSIC PROJECT, SEATTLE, WA

Joyce's House of Glamour, Nashville, circa 1963. Jimi, Billy Cox, and Alphonso Young lived in rooms upstairs, while performers at the Club Del Morocco. COURTESY OF THE COUNTRY MUSIC HALL OF FAME ® AND MUSEUM/THEODORE ACKLEN JR.

The King Kasuals, January 1963, Club Del Morocco. Left to right: Jimi Hendrix, Billy Cox, Alphonso Young, unknown (drums), and Buford Majors (saxophone).

Jimi performing with Hank Ballard and the Midnighters, March 14, 1963, Charleston, South Carolina.

The King Kasuals at Nashville's Jolly Roger Club, May 1963. Left to right: Jimi Hendrix (guitar), Billy Cox (bass), Harold Nesbit (drums), Leonard Moses (guitar), Buford Majors (saxophone), Harry Batchelor (vocals). DAVID PEARCY COLLECTION

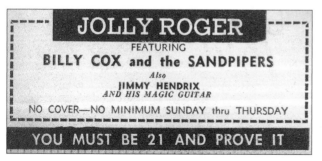

Jimi's first credited club billing. July 1963, Jolly Roger Club, Nashville.
STEVEN ROBY/STRAIGHT AHEAD ARCHIVES COLLECTION

Jimi and Little Richard, February 21, 1965. Fillmore Auditorium, San Francisco, California.

Little Richard and the Crown
Jewels, April 2, 1965, San Leandro
Roller Rink, San Leandro, California.

EMPLOYEE'S STATEMENT OF EARNINGS
AND DEDUCTIONS - DETACH AND RETAIN

LITTLE RICHARD'S PRODUCTIONS

PERIOD ENDING *May 27,* 19 *65*

EMP.
NAME *Maurice James*

TOTAL EARNINGS		*200 00*
SOCIAL SECURITY TAX	*7 25*	
WITHHOLDING U. S. INCOME TAX	*26 20*	
S. D. I.		
TOTAL DEDUCTIONS		*33 45*
NET PAY		*166 55*

Possibly Jimi's final paycheck
from Little Richard.
STEVEN ROBY/STRAIGHT AHEAD
ARCHIVES COLLECTION

Jimi with the Isley Brothers, August 5, 1965, Atlantic Studios, New York City.
COURTESY OF EXPERIENCE MUSIC PROJECT, SEATTLE, WA

In concert with the Isley Brothers, August 1965, Essex County Country Club, West Orange, New Jersey. COURTESY OF EXPERIENCE MUSIC PROJECT, SEATTLE, WA

Jimi with members of Joey Dee and the Starliters. Left to right: Jimi and Joey Dee. November 1965, McVans, Buffalo, New York. COURTESY PRIVATE COLLECTION OF LARRY MARION

Curtis Knight and the Squires publicity photo, 1965. Left to right: Jimi Hendrix, Marion Booker, Curtis Knight (front), and Horace "Ace" Hall.

Jimi's first arrangement credit. Released March 1966.

At Cheetah, New York City. May 1966. Left to right: Nate Edmonds Sr., Jimi Hendrix, Marion Booker (rear), Hank Anderson (kneeling), and Curtis Knight.

Wilson Pickett: "I will always remember Jimi being a very warm person, a superstar. In my opinion, he was a superstar from the day he was born."

PHOTOGRAPH BY: WILLIAM "POPSIE" RANDOLPH

Atlantic Records release party, May, 5, 1966, Prelude Club, New York City. Left to right: King Curtis, Percy Sledge, Cornel Dupree, and Jimi Hendrix.

PHOTOGRAPH BY: WILLIAM "POPSIE" RANDOLPH

Atlantic Records release party, May 5, 1966, Prelude Club, New York City.
"I used to dream in Technicolor that 1966 was the year that something would happen to me. So eventually, it's come true." —Jimi Hendrix

PHOTOGRAPH BY WILLIAM "POPSIE" RANDOLPH

Linda Keith, as a model, prior to helping Chas Chandler discover Jimi in Greenwich Village.
KEYSTONE/STRINGER/HULTON ARCHIVE /GETTY IMAGES

Café Wha?, Greenwich Village, New York, 1966, the venue where Jimi broke through.
MICHAEL OCHS ARCHIVES/GETTY IMAGES

March 1967, The Jimi Hendrix Experience, London, England. Left to right: Mitch Mitchell, Jimi Hendrix, Noel Redding, Chas Chandler. K & K ULF KRUGER OHG/REDFERNS/GETTY IMAGES

not the one playing Knight's Gretsch White Falcon guitar with gold sparkle trim and larger amp.

"I got a cheap guitar and a small amp," Jimi told Dean Courtney. "Curtis can't play good, and he turns his big amp up and my little amp down."

Shiroky joined the chorus of voices urging Jimi to go out on his own. "Jimi always used to say he was not from this planet. He was from somewhere out in space. That was his great line when he got in a crazy-ass mood: 'I'm not from this planet.'" When she told him Knight needed Jimi, not the other way around, Jimi admitted with shame that he stayed because he used a guitar Knight owned.

"So two days later," Shiroky said, "we went down to Manny's [Music Store] and I bought his first Strat [Fender Stratocaster]. It was all white with a rosewood neck. I watched him sit for a week—*a week*— before he played it. He was filing the frets so he could change the strings. For a week, that was like his baby. He gave birth. The first time he played it was on my birthday, and it was the first time they ever did 'Wild Thing' in public."

"Wild Thing" had been written by Chip Taylor and popularized by the British group the Troggs. When Jimi first heard "Wild Thing" played over the radio that summer, he immediately jumped out of the shower, hair in rollers, picked up his guitar, and gave Shiroky a performance, naked and dripping wet. Fortunately, his new Stratocaster was not plugged in at the time.

Jimi's spontaneity and lack of regularity in his life made Shiroky realize she could never have a long-term relationship with Jimi. "If you tried to hold him down, that's when you lost him," she said. "There were nights he didn't come home, and I knew he was in someone else's bed, and I would never question him, because if I did, he'd be gone." Shiroky, like other women, accepted his rules. When Jimi wasn't with Shiroky, he was spending the night with either Diana Carpenter, Lithofayne Pridgon, or a new lady he'd met, one who led him to the stardom he'd long dreamed of and worked for so completely.

Linda Keith was a striking, twenty-year-old, top London fashion model. She arrived in New York a month ahead of her boyfriend, Keith Richards of the Rolling Stones. Even though she had access to

Richards's reserved suite at the Holiday Inn, Linda preferred staying with her friends Roberta Goldstein and Mark Kaufman at their apartment on 57th Street.

One evening, they all wandered into Cheetah, where a lanky guitar player in Curtis Knight's band instantly captivated Linda's attention. "I asked Mark if he would see if Jimi wanted to come have a drink with us when he finished his set," recalled Linda. "Jimi came and we chatted, and I wanted to know everything, who he was and where he was from and what he was doing." Linda was shocked to learn that Jimi hadn't heard of many of the English bands she'd been exposed to, and she invited him back to Mark's apartment after the show. "I played him loads of my favorite tracks. We bonded."

Linda was amused by Jimi's charming innocence when it came to current drug jargon for a popular hallucinogen. "I asked him if he wanted to take any drugs, and he said that he wasn't sure. 'Like what?' And I said, 'Well, would you like some acid?' And he said, 'No. I don't think I want any acid. But I would like to try some of that LSD.' And we did."

Jimi's first LSD trip took place while the drug was still legal for personal use. It had been effective in certain psychotherapeutic cases. The Drug Abuse Control Amendments of 1965 went into effect on February 1, 1966. Sales and distribution of LSD merely required a license, until it was fully outlawed two years later.

Jimi's LSD experience with Keith at the Goldstein/Kaufman apartment had a profound effect upon him. The red velvet walls and decor influenced Jimi's writing of his classic electric blues number, "Red House." He began to regularly take the drug and encourage his inexperienced friends to try it as well.

Jimi was gone for days, but when he finally resurfaced, Carol Shiroky was given a rare glimpse of where Jimi went mentally, visually, and spiritually, under the influence of lysergic acid diethylamide-25. "I met these English people," he explained to Shiroky, "and this English chick gave me this drug called acid. At one point, I looked in the mirror, and I thought I was Marilyn Monroe."

Because his first band was the Jimi Hendrix Experience and his first album was *Are You Experienced*, it's apparent that he was interested not only in the sensation of being high but also a higher state of con-sciousness, one he attested to on his title track with the phrase "Not necessarily stoned but beautiful."

During the weeks that followed his first trip, Jimi and Linda Keith continued a romantic relationship, even though Keith Richards was due to arrive in New York on June 23. Jimi didn't bother to go into the details of his established relationship with Lithofayne Pridgon, whom he referred to as his "Auntie Faye." But Linda understood and did not confront him about it: "'Auntie Faye' was another way of him saying, 'I'm going to take care of some personal business that doesn't have to do with you.' It was almost code that he was going to see a girl and didn't want to hurt my feelings or upset me. I knew it was said with a twinkle in his eye. He was very loyal to Faye, loved her, and wanted to keep that side of his life very separate from what was happening."

When Jimi first met Keith, he introduced himself as Jimmy James, but then wanted to be known as "Jinx," a private nickname unknown to others, including Pridgon.

"It's made up of letters in sequence from his name," explained Keith.

He'd telephone and that would be the name he'd use. He would often write the name in capital letters, almost like a schoolboy thing, something you'd carve on your desk out of your name. It sort of said something about him. "I'm jinxed." He liked that whole voodoo effect and that his name incorporated that word. It was pleasing to him. I did have a guitar case at one time . . . battered and falling apart, that I actually had to use to get some of my stuff around. It had "Jinx" written on it, and it was from Jimi.

JIMI CONTINUED HIS SEEMINGLY IMPOSSIBLE TRANSITIONS BE-tween women and between groups. In June, he left Knight yet again, although it was to work in the studio with Squires saxophonist Lonnie Youngblood and producer Johnny Brantley, an influential figure on New York's soul music scene.

"Curtis started to lose interest in the band," explained Youngblood, "and at the same time, I had a couple of job offers to be a bandleader. I knew I didn't want to play in his band forever, so I told Jimi and a couple of the guys in the band about it and they said, 'Let's go!' From there, we started playing a few gigs as the Blood Brothers. I was an enterprising guy and wanted to cut me some records."

At the time, Jimi was less entrepreneurial than Youngblood. He still did not own an amplifier, and Youngblood and his wife took money out of their bank account to buy him one. Furthermore, they had to convince him to sing.

Several sessions at Abtone Recording Studio in New York yielded Youngblood two R&B singles, "Go Go Place" b/w "Go Go Shoes" and "Soul Food (That's a What I Like)" b/w "Goodbye, Bessie Mae."

Attempting to score a hit single turned out to be financially draining for Youngblood. "We ran out of money, and Jimi changed his way of thinking," remembered Youngblood. "His concept was changing in the middle of what we were about. I witnessed the transformation. I saw him as R&B and other blues kind of things. He loved that music, but after a while he didn't feel it anymore."

Jimi also did sessions for R&B singers the Icemen and singer-songwriter Jimmy Norman. Johnny Brantley was in charge of these sessions. He saw the potential for one unissued track left over from the Youngblood sessions called "Wipe the Sweat" and used it for singer Billy Lamont's single. Discarding Jimi's and Youngblood's vocal tracks, Brantley replaced them with Lamont's and added new lyrics. The song was now retitled "Sweet Thang." Had Jimi's vocals been used, it would have preceded his first official lead vocal track on "Hey Joe" by six months.

ON JUNE 10, THE SQUIRES, NOW MADE UP OF NAPOLEON ANDERson, Nathaniel Edmonds, Marion Booker, and Jimi, signed a contract with RSVP Records and recorded four instrumentals: "Station Break," "Flying on Instruments," "Hornet's Nest," and "No Such Animal." Jimi was still ignoring the implications of his deals with Juggy Murray and with Ed Chalpin, but he did make sure his new contracts included him as composer on "No Such Animal" and cowriter with Jerry Simon, president of RSVP, on "Station Break" and "Flying on Instruments."

In another major evolutionary step toward his new identity, at the end of the month Jimi put together a temporary group that became the house band at Ondine.

Singer Ronnie Spector of the Ronettes remembered: "Ondine's was a very exclusive East Side club on 59th Street. Bob Dylan used to come in, and all the English groups would drop by when they were in town. The house band was led by an unknown guitarist from Seattle named Jimi Hendrix, and I used to get up and sing with him all the time. We always had so much fun at Ondine's that we often wouldn't leave until dawn." Years later, Jimi invited Spector to sing background vocals on his song "Earth Blues."

Frustrated by his years of being a sideman, rejected by the black community in Harlem for his appearance and new musical approach, and buoyed by his experience with LSD and a rapidly evolving counterculture in America, Jimi was naturally drawn downtown. One of the first bohemians he encountered on his early visitations to Greenwich Village was Paul Caruso.

"He was starting to come out of his cocoon and becoming the butterfly," observed Caruso. "When we first started hanging out together . . . he was often sort of oddly dressed in calypso shirts and ratty bellbottom jeans because he didn't have any money yet. . . . He was actually very reserved in many ways until he got on stage. It took a great deal of courage for him to come out of himself. He was pathologically shy. He would stare at the ground and almost shuffle his feet when he met someone, but he had the courage to break through all that."

Until Jimi got a steady gig in the Village, he performed on street corners, playing an acoustic guitar for spare change with Paul Caruso and Linda Keith.

"Jimi continued to panhandle, which he had been doing prior to meeting me," said Keith. "And he would play the guitar on the street in Greenwich Village. Paul Caruso would play harmonica, and I think I sang, which is a horrible thought. But I think that was a little trio and I was the vocalist."

It was not a case of Jimi abandoning his musical roots as much as evolving into another kind of musician. And the treatment he received in the black community in New York City made his evolution an even more rapid one. "I used to go to the [Harlem] clubs, and my hair was really long then," Jimi later stated. "Sometimes I'd tie it up or do something with it and cats would say, 'Ah, look at that: Black Jesus.' Even in your own section [of town]. I had friends with me in Harlem, 125th Street, and all of a sudden, cats, old ladies, girls, anybody would say, 'Ooh, look at that. What is this, a circus or something?'"

One of the first songs Jimi ever wrote, "Stone Free," addressed in lyrics his resentment of this intraracial rejection. The song tells of people who "talk about me like a dog, talk about the clothes I wear," but the lyrics accuse them of being "square."

THE CHAMBERS BROTHERS ALSO EXPERIENCED THE SAME DIFFI-culties when they shifted away from their musical origins. "Like Jimi, we were never accepted by our own people in Harlem because they said we played white music," insisted Lester Chambers. "Even though we came from Mississippi and began by singing gospel, once we played the 1965 Newport Folk Festival and started hanging out with Bob Dylan, things changed for us."

Jimi, too, became so entranced with Bob Dylan's songwriting and hairstyle that he was later referred to in the music press as "Dylan Black." "When I first heard him I thought, 'You must admire the guy for having that much nerve to sing so out of key,'" said Jimi. "But then I started listening to the words. He is giving me inspiration. Not that I wanted to sound like him. I just wanted to sound like Jimi Hendrix." And crucially, when Jimi and Keith took their first trip together in the "Red House" apartment, Keith referred to Dylan's idiosyncratic vocals as the best reason Jimi should not be shy about his own singing voice.

When Dylan arrived in the city in 1961, the *New York Times* described him as a cross between a choirboy and a beatnik. And when his 1966 double album *Blonde on Blonde* hit the record stores toward the end of June, Jimi insisted those who were around him listen closely.

Jimi even shocked Lithofayne Pridgon when he spent their last few dollars for food on that record.

"We were living at Park West Village," said Pridgon, "when he came home from Colony Records with a record tucked under his arm." After taking one look at his purchase, Pridgon said in disbelief, "Bob who?" To many blacks at the time, Dylan's voice and music sounded too country, and that fact could often overshadow the power and craft of his lyrics.

Drummer Jimmy Mayes from Joey Dee and the Starliters provided Jimi cab fare to occasionally bring his guitar and amp down to Mayes's midtown apartment. But Jimi's obsession with practicing the Dylan song "Can You Please Crawl Out Your Window?" made Mayes want to do just that: "I think Jimi was trying to get his vocals together, but he used to get on my nerves with these different songs. After a while, I told him I don't want to hear no more of this Bob Dylan music."

But there was a place where Dylan's music could be heard playing in shops, clubs, and cafés on a regular basis. It was a place where the color of your skin, the style of your hair, or the mode of your dress did not matter as much as the newness of your sound and the passion and thought behind your lyrics. Prompted by Richie Havens and Linda Keith, Jimi was, at long last, ready to forge a new identity with his own band in the Greenwich Village music scene of 1966.

10

Downtown and Underground
(JULY—SEPTEMBER 1966)

JIMMY HENDRIX BECAME JIMI HENDRIX IN GREENWICH VILLAGE, and he scorched the perceptions of those in the music scene there like a lightning bolt.

To fully appreciate the freeing effect that Greenwich Village had on Jimi to create as never before, and the effect he had on acquaintances and audiences, one has to visualize the quality of the daily scene there. Dim, tiny-tabled coffeehouses, holdovers from the folk music era, still dotted the Village mainline, MacDougal Street, in 1966. A new crop of young people replaced the poetry-reading coffeehouse Beats and anti-A-bomb activists from the Eisenhower era. The tradition of folk singing in Washington Square Park that began in 1945 had fully blossomed by 1960 when hundreds of singers, players, and appreciative listeners congregated there on weekends.

Greenwich Village, by the mid-1960s, was New York's equivalent of San Francisco's Haight-Ashbury district, both perfect incubators for a bohemian cultural revolution. At night and on weekends, Village venues overflowed with locals and tourists listening to fresh and notable talent. James Taylor was a regular at one club that wanted but had no room for Jimi. Bob Dylan, Jimi's idol, would soon meet him at a Village hangout, although they would both be too drunk to have much of a conversation. And Richie Havens, who'd been gigging in the Village since 1959 and was dazzled by Jimi at Cheetah, finally convinced him to perform in the counterculture enclave of the Village.

More than half of the coffeehouses that featured folk music in 1964 had made the switch to rock and roll or folk-rock in 1966. Now, a new guitar player who went by the name Jimmy James accepted the challenge of making a living there.

Along with the newfound social mores of the time came economic desperation for the youthful counterculture, as well as once-in-a-lifetime freedom of expression. Impoverished hippies and creative artists huddled in doorways, smoking pot and begging for spare change. Greenwich Village folksinger Tom Rush, who lived at 19 West 8th Street, remembered the carnival-like street atmosphere. A young couple with a baby panhandled him successfully, "trying to get gas money to get home to Ohio. The next time, it was a different baby. I realized she was a babysitter using the *kid-du-jour* as bait. Then there was this guy who was six foot ten—and that's without his platform shoes—who wore nothing but a see-through raincoat and walked, at the end of a leash, an eighteen-inch-tall horse. I'm not making this up."

The surrealism and freedom of the Village, fueled by experimentation with LSD, proved fertile ground for Jimi and his music. Linda Keith expanded his consciousness with his first LSD experience and in the process unlocked his resistance to singing his own material. She became a devoted fan, catching as many Village appearances as she could. In a matter of weeks, she would be the unexpected force that transformed his career and his life.

"And I saw that my role," Keith said in an interview with the Experience Music Project, "was to convince him that he can sing as well as the next person, although, you know . . . he wasn't going to blow any minds with his singing. But it was perfectly good and adequate. And I convinced him by playing Bob Dylan songs and made him focus in on the actual vocal tones and to see that, you know, Bob Dylan couldn't 'sing,' but it came across wonderfully. And this is what I tried to let Jimi understand that he could achieve as well."

Jimi miraculously found a way to balance his time between Litho-fayne Pridgon uptown and Carol Shiroky and Linda Keith downtown. He had the unflagging energy of a gypsy and a stunning tolerance for LSD. During his career, he was seen to take a number of hits at the same time and perform with his usual inspired acumen.

Musician friend Lonnie Youngblood, one of Curtis Knight's Squires, received an invitation to drop acid with Jimi before Youngblood even knew what acid was: "He was wired up, man. He said, 'You ain't never felt nothing until you dropped a tab.' He'd seen beautiful things he'd never seen before that opened up his mind, but I didn't want none of that. He started writing some crazy songs, too, and then he'd run them down to me. I didn't want to offend him, but I said, 'That sounds kind of weird, man.'"

Jimi's access to LSD, marijuana, and other street drugs was made easier by fans as well as friends in New York City. One of Jimi's Village drug connections was, in the parlance of the day, a "speed freak," ad-dicted to amphetamines.

"Her name was Jonah," film critic Jeremiah Newton recalled. "She had beautiful white skin, blonde hair, German and looked like the Madonna. She had an occasional weight problem and took ampheta-mines to keep it down, but everybody took them back then. They were legal."

Tommy Butler, a bass player Jimi worked with in Greenwich Village, spent a day tripping with Jimi and Jonah. He claimed she had a virtual pharmacy of street drugs in her bag.

As Jimi began to use LSD more frequently, he also saw its growing influence on popular culture. "After I took it, it opened my eyes," Paul McCartney said of LSD in an interview in *Life*. "We only use one tenth of our brain. Just think what all we could accomplish if we could tap that hidden part. It would mean a whole new world. If politicians would take LSD, there wouldn't be any more war or poverty or famine."

The Beatles' seventh album, *Revolver*, was a forerunner of the psy-chedelia that would permeate more rock music in the near future. Re-leased in 1966 to great acclaim, it offered up the mind-altering, ethereal "Tomorrow Never Knows," with its highly compressed drums with reverse cymbals, reverse guitar, processed vocals, looped tape effects, and two East Indian instruments new to pop music: the sitar and the tamboura drone. John Lennon was inspired to write the song after reading Dr. Timothy Leary's *The Psychedelic Experience* . . . on LSD, of course.

That year, Jimi, who had been fascinated by science fiction as a boy in Seattle, read *Night of Light* by Phillip José Farmer. The "purplish haze" Farmer wrote about was caused by sunspots that had disorienting effects on a distant planet's inhabitants. It became the central image of Jimi's song "Purple Haze," which was further influenced by his dream of walking under the sea. Jimi wrote pages and pages of lyrics for "Purple Haze," creating a mythical land, including a history of wars on the planet Neptune. Other songs would also run pages in rough draft. The words were gushing out of him, and he scrambled to get them all down on paper.

"3rd Stone from the Sun," also on his first release, *Are You Experienced,* further exhibited his fascination with science fiction and psychedelic imagery. On that song, Jimi's voice is slowed down to portray an imagined extraterrestrial who plans to blow up the Earth and thinks chickens are the only creatures of any significant intelligence.

The Jimi who had been fired for objecting to routine R&B band outfits was now free to wear what he wanted, which included ruffled sleeves, brightly colored shirts and bellbottoms, jewelry, wide-brimmed hats, and capes. The music he'd heard for too long only in his mind was now finding a following. Jimi was exploring new lyrical territories.

The more time he spent in Greenwich Village, the more Jimi avoided the cognitive dissonance he experienced from members of his own race. Jimi rarely spoke on the record about the pain he felt when some in the black music establishment rejected his new musical ideas. Pridgon stood up for him when Harlem musicians and club owners rejected his radical new approach to the guitar, but it clearly hurt his psyche, as he once explained later: "In the Village, people were more friendly than in Harlem, where it's all cold and mean. Your own people hurt you more. I always wanted a more open and integrated sound."

Jimi had no qualms about singing songs with or by white performers, and he enjoyed flaunting his behavior a bit downtown, knowing he was among open-minded friends. Jeremiah Newton's friend Jonah showed up at a Village hangout one day with Jimi in tow. Jonah brought Jimi to Newton's table. Jimi had been working part-time as a bouncer and security guard at Salvation II, a Village discotheque. He typically wore a brightly colored shirt and was low key, until once, a sailor on leave, wearing his dress whites, sat down and joined them.

"He was telling us how he loved being on a ship," Newton claimed, "but couldn't stand those 'Village fags.' Hendrix immediately grabbed me around the waist, held my hand, and said, 'This is my boyfriend, and I really resent what you said to us. You have to leave our table now.' The sailor got up and ran for the door. We all started laughing."

Jimi had found the right environment to experiment and flourish. But now he needed a home base, a place where people could see him play regularly. And he found it in the first place Dylan had performed when he arrived in New York in January of 1961.

The Cafe Wha? was created when the owner of a small garage on West 3rd Street, a block south of Washington Square, took a threadbare wool couch with one leg missing and miscellaneous battered furnishings from neighborhood trash piles, tacked a "Folk Music" sign on the wall outside, and was in the coffeehouse business. Entrepreneur Manny Roth built, managed, and owned the Cafe Wha? throughout most of the 1960s. The basement had originally been a stable for horses, with a ramp running down from MacDougal Street. The trough that ran through the center of the long, narrow space had been the gutter for horse dung.

"I named it the Cafe Wha?" Roth, uncle of rock singer David Lee Roth, remembered, "because I couldn't think of anything else. Everyone would volunteer names, and I'd say, 'Wha?' People would walk in, look around, and say, 'Wha?'" With its burlap covered ceilings, weird wall fixtures, and cheap coffee, the popularity of the Cafe Wha? grew. It was where comedians Richard Pryor and Bill Cosby first captured audiences.

Visitors were herded down a steep staircase to a dark, dank basement filled with cast-off chairs and a miniscule stage. Candles in blue glass flickered at every table. At full capacity, the Wha? could hold 325 people.

Tim Dulaine, a solo guitarist at the club, witnessed Jimi's audition in July. He showed up dressed all in white, without a band or guitar, and played "Hey Joe," "Shotgun," and other R&B material. He turned up Dulaine's amp—with its clean sounding Altec Lansing speakers— so loud that Dulaine worried that it would blow up and he'd have to call his grandmother in Texas to send money for a replacement.

Tommy Butler, the house band bass player, returned from a break and walked into the middle of Jimi's audition. After seeing Jimi "eating" his guitar and playing staggering lines, Butler quickly plugged in his own bass and started jamming with the soon-to-be legend. Roth hired Jimi for Thursday, Friday, and Saturday, the best nights of the week.

Jimmy officially became Jimi. Carol Shiroky recalled the revised spelling of his first name on the chalkboard sign in front of the Wha? He even corrected her spelling of "Jimmy" in a card she sent him. Until his backup band, the Blue Flames, took shape, Jimi temporarily used drummer Chas Mathews and Butler, but they were let go when he recruited bassist Randy Palmer and drummer Danny Casey, both fill-ins for the Cafe Wha? house band. Jimi shared the bill with a hyp- notist named Martin St. James, Richard Pryor, and a then-unknown, blind folksinger named José Feliciano.

Mathews was on drums the night Jimi asked Tex, the stage manager, to lower the lights. Then, with a flourish, Jimi took off one of his shoes, laid down his guitar on the stage, and played the guitar with his foot. The crowd loved it. Jimi was not as pleased with Mathews' drumming and fired him for not getting the break right in the appro- priately titled "Wild Thing."

Jimi finally held the reins of his own musical vision and thrived in the club's casual atmosphere. He'd bum a Kool or a Salem cigarette on his way into the club, while Doug the doorman barked, "Hey folks, come on down and check out the talent at the fabulous Cafe Wha?!"

Danny Casey witnessed the joy and playful humor Jimi displayed with this major shift in his fortunes: "He was really into the *Batman* TV show at the time and watched it religiously. We'd be backstage getting ready, and right before we went on stage, he'd turn to me and say, 'Robin, are you ready?' I would answer, 'Yes, Batman,' and we went on stage that way most every night. He even wore a cape."

Casey and Jimi hit it off so well they became roommates at the Albert Hotel, a now historic building that had opened in 1883 at 11th Street and University Place. The Albert, with its red brick and white stone façade, and both squared and curved balconies, had been designed by Henry Hardenbergh, who simultaneously worked on the more renowned Dakota at 72nd Street and Central Park West. Jimi and Casey lived in the so-called penthouse of the Albert on the twelfth floor, wall to wall with people, thanks to owners who catered to the music scene and were reluctant to turn away anyone in need.

"It was so crowded," Casey warmly recalled, "Jimi often climbed out on the fire escape with a pillow to sleep. Some mornings, he'd wake up with his hair in rollers, grab a coke bottle, pretend it was a microphone, and act like a DJ. It was hysterical."

Jimi's residence was never permanent in the Village. From there, he and Casey found a basement apartment on 211 East Fifth Street across from ABC Studios. Tim Dulaine lived upstairs. "It was a filthy, rat-infested place with lots of cockroaches running around," remembered Dulaine. "Danny [Casey] used to help Jimi style his hair with these big, round yellow curlers and gel. Jimi had his hair straightened at the time and looked more like a pimp than a rock star. We'd all sit out on the steps while this was going on, and people looked at them like they were boyfriend and girlfriend."

Jimi also lived briefly on the third floor above the United Egg Company on the corner of Greenwich and Reade streets. Village regulars the Seventh Sons used the loft for music rehearsals and were often visited by guitarists Roger McGuinn and David Crosby from the Byrds. Sometimes their informal jams lasted for hours, according to Seventh Sons' guitarist Buzzy Linhart, but mainly it was a fun place to party and a convenient crash pad after the debauchery of the evening.

Jimi expanded the Blue Flames to a quartet. While searching for a new guitarist, Jimi met Randy Wolfe, a fifteen-year-old runaway from California who had played the Night Owl Cafe. Jimi was in the back of Manny's Music on 48th Street, trying out a Stratocaster.

"Our eyes caught each other," said Wolfe, "and I asked him if I could show him some things I learned on the guitar. He then gave me the Strat, and I played him slide guitar. He really liked it and invited me

161

down that night." And that very night, he was chosen by Jimi to join his band.

Because there were now two players named "Randy" in the band, Jimi christened Wolfe "Randy California" and Palmer "Randy Texas," in recognition of their home states.

"I didn't even know his last name was Hendrix," recalled California. "I always thought it was Jimmy James." California kept the name Jimi gave him and later went on to form the band Spirit, who created hits such as "Fresh Garbage," "Mechanical World," and "I've Got a Line on You."

Jimi had more musical experience than his fellow bandmates, so he often gave them quick lessons on song structures in the boiler room of the Cafe Wha? which served as their dressing room. This is where Jimi taught them "Hey Joe," "Wild Thing," and R&B standards like "Shotgun." While Jimi played lead and sang, California filled in with rhythm and occasionally used the neck of a broken 7-Up bottle for slide guitar effects.

From the start, Jimi chose to play "Hey Joe" slower, not like the Leaves' fuel-injected garage band version, but more like Tim Rose's soulful single, which Jimi had first heard on a jukebox. Other eyewitnesses reported hearing the band do a cover of the Beatles' then-current B side "Rain," with Jimi attempting, live, John Lennon's trippy, reversed vocal track. There was also an original called "Mr. Bad Luck," which years later morphed into "Look Over Yonder." The group also covered songs from John Hammond Jr.'s *So Many Roads* album, and most evenings, sets simply closed with disorienting amounts of feedback and tremolo, coupled with Jimi's seizurelike, onstage gyrations.

California used a Sears Silvertone amp that packed a lot of punch, and he sometimes swapped amps with Jimi, who had acquired a Fender Deluxe Reverb. It was during this period that Jimi finally perfected control of feedback by turning his guitar toward his new amp.

The Wha? attracted not only Jimi's fans and locals but also tourists and celebrities. It was not uncommon to see famous actors such as Sean Connery or James Coburn in the audience enjoying a late-night beverage, only to have their jaws drop when Jimi cranked his amp up and vibrated the floor and everyone's minds. Richie Havens, who was playing at the Night Owl, often brought English acts such as the Kinks and the Yardbirds around the corner to see and hear Jimi tear it up.

"They came away so visibly shaken and depressed from Jimi's awesome, powerful performance," Havens insisted, "that you could tell he had made these skilled musicians see that he was in another league, way above anything any of us ever thought to reach for."

Another musician who was adversely affected by Jimi's otherworldly skills was Chicago blues guitar legend Mike Bloomfield. After seeing Jimi at the Wha? Bloomfield admitted to having trouble even picking up his guitar for about one year.

As far as Jimi was concerned, the most important celebrity to attend his show was his idol. Dylan dropped in on a June night to see Jimi's last set.

After the show, a group went down MacDougal Street to the Kettle of Fish for drinks. Jimi was overwhelmed by Dylan's presence. Very drunk, both naturally shy men, Dylan and Jimi said very little to each other. But Dylan held forth, with stories like the time he met jazz great Thelonious Monk at the old Five Spot Club off Cooper Square. Dylan told them he introduced himself to Monk, informing him that Dylan played folk music. "We all play folk music," was Monk's joking reply, and the story brought a round of laughter from Dylan's rapt listeners.

Although Carol Shiroky and Jimi were no longer a couple, she still showed up at the Wha? to enjoy the band's cover songs of "Hang On Sloopy"; Don Covay's hit with Jimi, "Mercy, Mercy"; and his first tribute to Dylan, "Like a Rolling Stone." Later in his career, Jimi covered "All Along the Watchtower," which drew public praise from Dylan himself.

The love relationship with Shiroky had ended with a violent outburst from Jimi.

"Jimi had a fight with her one day," recalled Casey. "I happened to be there and saw him as he took his guitar and busted it over a bedpost, broke it in two, and then just walked out on her. That was the end of that relationship."

When Jimi destroyed Shiroky's gift guitar in a fit of pique at the Lennox Hotel, Linda Keith, who was so enamored of him, again came to his rescue. She "borrowed" Keith Richards's new white Stratocaster and gave it to Jimi to use at the club. According to Shiroky, when Richards discovered where his new white Strat was, he was furious.

"Keith Richards came down to the Cafe Wha? with a gun, wanting to blow Jimi's head off," said Shiroky. "He had Keith Richards gunning for him." Casey was onstage that night with Jimi's band and confirmed that the lead guitarist of the Rolling Stones angrily dragged Linda out of Cafe Wha? for giving away the guitar.

Although Linda was completely in love with Jimi, she could not manage to keep him to herself. Jimi had many girlfriends in the Village, and when a Polaroid instant camera was handy, he kept a little memento of them. "Jimi used to take pictures of girls going down on him and then put them in his guitar case," recalled Casey. "I never saw him with a suitcase. He put everything he owned in his guitar case. That was his briefcase. I still wonder what happened to those photos."

Charles Neville, sax player and future member of the Neville Brothers, was also playing in the Village at that time and verified Jimi's sexual charisma:

"Sometimes in the afternoon, we'd go for a sound check and Jimi would be over at the Cafe Wha? before it opened, just fooling around. I remember him sitting at the edge of the stage with his acoustic guitar, and there'd be a little semicircle of hippie girls gathered there, swooning."

Ever since he lost his guitar duel to Johnny Jones in Nashville due to a lack of amplification, Jimi had been committed to always playing as loud as possible. The volume of Jimi James and the Blue Flames was startling not only to some of the crowd but also to a certain band member. Casey recollected the night Randy California thought Jimi was playing too loud and reached around Jimi's back and turned his amp down.

"Jimi stopped, turned around, and started cussing him out," said Casey. "Boy, was he was mad. Jimi unplugged his guitar, threw it across the room, walked off stage and out of the club. We had to play the rest of the night without him." Jimi fired California the next day, and the group became a trio again.

Besides the folk and rock heard in clubs and coffeehouses in the Village, there was a strong jazz presence. John Coltrane, Miles Davis, and Rahsaan Roland Kirk all played at surrounding clubs during Jimi's gigs at the Wha? Legendary trumpeter Davis, whom Jimi would jam with years later, was said to have seen Jimi first perform at the Lighthouse Cafe.

Marion Booker, the drummer from Curtis Knight's Squires, introduced Jimi to John Coltrane's landmark jazz album *A Love Supreme* in 1966. "I may have contributed to some of Jimi's madness and genius," ventured Booker. Trane's sax work and Elvin Jones' drumming excited Jimi and inspired explorations into other musical directions.

Some of Jimi's jazz-influenced solos in the Greenwich Village era spilled over to his later work with the Jimi Hendrix Experience. Sans the science fiction dialogue and marvelously controlled feedback guitar, "3rd Stone from the Sun" (a tune developed at the Cafe Wha?) has a Wes Montgomery groove to it. "Up from the Skies," a smooth jazz shuffle, was sandwiched between two hard rock songs on Jimi's 1967 recording *Axis: Bold as Love* and sparked many musicians to cover it.

Jimi used all that he had learned from his R&B tours to give his new songs propulsion, a drive that made many of them danceable but also expanded the vocabulary of the electric guitar. Those who attended the Jimi James gigs recognized this. Even so, Jimi could not gain acceptance when he returned to his musical roots uptown.

In early August 1966, Jimi revisited Harlem to play an R&B dance at Connie's Ballroom. But after a few outrageously loud numbers, the organizer told him: "Don't you know any dance music? You all just pack this noise on up, and take it back downtown."

Because the money he made at Cafe Wha? was pitiful, Jimi auditioned at the Night Owl Cafe. Joe Marra, owner of the Night Owl, Roth's down-the-street competition at 118 West 3rd Street, paid his bands much better.

"Manny would pay these kids that performed at the Wha? as little as possible," Marra insisted. "Hendrix, if he was lucky, would get maybe twenty-five dollars a night, but he'd have to do five or six sets and then split it with his band. My club was much smaller, sat about 125, but I paid bands fifty dollars a night, and we usually had three bands a night."

Marra saw how difficult it was for a musician to survive, and he regularly ordered his kitchen to "donate" a burger, a cup of coffee, a coke, some ice cream, something to sustain the performers. In 1966, the rent for a two-bedroom apartment in the Village was ninety-five dollars a month. The groups at the Night Owl would get around three hundred dollars for an engagement, considerably more than the Wha?

"The groups who worked at the Wha?" Marra said resentfully, "would come into my club and pool their nickels and dimes just to get an order of French fries. I'd tell my waitress, 'Just give them the fucking fries.'"

Pop rock's the Lovin' Spoonful even dedicated the song "Night Owl Blues" to owner Marra and the club. Spoonful founder John Sebastian played there as well. It had transformed from an old beatnik, chess-playing hangout. Marra and Fred Neil (writer of the Grammy Award–winning Harry Nilsson hit "Everybody's Talkin,'" the theme song to *Midnight Cowboy*) decided that they could make it in the evolving landscape of Village folk music venues.

"Starting out," said Sebastian, "the Spoonful played a week there, and Joe told us we were terrible and better rehearse. He was right. We had tremendous confidence but weren't really that good." The public apparently didn't agree. "Summer in the City" went to number one on the *Billboard* charts that year.

Guitarist Pete Sando, who performed at the Night Owl in 1966 with his band the Rahgoos, described the club's colorful atmosphere: "The cast of characters included 'Jack the Rat' at the door, a frightening cat with teeth missing and dirty clothes. . . . The waitresses all used four-letter words that we had never heard from girls before, shocking to four straight, naïve, suburban rockers. There was Pepe, the openly gay cook. We had never seen anyone 'openly gay.'"

Guitarist Bob Kulick often saw men with bulges under their jackets come in and pick up "protection money" from Marra. Apparently, the owner of the Night Owl was big on security. He kept a sawed-off shotgun and a billy club under the cash register.

Initially, Marra's club manager suggested he check out a wild, new guitarist playing around the block. But Marra was not impressed. The Cafe Wha?'s floors were made up of broken pieces of marble, the walls were brick, and the ceiling was cement. Marra reacted to the loudness rather than the music.

Jimi, desperate for more work, went over to the Night Owl one Sunday afternoon, along with Kulick and others. After the audition was over, Marra told Jimi nicely, 'You're a phenomenal talent, but I can't hire you."

Marra was looking for performers who did original work only. He took down Jimi's phone number and promised to hire him if they had an open spot. James Taylor and his band the Flying Machine were in the middle of an eight-month gig at the Night Owl.

Jimi had spent years on the road, bouncing between groups and hotels, pawning and borrowing and losing guitars. His single-minded insistence on playing his own way repeatedly got him fired. But now there was a sea change in American music. He had a venue where he could regularly be heard. And Linda Keith simply would not give up on bringing music industry figures to witness his performance, searching for the person who would finally provide Jimi with the career he deserved.

Keith's relationship with the Rolling Stones' Keith Richards had been, in her own words, "running out." The Stones arrived in New York on June 23 for their North American tour. After a concert in Forest Hills, Queens, on July 2, the entire band saw Jimi perform at Ondine in midtown Manhattan. Her attraction and devotion to Jimi had begun then and never wavered.

While Jimi was performing at Cafe Wha? Linda managed to convince Andrew Loog Oldham, manager for the Stones, to come see Jimi. Oldham knew that Linda's involvement with Jimi threatened the well-being of the Rolling Stones and his own position as manager. He strongly suggested she give up on helping Jimi.

Next, Keith solicited the support of Seymour Stein, who cofounded Sire Records. Stein would eventually bring Fleetwood Mac to America. And years later, in his hospital room, recovering from an infection after heart surgery, he signed a new act he completely believed in named Madonna. But his assessment of Jimi, after seeing him perform at the Wha? was just as cold and indifferent as Oldham's.

Keith, completely by accident, ran into the person who launched Jimi into the upper reaches of rock stardom. The Animals, led by Eric Burdon, flew into New York from London to begin their final U.S. tour. They were to play the Rheingold Central Park Music Festival.

Bryan James "Chas" Chandler, bassist for the Animals, was looking to get into artist management and was searching for the right act to represent. The night before the Central Park gig for the Animals, Keith was walking out of Ondine as Chandler was walking in, and they spotted each other. Keith enthusiastically told him about Jimi playing at the Wha? Chandler agreed to come by. And on the afternoon of August 3, the beefy, six-foot-four-inch Newcastle native joined Keith to listen.

The first song Jimi launched into was "Hey Joe," and Chandler, sitting in the back with Keith, became so excited that he spilled his milkshake all over himself. The reason was that Chandler himself had heard Tim Rose's slower version of "Hey Joe" for the first time only hours before running into Keith at Ondine, and he was pondering producing a newer version. Jimi performed the very song in the style Chandler wanted to record it, and it was just days after Chandler had first heard it. The rest of Jimi's set merely reinforced Chandler's astonishment. Chandler later stated, "I remember thinking, 'This cat's wild enough to upset more people than [Mick] Jagger.'"

Chandler pitched Jimi on all the reasons he would succeed in England as a recording artist. Jimi was receptive but guarded in his enthusiasm. Chandler promised to offer Jimi a contract after the tour ended and Chandler returned to New York. Jimi replied, "Fair enough," and returned to the matter of keeping himself alive on starvation wages.

Word continued to spread about the groundbreaking performer over at the Wha? But Jimi needed more income and a more impressive venue. The person who helped bring Jimi to a more upscale environment was part of a remarkable American music family. John Hammond Jr., a noted blues man, was also the son of talent scout, critic, and producer John Hammond, who had been responsible for elevating the careers of Benny Goodman and Billie Holliday, signing Dylan to Columbia Records and producing his first album, and, later, working with Aretha Franklin, Bruce Springsteen, and Stevie Ray Vaughn.

"I was on this gig at the Gaslight in 1966," Hammond Jr. explained, "and my friend . . . came over and said, 'Man, there's this guy playing at the Cafe Wha? jamming over there, and he's playing this stuff off your *So Many Roads* album better than you, man!'"

When Hammond walked over and met Jimi shortly thereafter, Jimi was so desperate for paying work that he immediately asked Hammond if he could help find him a gig. Hammond convinced Cafe Au Go Go club owner Howard Solomon to book them for a week in September. Over the next few weeks, Hammond began rehearsing with Jimi.

To supplement his Cafe Wha? wages, Jimi grudgingly agreed to a Saturday gig with Curtis Knight and the Squires on August 20 at the Lighthouse Cafe on Broadway and 76th Street, on a tiny stage over a bar. Curtis criticized Jimi for playing too loud and for playing the guitar behind his head. At the end of the show, singer "King" George Clemons saw Jimi's disgust and his changed expectations.

Jimi snapped out his plugs and said, "That's the last time I play this shit. To hell with him. I'm going to England."

It would be his last performance with that group, a final slamming of a door on his backup guitarist past and a shifting away from the rhythm and blues he had been playing for so long.

Jimi relished the opportunity to be seen at a more fashionable club. Like the Wha? the Cafe Au Go Go, at 152 Bleecker Street, was in a basement, but the staircase circled down to a long, deep room. The food was good, the waitresses were sexy and friendly, and the lighting was certainly as decent as or better than most off-Broadway theaters of the day. Jimi was lead guitarist with a major musician accompanying him in a nice room, yet with all the advantages Hammond provided him, Jimi did not feel that he was on secure ground. To the surprise of those involved, he brought back the previously fired Randy California to play with the group.

They were booked to play two sets a night at the Cafe Au Go Go. Jimi received recognition in newspaper ads, albeit as "the Blue Flame." Jimi and Hammond were actually the opening act, listed fourth on the bill with the Times Square Two, folk icon Tim Hardin, and head-liner Judy Roderick. But finally, Jimi had a club where the sound system could do justice to his revolutionary guitar work.

When the Cafe Au Go Go transitioned from acoustic folk to electric rock, owner Howard Solomon upgraded the sound equipment, making it superior to other newly opened rock clubs, using Fender products and tube amps.

In mid-August, John Sebastian and the Lovin' Spoonful decided to drop by the Village hotspot and hear Hammond, with whom they had played. Like the rest of the crowd, they were amazed by the Blue Flame. He played an entire solo with one hand. He was doing hammer-ons, creating transcendent but carefully crafted feedback. And he was play-ing music louder than anyone had ever heard it played in Greenwich Village.

Jimi's mastery of many music styles also led to his unquenchable desire to play with a variety of musicians. Hanging out at the Au Go Go, he was impressed by singer-guitarist-pianist Ellen McIlwaine. He walked up and politely asked if he could sit in. McIlwaine started playing piano at the age of five, and she picked up guitar in 1963, arrived in the Village earlier in 1966, and bought a steel-stringed acoustic at Guild Guitars that was used as a loaner by Mississippi John Hurt and Richie Havens when repairs were done on their own.

"He was not the personality you'd see with the John Hammond act," McIlwaine reminisced, "like squirting toothpaste into the audience and fooling around like that. Jimi didn't do any of that when we played together. He played very quietly and seriously. I always played boogie-woogie piano and a couple of ballads. It was kind of bluesy."

As Jimi grew closer to the moment of his breakthrough, a gulf widened between him and the women who were closest to him in New York. He had broken up with Carol Shiroky, smashing the white Stratocaster she had given him to add a note of finality. Lithofayne Pridgon, who had lived with him on and off, lost him to a new direction in music that she could not abide. And then, one day at the Cafe Wha? Linda Keith was literally dragged away from him.

Keith Richards, when he returned to London that August, had called Keith's parents and warned them that she had become involved with a "black junkie." Keith's parents were utterly alarmed and assumed their twenty-year-old daughter would succumb to drugs in New York's growing youth counterculture. Keith's well-to-do father petitioned to make her a ward of the court, and after succeeding, he personally flew to New York and on August 24 marched into the Cafe Wha?

Keith recalled her actions and Jimi's unintentionally comical reaction:

> And I said to somebody, "Go tell Roberta [Goldstein] my father's here, and have her go and tell Jimi." And Roberta told me this story later, that she went backstage and she said to Jimi, "Jimi, Linda's father's arrived." And Jimi patted his hair and said, "Do I look all right?" Well, no matter how much patting of his hair he could have done, he was never going to look all right . . . to my father. It was very sweet and very amusing, and it indicates something about his own, again, that naiveté, that lack of worldliness, that he had no comprehension that my father might come from a culture that is so different and at the other end of the spectrum from him, that there was no way that there could be any relation there. And when Roberta told me that story, I cracked up.

But there was no laughter in the moment, as Mr. Keith dragged his daughter past stunned onlookers and forced her to fly with him back to their home in Hampstead, London.

The impact of this wrenching separation reverberated for both lovers. Jimi and Linda Keith had made a blood pact in honor of their special relationship. They cut themselves superficially, intermingling their blood, and Jimi promised that after his days of womanizing were over, he would return to her and only her.

CHAS CHANDLER CAME BACK TO NEW YORK IN SEPTEMBER TO find Jimi Hendrix. True to his word, he wanted to manage him. But Chandler searched for four days in every rundown hotel he could find in Greenwich Village, trying to locate Jimi. Undeterred, Chandler finally located Jimi and brought the Animals' manager Michael Jeffery down to see him perform. Jeffery agreed to come in as co-manager. They mutually decided that Chas would focus on producing the band's music and Jeffery would handle money and contractual matters.

Chandler chose the perfect Village bar for negotiating Jimi's move to London. It took place in the Kettle of Fish, where Jimi had spent a drunken evening in the company of his idol, Bob Dylan. Chandler said he was ready to bring Jimi into a heady brew of musical influences in the UK that would serve him perfectly.

The British appreciation for white blues, epitomized by Eric Clapton, John Mayall, and others, laid the groundwork for Jimi. Clapton later commented on Jimi's well-timed arrival: "The blues boom in London was dying, and it needed someone to bring it all back to life and cement it together."

Jimi, wanting his remarkable, young rhythm guitarist with him, called Randy California's stepfather to ask if he would give permission for Randy to accompany him to England. The answer was no.

However, Jimi did contact his old friend from the army and Nashville days. Billy Cox's name had been mentioned to Chandler. "I told Jimi I couldn't come," Cox said, "because I had fallen on bad times; I had only three strings on my bass, and I'm renting an amplifier. I was poor. He told me he'd make it and send for me, and that's just what he did." Jimi, fiercely loyal to his friends, eventually brought Cox into his Band of Gypsys.

Inevitably, Chandler didn't want the Blue Flames. He wanted to represent Jimi and build a new band around him. Jimi's remorse for leaving his newly formed band was noticed by other Village musicians he had come to know and admire, including Ellen McIlwaine. "Jimi felt guilty, but he was going through with it," McIlwaine said. "'I don't feel too good about it,' he said, 'but I think I'll do it.' He was flippant, but he was always very measured."

John Hammond witnessed this side of Jimi, his need for connectedness, despite his itinerant lifestyle and lack of romantic commitment. Directly after the last time they played together at the Cafe Au Go Go, Jimi took Hammond aside and told him he'd been offered an airline ticket, money, and a contract to go to England.

Hammond recalled the bittersweet moment: "And I said, 'Well, listen, it's about time. I know you're going to be a big star and just have a great time.' I saw him a year later, and he came and hung out with me for a week. And he didn't have to do that, you know? He was just a great guy. He was a human being."

Jimi and Chas stepped off their first-class Pan American flight and entered London's Heathrow Airport at 9:00 a.m., September 24, 1966. In his guitar case, Jimi carried all his possessions: a Fender Stratocaster, a change of clothes, and a jar of Valderma skin cream for his acne.

For all the struggles Jimi had been through, his acceptance in England and other parts of Europe in the first few months would be the complete opposite of his previous career trajectory: immediate and astonishingly swift. But there was one more impediment to his final ascent to rock stardom, and it would occur the moment he got off the plane in London.

Epilogue

JIMI WAS ALMOST NOT ALLOWED INTO ENGLAND. HE WAS GRANTED a seven-day, nonwork permit and had to get an extension on his visa.

Michael Jeffery was instrumental in getting Jimi into London, and he would turn out to be both a boon and a huge impediment to Jimi's career. It was Jeffery's undisclosed British government connections that helped get Jimi a travel visa to England on such short notice. Correspondence was forged, and the English government was told Jimi was a well-respected musician who had to enter the country to pursue unpaid royalties. It took six hours of negotiations in London with immigration officials to allow Jimi into the country.

But everything else about Jimi's career in the UK took place with dizzying speed. It took one day for Jimi to begin an affair with Kathy Etchingham. She lived upstairs at the house of musician Zoot Money, where Jimi jammed on the evening of his arrival. He met Etchingham at his first public jam that very night, at the Scotch of St. James Club, amid the cobbled streets and alleyways near the Houses of Parliament. They spent the night together and then moved in together.

Days later, Jimi called his father, Al, collect, to tell him of his good fortune in London. Al's first inquiry was from whom Jimi had stolen money in order to get to the UK. Jimi passed the phone to Etchingham to convince his father that his musical career had finally taken flight. According to Etchingham, Al's reaction was: "You tell my boy to write me. I ain't paying for no collect calls." And he promptly hung up.

Typically, Jimi's time with Etchingham was rife with fighting and volatility. But one violent disagreement about Etchingham's cooking, which resulted in her hurling a plate and storming out, yielded one of the most beautiful ballads in the history of rock music, "The Wind Cries Mary." They would live together longer than Jimi did with any other woman.

It took him a week to perform alongside his hero, Eric Clapton, while the newly formed Cream played at the Regent Street Polytechnic (now University of Westminster). It was the college where, in 1963, architecture students Roger Waters, Richard Wright, and Nick Mason had founded an early version of what later became a true pioneer of psychedelia, Pink Floyd.

British fans affectionately scrawled the graffiti "Clapton Is God" on walls throughout London, praising the former guitarist of the Yardbirds and John Mayall's Blues Breakers. At the time of the Regent Polytechnic show, Clapton, along with Jack Bruce and Ginger Baker, as the blues-rock trio called Cream, had just started playing live shows in July 1966. Their first single was yet to be released when Jimi, thanks to Chandler's entreaties, joined them onstage, October 1. No one had jammed with Cream before.

Chandler, during his negotiations with Jimi in Greenwich Village, promised he would get to meet Eric Clapton. After Chandler got Cream to initially agree to jam with Jimi, he thought better of it, not wanting to be accused of blindsiding the band. But Cream was intrigued by Chandler's confidence in his new client.

At the Poly, Jimi held nothing back onstage. He suggested Cream join him on a version of Howlin' Wolf's "Killing Floor." Jimi's speed, tone, and flair were so overwhelming that Clapton ceased playing, stunned, and exited the stage.

Chandler immediately made his way to Clapton to talk with him: "I went backstage and he was trying to get a match to a cigarette. I said, 'Are you all right?' and he replied, 'Is he that fucking good?' He had heard ten bars, at most."

Jimi's aftereffect on the supergroup Cream was profound. Jack Bruce remembered an incident right after the Regent Polytechnic gig with Jimi: "There is a Cream demo that was recorded the day after, which has Eric playing with his teeth, like Jimi."

Jimi's friendship with Clapton and Cream was not fleeting. Clapton attended many of Jimi's UK shows. On February 20, 1968, their paths crossed back in America.

"I remember when we were recording "White Room" in New York, at Atlantic Studios," Bruce said. "Jimi came down to the session, and he said, 'I wish I could write things like that.' But I pointed out to him that I probably ripped it off of him, anyway."

It was cross-fertilization and the highest of musical compliments. Clapton, as a master of the blues, like Jimi, explored the outer reaches of psychedelic rock, along with his bandmates, while Jimi did the same. Jimi visited the "3rd Stone from the Sun." Cream told "Tales of Brave Ulysses" on its album *Disraeli Gears*, one of the earliest uses of the "wah-wah" pedal in rock music. Jimi, inspired, further explored the wah-wah effect, most notably on "Voodoo Child (Slight Return)" on his third and final studio album, *Electric Ladyland*.

After two weeks in England, Jimi and Chas Chandler assembled Mitch Mitchell and Noel Redding and the Jimi Hendrix Experience. Redding was assigned bass guitar, though lead was his previous instrument. Mitchell's selection was even more curious.

Shortly after arriving, Chandler asked keyboardist Brian Auger to bring Jimi into the Brian Auger Trinity. Auger, loathe to make such a decision, especially without even having heard Jimi, was finding a way, with vocalist Julie Driscoll and guitarist Vic Briggs, to bridge the worlds of jazz and rock, well before "fusion" became a title for a musical genre.

Auger eventually played numerous shows with Jimi, and that first jam, on September 29 at Blaises Club in Kensington, an upscale venue in the basement of the Imperial Hotel, was one of the most important. The most popular act in France, Johnny Hallyday, saw the performance and later asked Jimi and Chandler to have Jimi join Hallyday's up-coming engagement at the Olympia, the premiere venue in Paris.

Chandler recalled Hallyday's only concern, after the jam: "'Has he got a band?' And we said yeah, and the next day we actually flipped a coin to decide who was the drummer for the outfit. We spun a coin between Aynsley Dunbar and Mitch Mitchell. Came up Mitch."

After two months, on November 25, 1966, Jimi played the Bag O' Nails Club in London, at 9 Kingly Street, near Carnaby Street, near all the top gear shops. Boutiques like "I Was Lord Kitchener's Valet," "Granny Takes a Trip," "Hung on You" "The Antiques Supermarket," and "Gear" stocked some psychedelically inspired fashions that not only affected the sartorial splendor of "Swinging London," as it was dubbed. It also had an impact on Jimi's appearance. In addition to the scarves, rings, capes, and hats he incorporated into his Greenwich Village look, he now added period military jackets and vividly colored, daringly patterned shirts in particular.

Members of the Beatles, the Rolling Stones, the Who, and other major British music acts had already seen Jimi onstage during the brief time he had been in England. Thus, the Bag O' Nails became her-alded as Jimi's official coming out party. It was an afternoon that fea-tured a press conference as well as a performance. It was witnessed by a truly unprecedented gathering of British rock icons: Paul McCartney, John Lennon, Pete Townshend, Mick Jagger, Brian Jones, Jeff Beck, Donovan, and many other British music luminaries.

The crowd also included Roger Mayer, who had already supplied friends Jeff Beck and Jimmy Page of Led Zeppelin with sound effects gadgets for their guitars. Two weeks later, Mayer introduced Jimi to an electronic device—a complex version of a frequency doubler—Mayer called the Octavia.

Mayer had joined the Royal Naval Scientific Service as an assistant experimental officer. Before he helped Jimi find stunning new sound effects, Mayer did vibration and acoustic analysis to help make British Navy boats quieter for underwater warfare.

Mayer and Jimi worked together for the rest of his career to develop equipment to further extend his palate of guitar sounds and effects. Mayer was present for most of the sessions for Jimi's second album,

Axis: Bold as Love, to consult on the creation of sound that simulated the effect of being in outer space. Mayer had begun work on the first Octavia in 1964, the same year Jimi set his guitar on fire while touring with Gorgeous George and the same year Pete Townshend had smashed his guitar to bits and Kit Lambert had told him to keep that in the act.

After three months, the song Chandler planned to produce himself, the first song Jimi had performed at the Cafe Wha? when Chandler first saw him, "Hey Joe," became the first single from the Jimi Hendrix Experience. Two months later, it was in the top ten in the UK.

British journalist Keith Altham recognized that in addition to Jimi's captivating style and sound, the press in England was well suited to the creation of a rock star. Despite inherently racist descriptions of Jimi as "Mau-Mau" and "the Wild Man of Borneo," epithets he gladly took in stride, the reviews and stories reached a wider public very quickly.

"Nowhere in the world," explained Altham, "were you getting the amount of coverage that you got in England, in national newspapers abroad. You were lucky if you got like a sort of six-paragraph review in the *New York Times* for your gig. In England, you could get a two-page spread in the *Daily Mirror,* which was probably selling 4 million copies."

BUT JUST AS MICHAEL JEFFERY MADE JIMI'S TRAJECTORY TO STAR-dom possible, he also haunted the rock icon. Jeffery's deal with Jimi extracted a whopping and disproportionate 40 percent for himself and Chandler. And Ed Chalpin's binding PPX contract siphoned off a further 2 percent of Jimi's back catalog. At the apex of his career, Jimi Hendrix was making $100,000 a night, and yet he was always in arrears on bills.

Jeffery had been a part of Britain's MI-5 intelligence service and spoke Russian. He kept money in an offshore Bahamas account, under the corporate name Yameta, that was untraceable, and it is alleged he had a set of financial books in London written in Russian to avoid scrutiny. He refused to deflate rumors that he had mobster connections or that he had killed other men in the service of Her Majesty.

To enhance his clandestine reputation, he always wore dark glasses and sometimes carried a Beretta.

Even with his newfound fame, Jimi remained loyal to those who had believed in him from the start. Jimi eventually reunited with his old army friend and fellow King Kasual member Billy Cox and recorded and toured with him. Jimi added fellow Nashville guitarist Larry Lee to the mix, and they both stood proudly with him on the stage at Woodstock.

Jimi formed the first all-black power rock trio in late 1969 with Cox and Buddy Miles, the teenage drummer he had met while on tour with the Isley Brothers in 1964. They were called the Band of Gypsys, but never really had the chance to fully develop before coming to a crashing halt in January 1970, partly due to Michael Jeffery's powerful control.

Jeffery had taken over as sole manager and wanted the hit singles his star had created before Experience sidemen Noel Redding and Mitch Mitchell left the band. Tragically, Chandler quit after two albums, frustrated by the presence of too many hangers-on, too many drugs, and Jimi spending far too much time and money in the studio.

The last official gig of the original Jimi Hendrix Experience was an utter disaster at the Denver Pop Festival in Mile High Stadium in June 1969. Rioting and tear gas disrupted the three-day event, and Jimi, Redding, and Mitchell had to be smuggled out backstage into a rented equipment van. Angry fans leaped onto it and crushed in the roof, threatening the lives of those inside. Shortly thereafter, a reporter who Redding encountered in a bar told the bassist of the rumor that he had been replaced. Disgusted, Redding jumped on the next plane and headed back to England.

Jimi withstood social pressures—like the Denver Pop Festival— that no rock star ever faced. In another disaster at a concert on the isle of Fehmarn, off the coast of Germany, an unruly crowd jeered him. With typical Hendrix humor, Jimi announced, "I don't give a fuck if you boo, as long as you boo in key." Money was stolen from Jimi's dressing room, and as soon as he and his band left the stage, looters burned a trailer used by the organizers.

In addition to Jeffery siphoning off money to his Bahamas account, creating exhausting and inconvenient tour schedules, and encouraging Jimi's out-of-control spending, he also did business with Phil Basile, reputed member of New York's Lucchese crime family. Basile managed the group Vanilla Fudge and forced Jeffery to take that band as an opening act for Jimi. Unbeknown to others, Jeffery had borrowed mob money to pay for his half of Electric Lady Studios. The Experience was not a particular fan of Vanilla Fudge, and when Noel Redding, the only member of the group willing to confront Jeffery, demanded to know why Vanilla Fudge had been added as an opening act, Jeffery's vague but telling reply was, "It's out of my hands."

Jimi complained to many people about wanting to get out of his deal with Jeffery, and yet he feared the unpredictability of taking on new management. Certainly, many in the music industry, such as Eric Burdon and Brian Auger, knew that Jeffery had a corrupt reputation. But cost overruns at Electric Lady Studios and his famously profligate spending also meant Jimi was saving very little of the money he made and a change of management posed a risk of Jimi becoming broke again. The memory of his abject poverty, the unwillingness to create strong emotional ties, and the lack of attention to contractual commitments all created psychological stumbling blocks that prevented Jimi from breaking the contract with Jeffery and taking him on in court.

In desperation, Jimi returned to the man who helped elevate him, Chas Chandler, explaining that he wanted to work with him again, that he needed the critical input from Chandler for the material he was currently developing. "He said he had no confidence in what he'd done," Chandler recalled mournfully. "There was nobody telling him, arguing with him, if you like. And that was on a Wednesday night. And on the Friday morning, he was dead, you know."

Linda Keith saw that Jimi's childlike, creative spirit did not protect him from threats to his genius: "And I think it was the theme of Jimi that runs through everything that he touches and touches his life, is his naïveté. I think that's what killed him, in fact, for which I have huge resentment, because those who knew him should know better."

The last time Jimi saw Keith was in London. Jimi brought a girl, and Keith was with her fiancé at Tramp, a members-only club in Jermyn Street. Jimi wanted to talk about their love affair and the blood pact they had made. Keith was upset by this, about to leave on a trip to the Mediterranean with her fiancé. Upstairs, in the privacy of a cloakroom, Jimi gave her a battered guitar case, one that contained his code name: Jinx. She asked why he was giving it to her. Jimi murmured that he owed it to her.

Inside the case was a Stratocaster guitar and an envelope. Jimi had not included the letter but still had the envelope that had contained the only letter Keith wrote to him after her father had dragged her out of the Cafe Wha? and made her a ward of the court back in London. Jimi had saved the envelope for four years. It's unknown whether he had lost the letter or simply could not part with it.

When Jimi played the Isle of Wight concert in 1970, he verbally dedicated "Foxy Lady" to Keith. And to the lyrics of "Red House," confirming the importance of Keith and his first acid trip at the red Goldstein/Kaufman apartment, he sang, "I got to get out of here / because my Linda don't live here no more."

JIMI'S DEATH IN LONDON IN 1970 AT THE AGE OF TWENTY-SEVEN was officially attributed to choking on his own vomit and acute barbiturate intoxication. Seemingly, it was an accidental overdose of nine tablets of the powerful German sedative Vesparax combined with red wine.

But the case has forensic anomalies that some connect with Jeffery. The autopsy revealed an abnormally large amount of red wine in Jimi's lungs, suggesting that it was forced down his throat. There was a relatively low blood-alcohol level and little wine in his stomach. And Monika Dannemann, the German competition ice skater with whom he was staying, suspiciously changed her story more than once about the circumstances of his demise. In fact, when the ambulance arrived, her door was open and no one other than Jimi, already deceased, was in the flat she rented at the Samarkand Hotel.

Jeffery died March 5, 1973, in a midair collision between two planes. He was flying back to London to testify at a lawsuit regarding his misuse of funds.

ERIC BURDON WAS ONE OF THE FIRST TO ARRIVE AT THE SAMarkand Hotel on the morning Jimi died. Having been called by Dannemann in a panic, he rushed over, and before entering the premises, he noticed on the window of a car a word written in the condensation. It resembled Jimi's handwriting.

"It was written in the humidity, the mist on the window . . . on an Opel, a copy of a Corvette. I figured it must have been him, coming in late at night from a party."

The word was "LOVE."

Jimi's politics was the politics of love, music, spirit, and transcendence. The Black Panthers in New York put pressure on him to actively support their cause, even using his name without permission in the promotion of a benefit concert. Jimi was no more willing to come out in support of the Panthers than he was to talk about his feelings about serving in—and getting a discharge from—the 101st Airborne. He spoke sometimes in riddles, in images, in parables. When Keith Altham once asked him what he would change in the world, Jimi's typically atypical reply was, "The colors in the street."

"He had a kind of alchemist's ability," Pete Townshend said of Jimi. "When he was on the stage, he changed. He physically changed. He became incredibly graceful and beautiful. It wasn't just people taking LSD, though that was going on, there's no question. But he had a power that almost sobered you up if you were on an acid trip. He was bigger than LSD."

AFTER LONDON, AFTER EUROPE, AFTER SETTING HIS GUITAR ON fire at the Monterey Pop Festival, after the iconic, daring, spontaneous performance of "The Star Spangled Banner" at Woodstock, after the sonic experimentations and musical genre explorations are taken into account, there is, perhaps, no better description of what Jimi created than his own words: "Electric church music."

He explained it further in an interview: "It's just a belief that I have. . . . We're planning for our sound to go inside the soul of a person and see if it can awaken some kind of thing in their minds, because there are so many sleeping people. . . . Our scene is to wash peoples' souls."

Novelist Tom Robbins, when he worked as a Seattle arts journalist, referred to Jimi's arrival in popular culture as "the new music spacequake."

The greatest testimony to how truly revolutionary Jimi was may be that just before the master tape of the single "Purple Haze" was sent from London's Track Records to Burbank's Warner Bros./Reprise Records for remastering, the following words were written on the tape box: "DELIBERATE DISTORTION. DO NOT CORRECT." The music industry itself was adapting to the influence of Jimi Hendrix.

Jimi had learned to play the guitar upside down, to play in every style imaginable. He couldn't write music, but he learned the structure of songs with stunning speed. He was afraid to sing, and yet he learned to use his voice to express charm, sexuality, and even despair. He lived through abject poverty, abandonment by his family and by the leaders of the bands in which he played. Time after time, he was told to stop playing guitar in a style that would revolutionize and redefine the instrument forever. He refused to give in, in the face of racism from whites, the limitations of equipment, and rejection from the black music establishment and startled audiences and bandleaders who could not appreciate his inventiveness.

He had to go to England to initially receive the level of acclaim he deserved, and at long last, he was about return to the United States to conquer his homeland. Paul McCartney recommended Jimi to Lou Adler and John Phillips of the Mamas & the Papas, who spearheaded the historic Monterey Pop Festival in 1967.

On the way to the stage in Monterey, he passed by producer Jerry Wexler, the man who had coined the term "rhythm and blues" to replace the term "race records" back in the 1940s and had known Jimi from his backup days. "There he was," said Wexler, "a veteran of the soul circuit, in crazy feathers and psychedelic regalia. He looked at me almost apologetically, knowing I knew where he came from. 'It's only for show,' he whispered in my ear before going out there and blowing up the star-spangled night."

Bibliography

Books

Altham, Keith. *The PR Strikes Back*. John Blake, London, 2001.

Altschuler, Glenn C. *All Shook Up: How Rock 'n' Roll Changed America*. Oxford University Press, New York, 2004.

Bego, Mark. *Aretha Franklin: The Queen of Soul*. St. Martin's Press, New York, 1989.

———. *Tina Turner: Break Every Rule*. Taylor Trade, New York, 2003.

Black, Johnny. *Jimi Hendrix: The Ultimate Experience*. Thunder's Mouth Press, New York, 1999.

Bockris, Victor. *Keith Richards: The Biography*. Poseidon Press, New York. 1992.

Bowman, Rob. *Soulsville U.S.A.: The Story of Stax Records*. Schirmer Books, New York, 1997.

Brown, James, with Bruce Tucker. *The Godfather of Soul: James Brown*. Da Capo Press, New York, 1997.

Brown, Tony. *Jimi Hendrix Concert Files*. Omnibus Press, London, 1999.

Burdon, Eric, with J. Marshall Craig. *Don't Let Me Be Misunderstood.* Da Capo Press, New York, 2001.

Carpenter, Diana Lynn. *Don't You Know Queens Don't Stand on the Corner?* Nystrom, Maple Grove, MN, 1999.

Chepesiuk, Ron. *Gangsters of Harlem: The Gritty Underworld of New York's Most Famous Neighborhood.* Barricade Books, New York, 2007.

Cohn, Lawrence. *Nothing But the Blues: The Music and the Musicians.* Abbeville Press, New York, 1993.

Cohn, Nik. *Rock, from the Beginning.* Stein and Day, New York, 1969.

Collis, John. *Ike Turner, King of Rhythm.* Do-Not Press, London, 2004.

Cooper, Ralph, with Steve Dougherty. *Amateur Night at the Apollo: Ralph Cooper Presents Five Decades of Great Entertainment.* HarperCollins, New York, 1990.

Crampton, Luke, and Dafydd Rees. *Rock and Roll Year by Year.* DK Publishing, London, 2003.

De Barros, Paul. *Jackson Street After Hours: The Roots of Jazz in Seattle.* Sasquatch Books, Seattle, 1993.

Deffaa, Chip. *Blue Rhythms: Six Lives in Rhythm and Blues.* University of Illinois Press, Champaign, 1996.

Dickerson, James L. *Mojo Triangle: Birthplace of Country, Blues, Jazz, and Rock 'n' Roll.* Schirmer Trade Books, New York, 2005.

Dolenz, Micky, and Mark Bego. *I'm a Believer: My Life of Monkees, Music, and Madness.* Hyperion, New York, 1993.

Doyle, Don H. *Nashville Since the 1920s.* University of Tennessee Press, Knoxville, 1985.

Einarson, John. *Forever Changes: Arthur Lee and the Book of Love.* Jawbone Press, London. 2010.

———. *Mr. Tambourine Man: The Life and Legacy of the Byrds' Gene Clark.* Backbeat Books, San Francisco, 2005.

Ertegun, Ahmet. *What'd I Say: The Atlantic Story 50 Years of Music.* Welcome Rain, New York, 2001.

Etchingham, Kathy, with Andrew Cofts. *Through Gypsy Eyes.* Orion, London, 1998.

Fein, Art. *The L.A. Musical History Tour: A Guide to the Rock and Roll*

Landmarks of Los Angeles. 2.13.61 Publications, Los Angeles, 1993.

Fisher, Robert W. *My Jimi Hendrix Experience.* Vantage Books, New York, 2003.

Floyd, Samuel A. Jr. *The Power of Black Music: Interpreting Its History from Africa to the United States.* Oxford University Press, New York, 1995.

Fong-Torres, Ben. *The Hits Just Keep On Coming: The History of Top 40 Radio.* Miller Freeman Books, San Francisco, 1998.

——. *Not Fade Away: A Backstage Pass to 20 Years of Rock & Roll.* Miller Freeman Books, Berkeley, CA, 1999.

Fox, Ted. *Showtime at the Apollo: The Story of Harlem's World Famous Theater.* St. Martin's Press, New York, 1983.

Freeman, Scott. *Otis! The Otis Redding Story.* St. Martin's Griffin, New York, 2001.

Garland, Phyl. *The Sound of Soul.* Henry Regnery, Chicago, 1969.

Geldeart, Gary, and Steve Rodham. *Jimi Hendrix: The Studio Log.* Jimpress, Warrington, UK, 2007.

George, Nelson. *The Death of Rhythm and Blues.* Pantheon Books, New York, 1988.

——. *Where Did Our Love Go? The Rise and Fall of the Motown Sound.* St. Martin's Press, New York, 1986.

Greenfield, Robert. *Timothy Leary: A Biography.* Harcourt, New York, 2006.

Grof, Stanislav. *LSD Psychotherapy: The Healing Potential of Psychedelic Medicine.* MAPS, Santa Cruz, CA, 2008.

Guralnick, Peter. *Dream Boogie: The Triumph of Sam Cooke.* Little, Brown, New York, 2005.

Hajdu, David. *Positively 4th Street: The Lives and Times of Joan Baez, Bob Dylan, Mimi Baez Farina, and Richard Farina.* Farrar, Straus and Giroux, New York, 2001.

Halberstam, David. *The Children.* Random House, New York, 1998.

Havens, Richie, with Steve Davidowitz. *They Can't Hide Us Anymore.* Avon Books, New York, 1999.

Heide, Robert, and John Gilman. *Greenwich Village: A Primo Guide to Shopping, Eating, and Making Merry in True Bohemia.* St. Martin's Griffin, New York, 1995.

Henderson, David. *'Scuse Me While I Kiss the Sky: Jimi Hendrix, Voodoo Child*. Atria Books, New York, 2008.

Hendrix, James A., with Jas Obrecht. *My Son Jimi*. Aljas Enterprises, Seattle, 1999.

Hirshey, Gerri. *Nowhere to Run: The Story of Soul Music*. Times Books, New York, 1984.

Hoskyns, Barney. *Arthur Lee: Alone Again Or*. Mojo Books, Edinburgh, UK, 2002.

———. *Waiting for the Sun: Strange Days, Weird Scenes, and the Sound of Los Angeles*. St. Martins Press, New York, 1996.

James, Etta, with David Ritz. *Rage to Survive: The Etta James Story*. Villard Books, New York, 1995.

Jarrett, Ted, with Ruth White. *You Can Make It if You Try: The Ted Jarrett Story of R&B in Nashville*. Hillsboro Press, Franklin, TN, 2005.

King, B. B., with David Ritz. *Blues All Around Me: The Autobiography of B. B. King*. Avon Books, New York, 1996.

Lawrence, Sharon. *Jimi Hendrix: The Intimate Story of a Betrayed Legend*. Harper Paperbacks, New York, 2005.

Leary, Timothy. *Flashbacks: A Personal and Cultural History of an Era*. Putnam, New York, 1983.

Mann, May. *Jayne Mansfield: A Biography*. Drake, New York, 1974.

McDermott, John, with Eddie Kramer. *Hendrix: Setting the Record Straight*. Warner Books, New York, 1992.

———. with Eddie Kramer and Billy Cox. *Ultimate Hendrix: An Illustrated Encyclopedia of Live Concerts and Sessions*. Backbeat Books, New York, 2009.

Murray, Charles Shaar. *Crosstown Traffic: Jimi Hendrix and the Post-War Rock 'n' Roll Revolution*. St. Martin's Press, New York, 1989.

Nager, Larry. *Memphis Beat: The Lives and Times of America's Musical Crossroads*. St. Martin's Press, New York, 1998.

Oakley, Giles. *The Devil's Music: A History of the Blues*. Taplinger, New York, 1977.

Oliver, Paul. *The Story of the Blues*. Chilton, Radnor, PA, 1969.

Phinney, Kevin. *Souled American: How Black Music Transformed White Culture*. Billboard Books, New York, 2005.

Pinkney, Alphonso, and Roger Woock. *Poverty and Politics in Harlem.* College and University Press Services, New Haven, CT, 1970.

Priore, Domenic. *Riot on Sunset Strip: Rock 'n' Roll's Last Stand in Hollywood.* Jawbone Press, Berkeley, CA, 2007.

Pryor, Richard, with Todd Gold. *Pryor Convictions and Other Life Sentences.* Pantheon Books, New York, 1995.

Redd, Lawrence N. *Rock Is Rhythm and Blues: The Impact of Mass Media.* Michigan State University Press, East Lansing, 1974.

Roby, Steven. *Black Gold: The Lost Archives of Jimi Hendrix.* Billboard Books, New York, 2002.

Sales, Soupy, with Charles Salzburg. *Soupy Sez! My Zany Life and Times.* M. Evans, New York, 2001.

Saxton, Martha. *Jayne Mansfield and the American Fifties.* Houghton Mifflin, Boston, 1975.

Schiffman, Jack. *Harlem Heyday: A Pictorial History of Modern Black Show Business and the Apollo Theater.* Prometheus Books, Buffalo, NY, 1984.

Segrest, James, and Mark Hoffman. *Moanin' at Midnight: The Life and Times of Howlin' Wolf.* Pantheon Books, New York, 2004.

Shapiro, Harry, and Caesar Glebbeek. *Jimi Hendrix: Electric Gypsy.* St. Martin's Griffin, New York, 1995.

Shaw, Arnold. *Honkers and Shouters: The Golden Years of Rhythm & Blues.* Macmillan, New York, 1978.

Smith, Susan E. *Dancing in the Street: Motown and the Cultural Politics of Detroit.* Harvard University Press, Cambridge, MA, 1999.

Smith, Wes. *The Pied Pipers of Rock 'n' Roll: Radio Deejays of the 50s and 60s.* Longstreet Press, Marietta, GA, 1989.

Sounes, Howard. *Down the Highway: The Life of Bob Dylan.* Grove Press, New York, 2001.

Staff of the Country Music Hall of Fame & Museum. *Night Train to Nashville: Music City Rhythm & Blues, 1945–1970.* CMF Press, Nashville, 2004.

Strait, Raymond. *Here They Are: Jayne Mansfield.* SPI Books, New York, 1976.

Turner, Ike, with Nigel Cawthorne. *Takin' Back My Name: The Confessions of Ike Turner.* Virgin Books, New York, 1999.

Unterberger, Richie. *Eight Miles High: Folk-Rock's Flight from Haight-Ashbury to Woodstock*. Backbeat Books, San Francisco, 2003.

———. *Turn! Turn! Turn!: The '60s Folk-Rock Revolution*. Backbeat Books, San Francisco, 2002.

Weingarten, Marc. *Station to Station: The History of Rock 'n' Roll Television*. Pocket Books, New York, 2000.

Werner, Craig. *Higher Ground: Stevie Wonder, Aretha Franklin, Curtis Mayfield, and the Rise and Fall of American Soul*. Crown, New York, 2004.

Wexler, Jerry, and David Ritz. *Rhythm and the Blues: A Life in American Music*. Knopf, New York, 1993.

Whitburn, Joel. *The Billboard Book of Top 40 Hits*. Billboard Books, New York, 1996.

White, Charles. *The Life and Times of Little Richard: The Quasar of Rock*. Harmony Books, New York, 1984.

Willix, Mary. *Voices from Home*. Creative Forces, San Diego, 1995.

Woliver, Robbie. *Hoot!: A 25-Year History of the Greenwich Village Scene*. St. Martin's Press, New York, 1986.

Woolbridge, Max. *Rock 'n' Roll London*. St. Martin's Griffin, New York, 2002.

Womack, Bobby, with Robert Ashton. *My Autobiography: Midnight Mover, the True Story of the Greatest Soul Singer in the World*. John Blake, London, 2006.

Documents

U. S. Army Personnel Records 1961–1962, James M. Hendrix, National Personnel Records Center, St Louis, Missouri.

Report of Medical History, U.S. Army, James M. Hendrix, May 14, 1961–1962.

Soupy Sales, *Easter in Person* concert program, April 1965.

Jimmy Hendrix's recording contract for PPX, October 15, 1965.

Jimmy Hendrix's Popular Songwriters Contract for RSVP, March 30, 1966.

Jimi Hendrix's 1967 UK fan club press release bio.

Yameta Co. and Jimi Hendrix against Capitol Records, Inc., PPX Enterprises, Inc., Edward Chalpin, and Curtis Knight, pretrial examination testimony, March 7, 1968.

Jimi Hendrix's FBI files, 1969–1970.

DVDs

All You Need Is Love, Episode 10, *Good Times—Rhythm and Blues*. Produced by Rob Ayling, Isolde Films, 2008.

The American Experience: That Rhythm, Those Blues. Produced by George T. Niernberg, PBS, 1988.

American Masters: Atlantic Records: The House That Ahmet Built. Produced by Phil Carson, Atlantic Recording Corporation, and Educational Broadcasting, 2007.

Everybody Needs Somebody: The Definitive Fully Authorized Story of Solomon Burke. Produced by Paul Spencer, Snapper Music Group, 2008.

A Film About Jimi Hendrix, including the special feature *From the Ukulele to the Strat*. Produced by Joe Boyd, John Head, and Gary Weis, Warner Bros. Entertainment, 1973 and 2005.

Hollywood Backstage, various 1965 episodes from the author's collection including coverage of the Sunset Strip nightclub Ciro's Le Disc.

The Howlin' Wolf Story: The Secret History of Rock and Roll. Produced by Joe Lauro, the Reel Factory, 2003.

Jimi Hendrix by Those Who Knew Him Best. Produced by Andy Cleland and Rob Johnstone, Chrome Dreams Media, 2004.

Jimi Hendrix: The Uncut Story, vols. 1 and 2. Produced by Steve Vogel, Passport Video, 2004.

Nashville Roots, a special feature from *Jimi Hendrix at Woodstock*. Produced by Janie Hendrix and John McDermott for Experience Hendrix, MCA, 2005.

Night Train. Produced by WLAC-TV, Nashville, Tennessee, 1965. Three complete episodes from the author's private collection.

Sam Cooke Legend: The Life, the Legend, the Legacy. Abkco Music and Records, New York, 2003.

Periodicals

Aarhuus Stiftstidende, Amsterdam News, Bass Player, Beat Instrumental, Bergen Record, Billboard, Bravo, Broadcasting, Cashbox, Chicago Daily News, Clarksville Leaf Chronicle, Daily Mirror, Daily Planet, Dallas Observer, Down Beat, Ebony, Experience Hendrix, Eye, Gallery, Goldmine, Guitar Player, Guitar World, Guitarist, Hit Parader, Humo, Jazz Review, Jet, Jimpress, L.A. Free Press, Life, Los Angeles Herald-Examiner, Melody Maker, Mojo, New Musical Express, New York Magazine, New York Post, New York Times, Open City, Pasadena Star News, Post-Standard, Rat, Rave, Rolling Stone, Seattle Times, Shake!, Sky, Straight Ahead, Sunday Mirror, The Sun, Syracuse Herald Journal, Teen Set, Tennessean, Time, Ugly Things, Univibes, Variety, Village Voice, Vintage Guitar, Wax Poetics.

Liner Notes

Better Shred Than Dead: The Dick Dale Anthology. Rhino, 1997.
Knock Yourself Out: Jimi Hendrix with Curtis Knight and the Squires. Freud-Jungle Full, 2000.
Martin Scorsese Presents the Blues: Jimi Hendrix. MCA, 2003.
Night Train to Nashville: Music City Rhythm and Blues, 1945–1970. CMF Records, 2004.
T-Bone Walker: Classics of Modern Blues. BGO, 2002.
Two Great Experiences: Lonnie Youngblood Featuring Jimi Hendrix. BMG, 2003.
Where the Action Is: Los Angeles Nuggets, 1965–1968. Rhino, 2009.

Audio Interviews

Hans Carl Schmidt interview with Jimi Hendrix for German Radio, May 25, 1967.
Tom Lopez interview with Jimi Hendrix, December 1967.
Gus Gossert (KMPX) backstage interview with Jimi Hendrix, October 1968.
Curtis Knight interview on WMCA, October 1974.
Steven Roby interviews conducted for *Straight Ahead*, 1989–1996.

Barney Hoskyns interview with Arthur Lee, June 24, 1993.

Terry Gross interview with Dick Dale from NPR's *Fresh Air* program, July 26, 1993.

Web Sites

Possibly the best Web site that focuses on prefame Hendrix is www.earlyhendrix.com/. The Webmaster offers a complete discography of confirmed and unconfirmed Hendrix-related recordings and a timeline and is updated often.

To sample eighteen pages of Jimi's military records, see www.the smokinggun.com/archive/0803051jimi1.html.

Longtime Hendrix archivist Caesar Glebbeek is the editor of the international Jimi Hendrix fanzine *Univibes*. The fanzine's Web site, www.univibes.com, is packed with information on Hendrix's life, Hendrix's music, and subscription details.

Another great source for Hendrix-related articles and audio interviews is www.rocksbackpages.com.

Recommended Listening

Covay, Don. *Mercy!* Atlantic S104, released 1964.

Curtis, King. *Live at Small's Paradise*. Atco 33–198, released 1966.

Hendrix, Jimi. *The Authentic PPX Studio Recordings,* vols. 1–6. SPV, released 1996.

Isley Brothers. *In the Beginning*. T-Neck TNS 3007, released 1971.

———. *The Isley Brothers Story,* vol. 1: *Rockin' Soul, 1959–68*. Rhino R2 70908, released 1991.

James, Etta. *Etta James Rocks the House*. MCA CHD9184, recorded live at the New Era Club, Nashville, Tennessee, September 27 and 28, 1963.

Little Richard. *Little Richard: 20 Greatest Hits*. Deluxe DCD-7797, released 1987.

Mansfield, Jayne. *Jayne Mansfield: Too Hot to Handle*. Legend 6008, released 1994.

Mr. Wiggles. *Mr. Wiggles Again*. Sound of Soul, released 2002.

———. *Mr. Wiggles and His Sound of Soul Family*. Sound of Soul, released 2002.

Various Artists. *The Jimmy James Singles Collection*. Private release, released 2002.

Various Artists. *The Old Town and Barry Soul Survey*. Kent CDKEND
244, released 2005.
Various Artists. *The Roots of Jimi Hendrix: 15 Tracks That Inspired the
Legend*. Mojo, released 2005.
Youngblood, Lonnie. *Two Great Experiences: The Complete Record-
ings/Expanded Edition*. Empire Music Werks, released 2003.

THE JIMI HENDRIX EXHIBIT AT EXPERIENCE MUSIC PROJECT IN
Seattle, Washington, features Al Hendrix's record player, a Decca
DP-306 High Fidelity console. The following is a list of R&B and
blues records from Al's collection that Jimmy listened to in the
1950s and early 1960s:

Bobby "Blue" Bland, "Saint James Infirmary"

James Brown, "Please, Please, Please"

The Coasters, "Poison Ivy"

The Crests, "16 Candles"

Frankie Ford, "You Talk Too Much"

Jimmy Forrest, "Remember"

The Imperials, "Tears on my Pillow"

Etta James, "Don't Cry Baby"

Little Richard, "By the Light of the Silvery Moon"

Lloyd Price, "You Need Love"

Ray Bryant Combo, "Sack o' Woe"

Jimmy Smith, "I Got a Woman"

The Wailers, "Velva"

Sessionography/Discography and Television Appearances,

1962–1966

1962

BILLY COX

TITLE: Unknown

COMPOSER: Unknown.

LOCATION: Starday/King Sound Studios, Nashville

RECORDED: April

PRODUCER: William "Hoss" Allen

PERSONNEL: James Hendrix (guitar), Billy Cox (bass), and others unknown

During their service in the army, Hendrix and Cox entered Starday/King Studios in Nashville to record a demo. After the first take, producer Bill "Hoss" Allen thought something was wrong with the equipment, but it turned out to be just Hendrix feeding back on his guitar. Allen recorded the song but removed Hendrix from the mix.

1963

JOHNNY JONES

TITLE: "Feels So Bad, Like a Ball Game on a Rainy Day"

COMPOSER: Johnny Jones

LOCATION: Starday/King Sound Studios, Nashville

RECORDED: August

PRODUCER: William "Hoss" Allen

PERSONNEL: Johnny Jones (vocals, lead guitar), James Hendrix (rhythm guitar), and others unknown

Jones and Hendrix recorded this track with the aid of Hoss Allen. Allen is said to have pressed a demo version and played it on WLAC.

FRANK HOWARD AND THE COMMANDERS

TITLE: "I'm So Glad" b/w "I'm Sorry for You"

COMPOSER: Billy Cox

LOCATION: Starday/King Studios, Nashville

RECORDED: August–November

PRODUCER: Hoss Allen

RELEASE DATE: 1965

LABEL: Barry Records

MATRIX NUMBER: 1008

PERSONNEL: Frank Howard, Herschel Carter, and Charley Fite (vocals), Johnny Jones (lead guitar), James Hendrix (rhythm guitar), Billy Cox (bass), Freeman Brown (drums), and Harrison Callaway and others (horns)

Billy Cox and singer Frank Howard invited Hendrix to sit in on this session. Because producer Hoss Allen had had such a bad experience with Hendrix's wild feedback in 1962, he kept Hendrix very low in the mix.

GEORGE YATES AND SANDRA WRIGHT

TITLE: "I'm Crying"

COMPOSER: George Yates

LOCATION: Starday/King Studios, Nashville

RECORDED: August–November

PRODUCER: Hoss Allen

PERSONNEL: Sandra Wright (lead vocal), George Yates (rhythm guitar), James Hendrix (lead guitar), and Freeman Brown (drums)

Guitarist George Yates used Hendrix for a session he did with singer Sandra Wright. The song was never released, and Yates still has the recording.

THE BONNEVILLES

TITLES: "Snuff Dripper," "Ouch," and two unknown titles
COMPOSER: Unknown
LOCATION: Fidelity Recording, Nashville
RECORDED: August–November
PRODUCER: Robert Fisher
PERSONNEL: Robert Fisher (keyboards), James Hendrix (lead guitar), Larry Lee (rhythm guitar), unknown (bass), Issac MacKay (drums), Harrison Callaway (trumpet), and Aaron "Heinz Ketchup" Varnell (saxophone)

These recordings still exist and are in storage.

1964

DON COVAY

TITLE: "Mercy, Mercy"
COMPOSERS: Don Covay and Horace Ott
LOCATION: A1 Sound Studios, New York
RECORDED: May 13
PRODUCER: Herb Abramson
RELEASE DATE: August 1964
LABEL: Rosemart Records
MATRIX NUMBER: 45-801
PERSONNEL: Don Covay (lead vocals), George "King" Clemons (background vocals), Ronald Miller (lead guitar), James Hendrix (second guitar), Horace "Ace" Hall (bass), and Bernard Purdie (drums)

THE ISLEY BROTHERS

TITLE: "Testify (Parts 1 and 2)"
COMPOSERS: O'Kelly Isley, Rudolph Isley, and Ronald Isley
LOCATION: Atlantic Studios, New York
RECORDED: May 21

PRODUCERS: O'Kelly Isley, Rudolph Isley, and Ronald Isley

RELEASE DATE: June 1964

LABEL: T-Neck

MATRIX NUMBER: 45-501

PERSONNEL: Isley Brothers (vocals), James Hendrix (guitar), Al Lucas (bass), James Brown and/or Bobby Gregg (drums), Paul Griffin (piano), and Dickie Harris, Haywood Henry, Quentin Jackson, Jimmy Nottingham, and Eddie Williams (horns)

1965

ROSA LEE BROOKS

TITLE: "My Diary"

COMPOSER: Arthur Lee

LOCATION: Billy Revis's home recording studio, Los Angeles

RECORDED: March 27

PRODUCER: Billy Revis

ENGINEER: Elmer "Doc" Siegel at Gold Star Studios, Hollywood

RELEASE DATE: June 1965

LABEL: Revis

MATRIX NUMBER: 1013

PERSONNEL: Rosa Lee Brooks (lead vocal), "Maurice James" Hendrix (lead guitar and background vocals), "Big Francis" (drums), Alvin, surname unknown (bass), Arthur Lee, "Maurice James" Hendrix and two unknown female singers (background vocals), and unknown (horns)

The song received minor airplay on KDAY-AM in Los Angeles.

ROSA LEE BROOKS

TITLE: "Utee"

COMPOSERS: Rosa Lee Brooks and Billy Revis

LOCATION: Billy Revis's home recording studio, Los Angeles

RECORDED: March 27

PRODUCER: Billy Revis

ENGINEER: Elmer "Doc" Siegel at Gold Star Studios, Hollywood

RELEASE DATE: June 1965

LABEL: Revis

MATRIX NUMBER: 1013

PERSONNEL: Same as on "My Diary"

LITTLE RICHARD

TITLE: "I Don't Know What You've Got (But It's Got Me) (Parts 1 and 2)"

COMPOSERS: Don Covay and Horace "Ace" Hall

LOCATION: Bell Sound Studios, New York

RECORDED: June 2

PRODUCER: Calvin Carter

RELEASE DATE: October 1, 1965

LABEL: Vee-Jay Records

MATRIX NUMBER: VJ-698

PERSONNEL: Little Richard (vocal, piano), Jimmy Hendrix (guitar), Don Covay (vocal), Bernard Purdie (drums), Billy Preston (organ), Ronnie Miller (bass), and the Crown Jewels' horn section

There were only four tracks recorded at one Little Richard session that featured Hendrix on guitar.

LITTLE RICHARD

TITLE: "Dance A Go Go"

COMPOSERS: B. Mitchell and Little Richard

LOCATION: Bell Sound Studios, New York

RECORDED: June

PRODUCER: Calvin Carter

RELEASE DATE: October 1, 1965

LABEL: Vee-Jay Records

MATRIX NUMBER: VJ-698

PERSONNEL: Same as on "I Don't Know What You've Got"

LITTLE RICHARD

June 1965 Sessions

In addition to the abovementioned single and an alternate take of "I Don't Know What You've Got," there were two other tracks recorded with Hendrix at this session: "Something Moves in My

Heart" and "You Better Stop." In a promo-only release, "Dance a Go Go" was released as the B side to "I Don't Know What You've Got."

Little Richard's twenty-first original album, *Talkin' 'bout Soul* (released in 1974), featured tracks recorded for Vee-Jay Records from 1964 to 1965, including those mentioned here. In 2007, Vee-Jay released a digital version of *Talkin' 'bout Soul* with twenty-eight tracks that include both takes of "I Don't Know What You Got" and the other three songs from the June 1965 session. Hendrix's guitar, however, is less audible on these tracks when compared to the "I Don't Know What You've Got" single.

MR. WIGGLES AND THE WIGGLIN' MEN
TITLE: "Wash My Back" b/w "Home Boy"
COMPOSER: Mr. Wiggles
LOCATION: A-1 Sound Studios, New York
RECORDED: July
PRODUCER: Little Tommy
RELEASE DATE: 1966
LABEL: Golden Triangle
MATRIX NUMBER: 100
PERSONNEL: Mr. Wiggles (vocals), James Hendrix (guitar), and Grady Gaines (tenor saxophone), with other instruments provided by various members from Little Richard's original band, the Upsetters

MR. WIGGLES
TITLE: "Fat Back (Part 1)" b/w "Fat Back (Part 2)" (Instrumental)
COMPOSER: Mr. Wiggles
LOCATION: A-1 Sound Studios, New York
RECORDED: July
PRODUCER: Mr. Wiggles
RELEASE DATE: 1966
LABEL: Parkway Records
MATRIX NUMBER: P-104-A/B
PERSONNEL: Same as on "Wash My Back"

THE WORLD FAMOUS UPSETTERS

TITLE: "K. P." b/w "Cabbage Greens"

COMPOSER: Grady Gaines

LOCATION: A-1 Sound Studios, New York

RECORDED: July

PRODUCER: Mr. Wiggles

RELEASE DATE: 1966

LABEL: Sound of Soul

MATRIX NUMBER: 105

PERSONNEL: James Hendrix (lead guitar), Melvin Sparks (rhythm guitar), and Grady Gaines (tenor saxophone), with other instruments provided by various members from Little Richard's original band, the Upsetters

During the Mr. Wiggles sessions, Hendrix cut these two instrumental tracks with tenor saxophonist Grady Gaines.

THE ISLEY BROTHERS

TITLE: "Move Over Let Me Dance" b/w "Have You Ever Been Disappointed?"

COMPOSERS: O'Kelly Isley, Rudolph Isley, and Ronald Isley

ARRANGER/CONDUCTOR: Teachco Wilshire

LOCATION: Atlantic Studios, New York

RECORDED: August 5

PRODUCERS: O'Kelly Isley, Rudolph Isley, and Ronald Isley

RELEASE DATE: September 1965

LABEL: Atlantic

MATRIX NUMBER: 45-2303

PERSONNEL: Ronald Isley (lead vocal), Rudolph Isley and O'Kelly Isley (background vocals), Al Lucas (bass), Bobby Gregg (drums), James Hendrix (lead guitar), Douglas McArthur and/or Carl Lynch (rhythm guitar), Jimmy Nottingham and Eddie Williams (trumpet), Quentin Jackson and Dickie Harris (trombone), Seldon Powell (tenor sax), and Haywood Henry (baritone sax)

CURTIS KNIGHT

TITLE: "How Would You Feel" b/w "Welcome Home"

COMPOSER: "How Would You Feel," Curtis Knight; "Welcome Home," Curtis Knight and Dick Glass
ARRANGER: Jimmy Hendrix
LOCATION: Studio 76, New York
RECORDED: October 6 and December
PRODUCER: Ed Chalpin
RELEASE DATE: April 1966
LABEL: RSVP
MATRIX NUMBER: RSVP 1120
PERSONNEL: "How Would You Feel": Curtis Knight (lead and background vocals), James Hendrix (guitar, fuzz bass, drums, background vocals, and arrangement), and Johnny Star (background vocals)

"Welcome Home": Curtis Knight (lead vocals, guitar), James Hendrix (lead guitar), Horace "Ace" Hall or Napoleon Anderson (bass), Marion Booker or Ditto Edwards (drums), and crowd noise (all)

CURTIS KNIGHT AND THE SQUIRES

TITLES: "Don't Accuse Me," "You Don't Want Me," "Simon Says," "Welcome Home"
COMPOSER: Curtis Knight
LOCATION: Studio 76, New York
RECORDED: December
PRODUCER: Ed Chalpin
PERSONNEL: Curtis Knight (lead vocals), James Hendrix (guitar, fuzz bass), Horace "Ace" Hall or Napoleon Anderson (bass), Ditto Edwards or Marion Booker (drums), and Lonnie Youngblood (sax)

It is believed that these sessions took place sometime in December 1965. However, most of the tracks were released in 1967 after Hendrix became famous.

CURTIS KNIGHT AND THE SQUIRES/
THE LOVE LIGHTS
Live Recordings
TITLES: "Ain't That Peculiar"; "Baby, What You Want Me to Do"; "Bleeding Heart"; "Bo Diddley"; "Bright Lights, Big City"; "Califor-

nia Night"; "Come On (Part 1)"; "Day Tripper"; "Drivin' South"; "Get Out of My Life, Woman"; "Hang on Sloopy"; "Hold What You've Got"; "I Can't Help Myself (Sugar Pie, Honey Bunch)"; "I Got You (I Feel Good)"; "I'll Be Doggone"; "I'm a Man"; "Just a Little Bit"; "Killing Floor";* "Land of a Thousand Dances"; "Last Night";* "Let's Go, Let's Go, Let's Go"; "Mercy, Mercy"; "Money"; "Mr. Pitiful"; "One Night with You"; "Satisfaction"; "Shotgun"; "Something You've Got"; "Stand by Me"; "Sweet Little Angel"; "There Is Something on Your Mind"; "Twist and Shout"; "You Got What It Takes"; "Walkin' the Dog"; "What I'd Say"; and "Wooly Bully"

COMPOSERS: Various

LOCATIONS: George's Club 20 in Hackensack, New Jersey, and other unidentified locations

RECORDED: December 26 and other undetermined dates

PRODUCER: Unknown

PERSONNEL: Curtis Knight (lead and background vocals and rhythm guitar), James Hendrix (lead and background vocals and lead guitar), Horace "Ace" Hall (bass/tambourine on some songs), Harry Jensen (bass on some songs), Ditto Edwards (drums on some songs), and Lonnie Youngblood (saxophone)

Occasionally, the band billed itself as the Love Lights.

It's doubtful that these club recordings were ever meant to be released; rather, they were probably meant to be used as a reference tape for the group and as a sample for potential club owners of what the band sounded like live.

These tracks (and possibly a few others) are not live recordings but have crowd noise added, giving them a "live recording" sound.

1966

RAY SHARPE WITH THE KING CURTIS ORCHESTRA
TITLE: "Help Me (Get the Feeling)" Parts 1 & 2
COMPOSERS: Curtis Ousley, Ray Sharpe, and Cornell Dupree
LOCATION: Atlantic Studios, New York
RECORDED: January 21
PRODUCER: King Curtis

RELEASE DATE: Spring 1966
LABEL: Atco Records
MATRIX NUMBER: 45-6402
PERSONNEL: Ray Sharpe (vocal and lead guitar), King Curtis (sax), Ray Lucas (drums), Bernard Purdie (drums), Cornel Dupree (guitar), James Hendrix (guitar), Melvin Laste (trumpet), and Willie Bridges (sax)

RAY SHARPE WITH THE KING CURTIS ORCHESTRA
April 28, 1966, Session
LOCATION: Atlantic Studios, New York
One final session with Hendrix took place on April 28, 1966. These master tapes were destroyed, however, in an Atco/Atlantic warehouse fire in 1978. No other copies are known to exist.
MATRIX/TITLE/STATUS:
66C-10190 "Linda Lou," unissued
66C-10191 "I Can't Take It," unissued
66C-10192 "Baby How About You," unissued

JAYNE MANSFIELD
TITLE: "Suey"
COMPOSERS: Edward Chalpin and Douglas "Jocko" Henderson
LOCATION: Studio 76, New York
RECORDED: Late January or early February
PRODUCER: Edward Chalpin
RELEASE DATE: 1967 in the UK
LABEL: London
MATRIX NUMBER: HL 10147
PERSONNEL: Jayne Mansfield (vocals), James Hendrix (guitar, bass), Douglas "Jocko" Henderson (drums), unknown (organ), and unknown (horns)

While performing in New York, producer Ed Chalpin asked Jayne Mansfield to record a single at his studio. The heavily arranged A side, "As the Clouds Drift By," has no Hendrix involvement and is mostly strings and background singers backing up Mansfield's lead vocal. The Mansfield single (London HL 10147) wasn't released until after her tragic death in 1967.

CURTIS KNIGHT AND THE SQUIRES

TITLES: "Strange Things," "Better Times Ahead," "Everybody Knew but Me," and "If You've Got to Make a Fool of Somebody"
COMPOSERS: "Strange Things," Ed Dantes; "Better Times Ahead," Ed Dantes; and "Everybody Knew but Me" and "If You've Got to Make a Fool of Somebody," unknown
LOCATION: Studio 76, New York
RECORDED: March
PRODUCER: Ed Chalpin
PERSONNEL: Curtis Knight (vocals) Jimmy Hendrix (guitars), unknown (bass), unknown (drums), and Nathaniel Edmonds Sr. (organ).

BMI's database credits Ed Dantes (a pseudonym that Ed Chalpin occasionally used) as composer for several of the Curtis Knight and the Squires songs.

"Strange Things" features new member "Nate" Edmonds Sr. on organ. The song will later surface on the 1967 LP *Get That Feeling.* "Better Times Ahead" and "Everybody Knew but Me" appear to be in demo form, with only Hendrix playing guitar and Knight singing. "If You've Got to Make a Fool of Somebody" probably has no Hendrix involvement. There's also a possibility that an early demo of "I Ain't Taking Care of No Business" was recorded during these sessions.

CURTIS KNIGHT AND THE SQUIRES
The RSVP Sessions
RSVP producer Jerry Simon organized and produced three separate sessions with Curtis Knight and the Squires.

TITLES (FIRST SESSION): "I'm a Fool for You Baby," "Gotta Have a New Dress," and "U.F.O."
COMPOSERS: "I'm a Fool for You Baby," Curtis Knight; "Gotta Have a New Dress," Sampson Horton and Curtis Knight; and "U.F.O.," Curtis Knight

LOCATION: Allegro Sound Studios, New York
RECORDED: June
PRODUCER: Jerry Simon
PERSONNEL: Curtis Knight (vocals), Jimmy Hendrix (guitar), Napoleon Anderson (bass), Marion Booker (drums), and Nathaniel Edmonds Sr. (organ)

TITLES (SECOND SESSION): "Hornet's Nest" (aka "Kato's Special"), "Flying on Instruments" (aka "Knock Yourself Out"), "No Such Animal," and "Station Break"
COMPOSERS: "Hornet's Nest," Jimi Hendrix and Jerry Simon; "Flying on Instruments," Jimi Hendrix and Jerry Simon; "No Such Animal," Jimi Hendrix; and "Station Break," Jimi Hendrix and Jerry Simon
LOCATION: Allegro Sound Studios, New York
RECORDED: June
PRODUCER: Jerry Simon
PERSONNEL: Jimmy Hendrix (guitar), Napoleon Anderson (bass), Marion Booker (drums), and Nathaniel Edmonds Sr. (organ)

TITLES (THIRD SESSION): "My Love" (aka "My Heart Is Higher") and "The Ballad of Jimmy" (aka "My Best Friend")
COMPOSERS: "My Love," Tony Hatch; and "The Ballad of Jimmy," Curtis Knight
LOCATION: Allegro Sound Studios, New York
RECORDED: June
PRODUCER: Jerry Simon
PERSONNEL: Curtis Knight (vocals), unknown (guitar), unknown (bass), unknown (drums), and Nathaniel Edmonds Sr. (piano/organ)

Based on the quality of the playing, it's doubtful that Hendrix appears on this third session.

CURTIS KNIGHT AND THE SQUIRES
TITLES: "Hornet's Nest" b/w "Knock Yourself Out"
COMPOSERS: Jimmy Hendrix and Jerry Simon
LOCATION: Allegro Sound Studios, New York
RECORDED: June

PRODUCER: Jerry Simon
ENGINEER: Bruce Staple
RELEASE DATE: late 1966
LABEL: RSVP
MATRIX NUMBER: RSVP 1124
PERSONNEL: Jimi Hendrix (guitar), Napoleon Anderson (bass), Marion Booker (drums). Nathaniel Edmonds Sr. (organ), and unknown (screaming on "Hornet's Nest")

Both tracks are instrumentals. "Hornet's Nest" is based on the song "Flight of the Bumble Bee" written by Nikolai Rimsky-Korsakov for his opera *The Tale of Tsar Saltan.* "Knock Yourself Out" showcases Jimi's guitar work, but the single release of this song is in edited form.

JIMI HENDRIX

TITLE: "No Such Animal (Parts I and II)"
COMPOSER: Jimi Hendrix
LOCATION: Allegro Sound Studios, New York
RECORDED: June
PRODUCER: Jerry Simon
RELEASE DATE: 1971
ENGINEER: Bruce Staple
LABEL: Audio Fidelity
MATRIX NUMBER: AF-167
PERSONNEL: Jimi Hendrix (guitar), Napoleon Anderson (bass), Marion Booker (drums), Nathaniel Edmonds Sr. (organ), and unknown (shouting)

The song is edited into two parts due to its length.

LONNIE YOUNGBLOOD

TITLE: "Go Go Shoes" b/w "Go Go Place"
COMPOSERS: May Thomas, Lonnie Thomas (aka Lonnie Youngblood), and Horace "Ace" Hall
ARRANGER: Lonnie Youngblood
LOCATION: Abtone Studios, New York
RECORDED: June 10

PRODUCER: Lonnie Youngblood
RELEASE DATE: 1966
LABEL: Fairmount Records
MATRIX NUMBER: F-1002
PERSONNEL: Same personnel on both recordings—Lonnie Youngblood (lead vocal and horns), May Thomas (backing vocals), unknown (drums), Horace "Ace" Hall (bass), and James Hendrix (guitar)

The June sessions yielded two singles for Youngblood and a backing track used for other artists.

LONNIE YOUNGBLOOD

TITLE: "Soul Food (That's a What I Like)" b/w "Goodbye Bessie Mae"
COMPOSERS: "Soul Food," Lonnie Thomas (aka Lonnie Youngblood) and Napoleon Anderson (aka Hank Anderson); "Goodbye Bessie Mae," Lonnie Thomas
LOCATION: Abtone Studios, New York
RECORDED: June 10, 1966
PRODUCER: Lonnie Youngblood
ARRANGER: Lonnie Youngblood
LABEL: Fairmount
MATRIX NUMBER: F-1022
RELEASE DATE: 1967
PERSONNEL: Same as on "Go Go Shoes"

In 1970, Hendrix revisited Youngblood's "Goodbye Bessie Mae" melody while recording the song "Sugar Daddy" with the vocal group the Ghetto Fighters.

LONNIE YOUNGBLOOD

TITLES: "Under the Table" and "Wipe the Sweat"
COMPOSERS: "Under the Table," Lonnie Youngblood and Wes Wesley; "Wipe the Sweat," Lonnie Youngblood and James Hendrix
LOCATION: Abtone Studios, New York
RECORDED: June

Take three of "Wipe the Sweat" features the first known studio recording of Hendrix singing lead, preceding his version of "Hey Joe" by six months. Unfortunately, both Hendrix and Youngblood's vocal tracks for this song are merely guide tracks and are discarded when other singers overdub their vocals.

THE ICEMEN

TITLES: "(My Girl) She's a Fox" b/w "(I Wonder) What It Takes"
COMPOSERS: "(My Girl) She's A Fox," Richard Poindexter, Robert Poindexter, and Charles Harper; "(I Wonder) What It Takes," Gino Armstrong, James Stokes, and Robert Poindexter
ARRANGER: Lonnie Youngblood
LOCATION: Abtone Studios, New York
RECORDED: June
PRODUCER: Johnny Brantley
RELEASE DATE: Late 1966
LABEL: Samar
MATRIX NUMBER: S-111

This single featuring Hendrix on guitar is arranged by Lonnie Youngblood and released in 1966.

JIMMY NORMAN

TITLES: "You're Only Hurting Yourself " b/w "That Little Old Groove-maker"
COMPOSER: Jimmy Norman
LOCATION: Abtone Studios, New York
RECORDED: June
PRODUCER: Johnny Brantley
RELEASE DATE: Late 1966
LABEL: Samar
MATRIX NUMBER: S-112
PERSONNEL: Jimmy Norman (vocals), James Hendrix (guitar), Gino Armstrong, James Stokes, and a girl group called the Thrills (background singers), and the rest unknown.

Nashville born singer-songwriter Jimmy Norman noted that Jimi played on two of his unreleased songs: 'On You Girlie That Looks Good" and "Family Tree."

The original mixes for the Icemen and Jimmy Norman singles are available only on the Samar 45s released in 1966. Versions that appear on later compilations, titled either "Groovemaker," "Groove," or "Two in One Goes," are all drastically different. Another Jimmy Norman single, "Gangster of Love," which is often featured on many posthumous compilations, has no Hendrix involvement.

JIMI JAMES AND THE BLUE FLAMES

LOCATION: Cafe Wha?
RECORDED: July—August

According to several eyewitnesses, Hendrix is encouraged to make a demo tape of his new band to share with potential managers and producers. After several attempts, the project is aborted when the tape deck continues to malfunction. It's believed that the recording is trashed.

Television Performances: 1965

LITTLE RICHARD

SHOW: *Hollywood A Go Go* (syndicated)
DATE: February 20
SONGS PERFORMED: Unknown, lip-synched

Hollywood A Go Go was a nationally syndicated nightly half-hour program, hosted by Sam Riddle. It was taped on a set that resembled a "dank basement turned seedy speakeasy." "*Hollywood A Go Go* was the loudest, nastiest, and funkiest show," said its producer Al Burton, "but it was primitive on purpose." It's unknown if Hendrix appeared with Little Richard on this show.

LITTLE RICHARD

SHOW: *New American Bandstand* (ABC-TV syndicated)
DATE: March 6, episode 1669
SONGS PERFORMED: "Lucille" and "Ain't What You Do," lip-synched.
American Bandstand broadcasted weekly from Los Angeles beginning in 1964. While Hendrix and Little Richard were in Los Angeles, Richard made a solo appearance on this teen dance show. Richard shared the bill with TV/film actor Chad Everett and J. Frank Wilson and The Cavaliers ("Last Kiss"). Unfortunately, only the Royal

Company guards, not the Crown Jewels, appeared with Little Richard on this broadcast.

LITTLE RICHARD
SHOW: *Channel 7 News* (WABC-TV, New York)
DATE: April 16

New York City's ABC affiliate covered opening day of the *Soupy Sales Easter Show* at the Paramount Theater. It's believed footage may still exist of a short clip of Little Richard's show.

BUDDY AND STACY WITH THE CROWN JEWELS
SHOW: *Night Train* (broadcast on WLAC-TV, Nashville)
DATE: Recorded July 6; broadcast in September
SONG PERFORMED: "Shotgun"

The artists on this episode of *Night Train* included Buddy and Stacy backed by the Crown Jewels, the Avons, the Spidells, Jimmy Church, and Pamela Releford. During a stopover in Nashville, Richard let his band and opening act perform while he stayed back at his hotel room.

This clip has appeared in numerous documentaries and can also be viewed on YouTube.

JOEY DEE AND THE STARLITERS
SHOW: TV commercial for McVans, Buffalo, New York
DATE: November 2 or 3
SONG PERFORMED: "Peppermint Twist"

In an effort to promote the six-night run at McVans, the club hired a film crew to make a TV commercial of Joey Dee and the Starliters performing "Peppermint Twist." According to Dee, Hendrix made some unexpected feedback with his guitar during the song.

Chronology of Tours and Events, 1962–1966

1962

JANUARY

Fort Campbell, Kentucky

Hendrix forms the group the King Kasuals with Billy Cox (bass), Gary Ferguson (drums), and, on occasion, Major Charles Washington (saxophone). They play Service Clubs No. 1 and 2 at Fort Campbell Military Reservation and occasionally in nearby Clarksville, Tennessee.

Thursday, 1/11

Fort Campbell, Kentucky

Hendrix has successfully completed training and is rated a qualified parachutist and authorized to wear the wear parachutist badge as declared by Major General C. W. G. Rich. As he was a high school dropout, Hendrix begins taking his GED (General Educational Development) tests today.

Friday, 1/12

Fort Campbell, Kentucky

Second round of GED testing occurs for Hendrix.

Monday, 1/13
Fort Campbell, Kentucky
Hendrix takes the third part of his GED tests.

Tuesday, 1/16
Fort Campbell, Kentucky
Hendrix takes part four of his GED tests.

Wednesday, 1/17
Fort Campbell, Kentucky
Hendrix writes home and asks his father to send his guitar.

Monday, 1/22
Fort Campbell, Kentucky
Hendrix takes his final GED test.

Tuesday, 1/30
Fort Campbell, Kentucky
Hendrix is promoted to private first class.

FEBRUARY
Wednesday, 2/7
Fort Campbell, Kentucky
Hendrix makes another successful parachute jump.

Thursday, 2/8
Fort Campbell, Kentucky
Hendrix writes home to his father about his recent promotion and his receipt of a Screaming Eagles patch.

Friday, 2/16
Fort Campbell, Kentucky
Captain Gilbert H. Batchman orders physical and psychiatric examinations for Hendrix because "the individual is unable to conform to military rules and regulations. Misses bed check; sleeps while supposed to be working; unsatisfactory duty performances." In prepara-

tion for board proceedings, Hendrix signs a statement declining counsel and does not submit a statement on his behalf.

MARCH
Thursday, 3/22
Fort Campbell, Kentucky

Hendrix logs another parachute jump on his individual jump record.

Saturday, 3/31
Fort Campbell, Kentucky

Hendrix fails to report for bed check and as a result is reduced to general private status. His excuse: "delay due to payday activities and weekend."

APRIL
Saturday, 4/14
George's Bar, Indianapolis, Indiana

During a weekend furlough, Hendrix and fellow soldier Billy Cox go to Indianapolis to enter a talent contest. After many delays in getting back to base, Hendrix fails to report for bed check. He is given fourteen days of restriction in building 6781 between April 16 and 29.

MAY
Tuesday, 5/22
Fort Campbell, Kentucky

Hendrix receives a mental hygiene consultation. Lieutenant Lanford H. DeGeneres reports: "There are no disqualifying mental defects sufficient to warrant disposition through medical channels. . . . The individual . . . has the mental capacity to understand and participate in the board proceedings."

Squad Leader Gerd H. K. Klepper files a report against Hendrix.

Wednesday, 5/23
Fort Campbell, Kentucky

Hendrix fails to report for bed check and is given fourteen days of restriction in building 6781 between May 24 and June 6.

Specialist Fourth Class James W. Mattox files a report against Hendrix for not working and for masturbating in a latrine.

Thursday, 5/24
Fort Campbell, Kentucky
Platoon Sergeant James C. Spears files a report against Hendrix for missing bed check.

Monday, 5/28
Fort Campbell, Kentucky
Sergeant Louis J. Hoekstra files a statement against Hendrix for missing bed check and being obsessed with his guitar.

Thursday, 5/31
Fort Campbell, Kentucky
A request is filed by Captain John T. Halbert to the commanding officer of the 101st Airborne Division that Private James M. Hendrix be discharged from the army. In his report, Captain Halbert writes: "The individual's behavior problems are not amendable to hospitalization and or counseling. Unit punishment has no effect on individual. . . . Apprehended masturbating. Poor character. No known good characteristics. Appears to be an extreme introvert."

Lieutenant Colonel Francis J. Myers also recommends that Hendrix be eliminated from the service and issued an undesirable discharge certificate.

JUNE
Friday, 6/1
Fort Campbell, Kentucky
Supply officer Lyndon D. Williams files a report against Hendrix for lack of interest and inability to concentrate.

Saturday, 6/2
Fort Campbell, Kentucky
Sergeant William R. Bowman files a report against Hendrix for

sleeping on duty, masturbating in the latrine, and owing money for a laundry bill.

Monday, 6/4
Fort Campbell, Kentucky
Private Raymond S. Stroble files a report against Hendrix for the same masturbation incident.

Wednesday, 6/27
Fort Campbell, Kentucky
Hendrix receives his general discharge certificate from the army. The reason given is "unsuitability—under honorable conditions." The discharge will be effective on July 2, 1962, and he will receive twenty-one days of pay and the clothing he wore when he began service.

JULY
Monday, 6/ 2
Clarksville, Tennessee
After being discharged, Hendrix moves into 411 Glenn Street, Clarksville. During the month of July, the King Kasuals play the Elks Lodge, the Disabled American Veterans Hall, and the Pink Poodle Club in Clarksville.

SEPTEMBER
Saturday, 9/1
Collins Music Store, Clarksville, Tennessee
Billy Cox cosigns a loan for Hendrix's Ibanez Japanese electric guitar, strap, and case. After a deposit, Hendrix agrees to make weekly installments of $10 to Collins Music Store until the balance of $95.87 is paid off.

OCTOBER
Thursday, 10/18
Clarksville, Tennessee

Billy Cox is discharged from the army. Cox, Alphonso Young, and Hendrix rent a house at 610 Ford Street in Clarksville. After three weeks there, they try their luck in Nashville and eventually work at the Club Del Morocco. The club owner buys Hendrix a new Silvertone amp and gives him a room to stay in above Joyce's House of Glamour.

NOVEMBER

Tuesday, 11/13

Collins Music Store, Clarksville, Tennessee

Hendrix voluntarily returns the Ibanez guitar he got on loan from Collins Music Store in Clarksville because he cannot continue payments.

Hendrix meets guitarist Lawrence H. Lee Jr. at the Club Del Morocco in Nashville. "Larry" will later join Hendrix's band Gypsy Sun and Rainbows in 1969.

Midmonth

The King Kasuals

Club Del Morocco, Nashville, Tennessee

The King Kasuals now feature Harry Batchelor (vocals), Billy Cox (bass), Jimmy Hendrix (guitar), Buford Majors (saxophone), Alphonso "Baby Boo" Young (guitar), and Harold Nesbit (drums), and they play at the Club Del Morocco.

Tuesday, 11/27

Jimmy Hendrix turns twenty years old.

DECEMBER

Sunday, 12/23

The King Kasuals

Club Del Morocco, Nashville, Tennessee

The King Kasuals perform at the Del Morocco two nights before Christmas. The lineup now includes Jimmy Hendrix (guitar), Alphonso "Baby Boo" Young (guitar), Billy Cox (bass), Buford Majors (sax), Raymond Belts (dancer), and an unidentified drummer. Belts also acts as MC.

1963

JANUARY-FEBRUARY
The Continentals
Club Del Morocco, Nashville, Tennessee

Hendrix is used as a replacement guitarist for the Continentals, a six-piece band, during their four-week engagement at the Del Morocco. On the weekends, the Continentals back up popular R&B acts at the club. Hendrix continues his regular Wednesday-Thursday night gigs with the King Kasuals at the Del Morocco.

MARCH
Early March
Hendrix is recruited by MC-singer "Gorgeous" George Odell and joins a tour of the South with singer Aretha Franklin and Hank Ballard and the Midnighters. Hendrix is part of Gorgeous George's back-up band and later plays with the Midnighters.

Wednesday, 3/13
Hank Ballard and the Midnighters
Unknown venue, Columbia, South Carolina

Hendrix sends a postcard home to his father from Columbia.

Thursday, 3/14
Hank Ballard and the Midnighters
Unknown venue, Charleston, South Carolina

APRIL
Knoxville, Tennessee

Hendrix is left stranded in Knoxville when he is abruptly fired from the Hank Ballard and the Midnighters tour.

MAY
Nashville, Tennessee
Hendrix and Cox re-form the King Kasuals with Leonard Moses on guitar, Harold Nesbit on drums, Buford Majors on saxophone, and Harry Batchelor on lead vocals.

Sunday, 5/19
The King Kasuals
Club Del Morocco, Nashville, Tennessee
The King Kasuals play regular gigs at the Club Del Morocco in Nashville. The lineup includes Harry Batchelor (vocals), Alphonso "Babe Boo" Young (guitar), Billy Cox (bass), Jimmy Hendrix (guitar), Frank Sheffield (drums), Tee Howard Williams (saxophone), and Tommy Lee Williams (saxophone).

JUNE
The King Kasuals shorten their name to the Casuals.

JULY
Thursday 7/6–Sunday 7/21
The Casuals
Black Poodle Club, Nashville, Tennessee
The Casuals play the Black Poodle Club in Nashville for a two-week run. Cox and Hendrix and Cox by himself play two separate gigs on the 21st.

Sunday 7/21–Thursday 7/25
Billy Cox and the Sandpipers/Jimmy Hendrix and His Magic Guitar
Jolly Roger Club, Nashville, Tennessee
Billy Cox and the Sandpipers headline at Jolly Roger Club along with Jimmy Hendrix and His Magic Guitar. The Sandpipers are an off-shoot of the Casuals.

Saturday 7/27
Curtis Mayfield and the Impressions play the Jolly Roger Club in Nashville. Negotiations take place in Nashville with promoter Isaac Washington, who is looking for a band that will back the singers on an upcoming tour of the South. The Bonnevilles accept his offer.

Sunday 7/28–Thursday 8/1
Billy Cox and the Sandpipers/Jimmy Hendrix and His Magic Guitar
Jolly Roger Club, Nashville, Tennessee

Hendrix performs double duty, as opening act and with the Sandpipers.

AUGUST

Frank Howard and the Commanders
Starday/King Studios, Nashville, Tennessee
With producer Bill "Hoss" Allen, Billy Cox presents two of his songs he feels singer Frank Howard and his group should record.

Billy Cox
Starday/King Studios, Nashville, Tennessee
With producer Bill "Hoss" Allen, Hendrix and Cox record an unidentified song that may have been erased.

Johnny Jones
Starday/King Studios, Nashville, Tennessee
With producer Bill "Hoss" Allen, Jones uses Hendrix on his composition "Feels So Bad, Like a Ball Game on a Rainy Day."

George Yates and Sandra Wright
Starday/King Studios, Nashville, Tennessee
With producer Bill "Hoss" Allen, guitarist George Yates uses Hendrix on the song "I'm Crying" with singer Sandra Wright.

SEPTEMBER–OCTOBER

The Bonnevilles
Unknown venue, Huntsville, Alabama
Bonnevilles bandleader Robert Fisher hires Hendrix as a guitarist for his group. The lineup includes A. W. Davis (alto sax), Jimmy Hendrix (guitar), Don Nunnelly (tenor sax), Isaac McKay (drums), Aaron "Heinz Ketchup" Varnell (tenor sax), Willie Young (bass), and, occasionally, Joe Fisher (organ). Larry Lee will be added as a second guitarist, and for a brief period George Yates is hired as a third guitar player.

The Bonnevilles' sets include covers of songs by Ray Charles, Bobby "Blue" Bland, Rufus Thomas, and Johnny Taylor.

The Bonnevilles
Unknown venue, Parsons, Tennessee
Larry Lee is added as second guitarist to the tour. He and Hendrix
will trade off solos.

The Bonnevilles
American Legion Hall, Clarksville, Tennessee
Hendrix, Robert Fisher (drums), and Jimmy Scott (saxophone) have
to improvise for twenty minutes because the rest of the band shows
up late for the gig.

The Bonnevilles
Searcies, Bells, Tennessee
At the request of the club's owner, Hendrix and Larry Lee, along
with a bass player and drummer, perform without the Bonnevilles
horn section.

The Bonnevilles/the Impressions
Unknown venue, Clarksville, Tennessee
The Bonnevilles begin a tour with the Impressions as the opening
act and backup for the Impressions. Other acts on the tour include
the Avons and Peggy Gains, and Harry Batchelor serves as MC. On
opening night in Clarksville, Tennessee, Hendrix accidentally dam-
ages guitarist Curtis Mayfield's amplifier by turning it up too loud.
The tour will conclude in Knoxville, Tennessee.

The Bonnevilles
Fidelity Recording, Nashville, Tennessee
The Bonnevilles record four demos.

NOVEMBER
Early November
Hendrix and concert promoter Carl Fisher leave Nashville for
New York City. Upon arrival, they stay at the Hotel Theresa in
Harlem.

Friday 11/22-Wednesday 11/27
Apollo Theater, Harlem, New York
Hendrix meets Sam Cooke during the singer's weeklong engagement at the Apollo Theater. Cooke turns Hendrix down for a position in his band.

Wednesday 11/27
Jimmy Hendrix turns twenty-one.

1964

JANUARY
Early January
Apollo Theater, Harlem, New York
Hendrix wins first place at the Wednesday Night Amateur Competition.

End of the month
Palm Cafe, Harlem, New York
Singers Tony Rice and Ronald Isley meet Hendrix to discuss joining the Isley Brothers' band. The house band doesn't let Hendrix sit in, and audition arrangements are made for a later date.

FEBRUARY
Sunday, 2/9
Isley home, Englewood, New Jersey
Hendrix auditions for the Isley Brothers.

March–April

Hendrix joins the Isley Brothers as lead guitarist. The Isley Brothers' backing band, the I. B. Specials, consists of Al Lucas (bass), Bobby Gregg (drums), Eddie Williams (trumpet), Douglas MacArthur (saxophone), Marv Massey (baritone saxophone), and Gene Friday (organ).

The Isley Brothers begin a tour that covers Bermuda, Pennsylvania, Montreal, and Ottawa. While playing at the Grand National Club in Montreal, Hendrix meets drummer Buddy Miles, who is playing with Ruby and the Romantics.

MAY
Early May
The Isley Brothers
Unknown venue, Seattle, Washington
Hendrix's guitar is stolen after a performance. He stays an extra day in Seattle and misses the Isley Brothers' next show in Atlanta.

Saturday, 5/16
The Isley Brothers
Peter's Park, Atlanta, Georgia
The Isley Brothers perform at a street dance as part of the Georgia Institute of Technology's Greek Week festival. Without Hendrix, the Isleys find a substitute guitar player for this show.

Monday, 5/18
Don Covay and the Goodtimers
A-1 Sound, New York
Hendrix records "Mercy, Mercy" with Don Covay and the Goodtimers.

Thursday, 5/21
The Isley Brothers
Atlantic Studios, New York
Hendrix records "Testify (Parts 1 and 2)" with the Isley Brothers.

JUNE
Friday, 6/19
The Isley Brothers
Rockland Palace, New York
The Isley Brothers perform at Rockland Palace for a Farewell Dance

and Show to WWRL's "Magnificent Montague." The Isley Brothers are joined by thirty other performers. The lineup includes Solomon Burke, Billy Butler, King Curtis, Don Covay, Wilson Pickett, and the Tams. The show starts at 9 p.m. and ends at 3 a.m.

Friday, 6/26
The Isley Brothers
Apollo Theater, Harlem, New York
The Isley Brothers headline a bill at the Apollo with Dionne Warwick, the Five Royals, the Exciters, the Charades, and the Carletons.

AUGUST
Saturday, 8/1
The Isley Brothers
Macon Auditorium, Macon, Georgia
The Isley Brothers play with Carla Thomas, Joe Tex, Esther Phillips, and the Drifters.

Late August
Hendrix is fired from the Isley Brothers and joins Gorgeous George on another Supersonic Attractions tour, playing guitar for the Atlanta group the Tams.

SEPTEMBER
Thursday, 9/17
The Tams
Ponce De Leon Ball Park, Atlanta, Georgia
Playing with the Tams, Hendrix is on the same bill with Solomon Burke, Jerry Butler, the Drifters, Chuck Jackson, Johnny Thunder, Patti LaBelle & the Bluebelles, Jackie Ross, Betty Everett, the Chuck Jackson Orchestra, and Gorgeous George.

Saturday, 9/19
The Tams
Memorial Auditorium, Louisville, Kentucky

Sunday, 9/20
The Tams
The Sulfur Dell, Nashville, Tennessee

Tuesday, 9/22
The Tams
Unknown venue, Birmingham, Alabama

Saturday, 9/26
The Tams
Unknown venue, St. Louis, Missouri

Monday, 9/28
The Tams
Unknown venue, Columbus, Ohio
From Columbus, Ohio, Hendrix writes home to his father explaining that he is about halfway through a thirty-five-day tour that has passed through cities in the Midwest, East, and South. The tour also covers Jacksonville, Tampa, Miami, and Dallas.

OCTOBER
Thursday, 10/8
The Tams
Cincinnati, Ohio
In a postcard home, Hendrix tells his father that his new address is an apartment in Atlanta, Georgia. When the tour arrives in Kansas City, Missouri, Hendrix misses the bus. He's able to make his way back to Atlanta, where he reconnects with Gorgeous George.

Friday, 10/16
Gorgeous George Band
Unknown venue, Mobile, Alabama
With Gorgeous George's help, Hendrix joins the Sam Cooke Supersonic Attractions tour, which runs from October 16 through November 9. Cooke and Jackie Wilson are the headliners; other acts on the bill include Hank Ballard and the Midnighters,

Garnet Mims, Jimmy Hughes, Mittie Collier, the Upsetters,
the Valentinos, the Upsetters Orchestra, and MC Gorgeous
George.

Saturday, 10/17
Gorgeous George Band
Unknown venue, Knoxville, Tennessee

Sunday, 10/18
Gorgeous George Band
Circle Theater, Indianapolis, Indiana

Saturday, 10/24
Gorgeous George Band
Unknown venue, Chattanooga, Tennessee

Sunday, 10/25
Gorgeous George Band
City Auditorium, Birmingham, Alabama

Monday, 10/26
Gorgeous George Band
Municipal Auditorium, New Orleans, Louisiana

Tuesday, 10/27
Gorgeous George Band
Unknown venue, Charlotte, North Carolina

Wednesday, 10/28
Gorgeous George Band
Dorton Arena, Raleigh, North Carolina

NOVEMBER
Sunday, 11/1
Gorgeous George Band
Kiel Opera House, St Louis, Missouri

Monday, 11/2
Gorgeous George Band
Hippodrome, Nashville, Tennessee

Tuesday, 11/3
Gorgeous George Band
Ellis Auditorium, Memphis, Tennessee
While Sam Cooke and Jackie Wilson tape a duet on WHBQ-TV's
Talent Party, Hendrix meets guitarist/producer Steve Cropper at
Stax recording studios. Later, the Cooke/Wilson show plays Ellis
Auditorium.

Thursday, 11/5
Gorgeous George Band
Unknown venue, Greenville, South Carolina

Friday, 11/6
Gorgeous George Band
Norfolk Arena, Norfolk, Virginia

Saturday, 11/7
Gorgeous George Band
Unknown venue, Clemson, South Carolina

Sunday, 11/8
Gorgeous George Band
Mosque Theater, Richmond, Virginia

Monday, 11/9
Gorgeous George Band
Unknown venue, Greensboro, North Carolina

Mid- to late November
The Tams
Soul City Club, Atlanta, Georgia

After the Cooke/Wilson tour concludes, Hendrix resides in Atlanta and performs with the Tams.

Friday, 11/27
Jimmy Hendrix turns twenty-two.

DECEMBER
Tuesday, 12/15–Tuesday, 12/22
Domino Lounge, Atlanta, Georgia
Little Richard and the Crown Jewels play the Domino Lounge. During this time, Gorgeous George tells Little Richard that Hendrix is his guitar-playing cousin Maurice James and that he needs a job. Hendrix is hired.

Thursday, 12/31
Little Richard and the Crown Jewels
Unknown venue, Greenville, South Carolina
    Richard's band features Wade Jackson (drums), Eddie Fletcher (bass), Frank McCray and Boogie Daniels (tenor saxes), Glen Willings (rhythm guitar), and Maurice James, aka Jimmy Hendrix (lead guitar).

1965
JANUARY
Early–mid-January
Little Richard and the Crown Jewels
Royal Peacock, Atlanta, Georgia

Little Richard and the Crown Jewels
Whisky a Go-Go (aka Whisk 'A Go-Go), Atlanta, Georgia

Little Richard and the Crown Jewels
Harlem Duke Social Club, Prichard, Alabama
Hendrix meets B. B. King and discusses guitar-playing techniques.

Tuesday, 1/25
Little Richard and the Crown Jewels
Unknown venue, Lafayette, Louisiana

Wednesday, 1/27
Little Richard and the Crown Jewels
Club 500, Houston, Texas
Hendrix jams with guitarist Albert Collins.

Thursday, 1/28
Little Richard and the Crown Jewels
Soul City Club, Dallas, Texas

Friday, 1/29
Little Richard and the Crown Jewels
Will Rogers Auditorium, Fort Worth, Texas

Saturday, 1/30
Little Richard and the Crown Jewels
Unknown venue, Tulsa, Oklahoma

Sunday, 1/31
Little Richard and the Crown Jewels
Diamond Ballroom, Oklahoma City, Oklahoma

FEBRUARY
Friday, 2/5-Saturday, 2/6
Little Richard and the Crown Jewels
Red Velvet, Hollywood, California

Sunday, 2/14
After Hendrix passes his audition with Ike and Tina Turner,
his former boss Little Richard leaves Los Angeles and performs
a solo Valentine Day's concert for disabled war veterans at the
Mountain Home in Kingsport, Tennessee. The Caprees, a four-

man group out of Mississippi, accompany him. Hendrix fills
in as a performer with the Turners while Richard performs solo
gigs.

Monday, 2/15
Ike and Tina Turner Revue
The 49er, El Monte, California

Tuesday, 2/16–Saturday, 2/20
Ike and Tina Turner Revue
Skol Lounge's Teen Show, Tarzana, California

Saturday, 2/20
Little Richard
Hollywood A Go Go, KHJ-TV, Los Angeles, California
Little Richard returns to Los Angeles and performs solo on the teen
dance show *Hollywood A Go Go*. Other advertised guests include
Johnny Crawford, the Challengers, Billy Strange, the Platters, Donnie
Brooks, and Toni Fisher.

Sunday, 2/21
Little Richard and the Crown Jewels
Fillmore Auditorium, San Francisco, California
Support act: Ike and Tina Turner
Hendrix performs with Little Richard and the Crown Jewels.

Thursday 25
Ike and Tina Turner Revue
Los Angeles Valley College, Van Nuys, California

MARCH
Monday, 3/1
Little Richard and the Crown Jewels
The 49er, El Monte, California

Friday, 3/5–Saturday, 3/13
Ike and Tina Turner Revue
Ciro's Le Disc, Hollywood, California
Support act: The Byrds

Saturday, 3/6
Little Richard (solo)
New American Bandstand, ABC-TV, Los Angeles, California

Monday, 3/8
Little Richard and the Crown Jewels
Pink Carousel, Downey, California

Friday, 3/12–Saturday, 3/13
Ike and Tina Turner Revue
Ciro's Le Disc, Hollywood, California
Support act: The Byrds
This may have been Hendrix's final show with the Turners.

Friday, 3/19
Wilcox Hotel, Hollywood, California
Hendrix writes home to his father: "Drop me a line as soon as possible. My address is 6500 Selma Ave., Hollywood, Calif. c/o Maurice James."

Friday, 3/19–Saturday, 3/20
Little Richard and the Crown Jewels
Ciro's Le Disc, Hollywood, California
Support act: The Byrds

Saturday 27
Rosa Lee Brooks
Producer Billy Revis's home recording studio, Los Angeles, California
Brooks, Hendrix, Arthur Lee, and members of Major Lance's band record "My Diary" and "Utee."

APRIL

Friday, 4/2
Little Richard and the Crown Jewels
San Leandro Roller Rink, San Leandro, California

Saturday, 4/3
Little Richard and the Crown Jewels
Golden Bear, Huntington Beach, California
After the show, Little Richard fines Hendrix and Glen Willings
for not wearing their standard costuming.

Friday, 4/9–Saturday, 4/10
Little Richard and the Crown Jewels
Ciro's Le Disc, Hollywood, California
Support act: The Byrds.

Friday, 4/16–Saturday, 4/17
Little Richard and the Crown Jewels
Paramount Theatre, New York
Little Richard is fired after the second day's performance for
exceeding his allotted time slot. Hendrix meets Chas Chandler
from the Animals for the first time at this venue.

Friday, 4/30
Little Richard and the Crown Jewels
Union College, Field House, Schenectady, New York
Support acts: Gary U.S. Bonds, the Shirelles

MAY

Sunday, 5/2
Hotel Theresa, Harlem, New York
Jimi takes a moment to write home and catch his father up with
his new location: "My address is Theresa Hotel, 2090 Rm, 416
7th Ave. NY."

Saturday, 5/8
Little Richard and the Crown Jewels
Syracuse College, Women's Building, Syracuse, New York

Wednesday, 5/12
Little Richard and the Crown Jewels
Donnelly Theater, Boston, Massachusetts
Support act: Jackie "Moms" Mabley

Mid-May
Little Richard and the Crown Jewels
Long Pond Inn, Greenwood Lake, New York

JUNE
Wednesday, 6/2
Little Richard and the Crown Jewels
Bell Sound Studios, New York
Sessions take place for an upcoming Little Richard single and album.

Saturday, 6/5
Billboard announces that Maylynn Products is releasing Rosa Lee
Brooks's single on Revis Records.

Mid-June
Hendrix writes his LA girlfriend Rosa Lee Brooks for money to get
his guitar out of the pawnshop.

JULY
Saturday, 7/3
Little Richard and the Crown Jewels
Acme Market, Wildwood, New Jersey
Little Richard performs at a record hop hosted by Philadelphia disc
jockey Jerry Blavat.

Tuesday, 7/6
Buddy and Stacy with the Crown Jewels

Night Train, WLAC-TV Studios, Nashville, Tennessee
The Crown Jewels along with Buddy Travis and Leroy "Stacy" Johnson Jr. perform "Shotgun." Little Richard is absent from the taping.

Little Richard and the Crown Jewels
New Era Club, Nashville, Tennessee
After the taping at WLAC-TV, Little Richard and band perform. Afterward, Hendrix, Glen Willings, George Yates, and Johnny Jones have a jam at the Del Morocco.

Friday, 7/9-Saturday, 7/10
Little Richard and the Crown Jewels
Flamingo Club, Newport, Kentucky
Singers Buddy and Stacy are terminated after these performances.

Monday, 7/12-Thursday, 7/15
Little Richard and the Crown Jewels
Apollo Theater, Harlem, New York
Hendrix either quits or is fired after these shows.

Late July
Mr. Wiggles
A-1 Sound Studios, New York
Hendrix meets Alexander Randolph, a singer-songwriter who goes by the stage name Mr. Wiggles. Wiggles and Hendrix record "Fat Back" and others with the Upsetters.

Tuesday, 7/27
Sue Records, New York
Hendrix signs his first recording contract. The two-year, exclusive recording artist contract with Sue Records and Copa Management of New York City provides an option for an additional three years.

AUGUST
Thursday, 8/5
The Isley Brothers

239

Atlantic Studios, New York
The Isley Brothers record "Move Over and Let Me Dance" and
"Have You Ever Been Disappointed."

Thursday, 8/5
The Isley Brothers
National Guard Armory, Gastonia, North Carolina

Sunday, 8/8
Hendrix writes a lengthy letter home explaining how tough the
music business is in New York City.

Mid-August to end of August
The Isley Brothers
Paterson Armory, Paterson, New Jersey

The Isley Brothers
Essex County Country Club, West Orange, New Jersey

SEPTEMBER
The single "Move Over And Let Me Dance" b/w "Have You
Ever Been Disappointed" (Atlantic 45-2303) is released in America.
This is the second Isley Brothers single featuring Hendrix.

Wednesday, 9/1
Hendrix writes a letter to Lithofayne Pridgon, explaining that
there may be trouble in their relationship.

Saturday, 9/4
The Isley Brothers
Route 59 Go Kart Speedway, West Nyack, New York
The Isley Brothers headline a Battle of the Bands event featuring
the Rogues and eleven other bands. The Isley Brothers band,
now known as the Modern Knights, performs "Driving South"
prior to the Isleys joining band members on stage.

The Isley Brothers
Hejazz Grotto Hall, New Haven, Connecticut

The Isley Brothers
Unknown venue, Waterbury, Connecticut

OCTOBER
Tuesday, 10/5
Lighthouse Cafe, New York
After Hendrix meets singer Curtis Knight in the lobby of the
America Hotel, Knight loans Hendrix a guitar. Hendrix later audi-
tions for him at the Lighthouse Cafe.

Wednesday, 10/6
Studio 76, New York
Knight takes Hendrix to meet his manager, Ed Chalpin, at Studio 76.
Knight is eager to record a civil rights—themed song he's just
penned, titled "How Would You Feel."

Saturday, 10/9
The Isley Brothers
Bowman Gymnasium, DePauw University, Greencastle, Indiana
The Isley Brothers and Booker T. & the MGs perform the Fall
Opener dance at DePauw University.

Friday, 10/15
America Hotel, New York
Nine days after Hendrix's recording session with Curtis Knight,
Ed Chalpin signs Hendrix to an exclusive three-year recording
deal.

Late October
Joey Dee's house, Lodi, New Jersey
Hendrix auditions for and joins Joey Dee and the Starliters after
their guitar player Gene Cornish quits and moves to California.

Dee's tour with Hendrix covers the tristate area of Connecticut, New York, and New Jersey, with a few gigs in Ohio and Wisconsin.

NOVEMBER
Monday, 11/1
Joey Dee and the Starliters
Ondine, New York
The Rolling Stones watch Hendrix perform at Ondine after their concert in Rochester, New York.

Tuesday, 11/2–Sunday, 11/7
Joey Dee and the Starliters
McVans, Buffalo, New York

Sunday, 11/7
Joey Dee and the Starliters
Club Commodore, Buffalo, New York
McVans shares Joey Dee and the Starliters with the Club Commodore for a Sunday afternoon show.

Tuesday, 11/23
Joey Dee and the Starliters
Castle Mar Motel, Revere Beach, Massachusetts
Four days before his twenty-third birthday, Hendrix writes home about the tour with Joey Dee.

Wednesday, 11/24
Joey Dee and the Starliters
Beach Ball Club, Revere Beach, Massachusetts
Support act: The Undertakers

Saturday, 11/27
Hendrix turns twenty-three years old.

Late November
Joey Dee and the Starliters
Unknown venue, Richmond, Virginia

DECEMBER
Thursday, 12/2–Saturday, 12/11
Joey Dee and the Starliters
Mario's Club Au Go-Go, Syracuse, New York

Mid-December
Curtis Knight and the Squires
Club Allegro, Garfield, New Jersey
While Hendrix auditions one afternoon, guitar legend Les Paul
walks into the club and is impressed by Hendrix's playing. Upon
his return about two hours later, Paul misses Hendrix and does
not learn his name.

Late December
Curtis Knight and the Squires
Studio 76, New York
The following songs are recorded: "Don't Accuse Me," "Welcome
Home," and "Simon Says." "Welcome Home" becomes the B side to
"How Would You Feel."

Sunday, 12/26
Curtis Knight and the Squires
George's Club 20, Hackensack, New Jersey
A recording is made of the Curtis Knight and the Squires' post-
Christmas show.

1966
JANUARY
Thursday, 1/6
Lithofayne Pridgon and Hendrix attend the Apollo Theater's Blues

Revue show, which features Sonny Terry and Brownie McGhee, T-Bone Walker, John Lee Hooker, Muddy Waters, and Bo Diddley.

Thursday, 1/13
Hendrix writes a postcard home to his father admitting his career hasn't improved.

Mid-January
King Curtis and the Kingpins
Small's Paradise, Harlem, New York
A vacancy opens in King Curtis's band, and Hendrix plays his first gig with them.

Friday, 1/21–Saturday, 1/22
Ray Sharpe with the King Curtis Orchestra
Atlantic Studios, New York.
Hendrix records with King Curtis and the All Stars for a session with singer Ray Sharpe. The track is titled "Help Me (Get That Feeling)." Because the song runs more than three minutes, the recording is broken up into two parts for a single release.

Late January
King Curtis and the Kingpins
Small's Paradise, Harlem, New York

FEBRUARY
Early February
Jayne Mansfield
Studio 76, New York
Hendrix records bass and guitar parts for Mansfield's song "Suey."

Mid-February
King Curtis and the Kingpins
Hendrix begins touring with King Curtis and the Kingpins.

Sunday, 2/27
King Curtis and the Kingpins
Pittsfield Boy's Club, Pittsfield, Massachusetts
Support acts: The McCoys and the Crystals

MARCH
Mid-March
Curtis Knight and the Squires
Studio 76, New York
The Squires now feature Nate Edmonds on organ. This session
yields "Strange Things" and Hendrix's original composition,
"I Ain't Taking Care of No Business."

Tuesday, 3/15
Producer Ed Chalpin secures a licensing deal with RSVP Records.
The label releases Knight's recording with Hendrix "How Would
You Feel" b/w "Welcome Home."

Wednesday, 3/30
Hendrix signs a publishing contract with RSVP Music for the track
"I Ain't Taking Care of No Business."

APRIL
Early April
Ham and Eggs Restaurant, New York
Hendrix meets Diana Carpenter, a sixteen-year-old prostitute
who is using the name Regina Jackson to avoid being found
by her parents. Hendrix moves in with her at the Lexington
Hotel, and they have a part-time relationship that lasts though
August.

Early April
Curtis Knight and the Squires
Lighthouse Cafe, New York
Support act: The Beats

Future Vanilla Fudge drummer Carmine Appice plays drums for the Beats.

Saturday, 4/16
Billboard lists Curtis Knight's single "How Would You Feel" in its R&B Spotlights column and predicts the record will reach the charts.

Thursday, 4/28
Ray Sharpe with the King Curtis Orchestra
Atlantic Studios, New York

The Chambers Brothers
Cheetah, New York
On opening night at Cheetah, Hendrix introduces himself to the Chambers Brothers. Willie Chambers invites Hendrix to sit in with group and lends him his guitar.

MAY
Thursday, 5/5
King Curtis and the Kingpins
Prelude Club, New York
Atlantic Records holds a private record release party for Percy Sledge in celebration of his hit "When a Man Loves a Woman." The show features Sledge, Esther Phillips, and Wilson Pickett. King Curtis and the All Stars are the house band.

Saturday, 5/7
King Curtis and the Kingpins
Sheraton Hotel, Metropolitan Ballroom, New York
King Curtis tells Hendrix he must wear a tuxedo or he can't play this gig. After Hendrix borrows a tux, King Curtis humiliates him on stage and fires him for being late and not adhering to a dress code.

Monday, 5/9
The Animals perform at New York's House of Liverpool Theater.

Toward the end of the week, Eric Burdon and Chas Chandler witness Hendrix playing at the newly opened Cheetah discotheque.

Early May
Sam & Dave
Unknown venue, New York
Hendrix is fired at his first gig with the soul duo.

Friday, 5/13–Thursday, 5/26
Curtis Knight and the Squires
Cheetah, New York
Hendrix rejoins Curtis Knight and the Squires and begins a two-week engagement at Cheetah as the opening band for the Denims. Hendrix also meets Linda Keith during one of his Cheetah performances.

During May, Jimi finds temporary work with singer Monti Rock III at Trude Heller's nightclub.

Friday, 5/27–Thursday, 6/2
Carl Holmes and the Commanders
Cheetah, New York
Support act: The 7 of Us
After joining the New York Musicians Union (Local 802), Hendrix finds work with Carl Holmes and the Commanders for a one-week gig at Cheetah. Folk singer Richie Havens meets Hendrix at the club and encourages him to visit Greenwich Village for better opportunities.

JUNE
Early June
Kettle of Fish, New York
During June, Hendrix meets his idol, Bob Dylan, in Greenwich Village.

Friday, 6/3–Thursday, 6/9
Little Charles and Sidewinders
Cheetah, New York

Singer Charles Walker, a friend of Hendrix's from Club Del Morocco in Nashville, hires Hendrix for this run at Cheetah.

Friday 6/10
Producer Ed Chalpin secures a second licensing deal with Jerry Simon's RSVP Records for more Curtis Knight recordings. The label releases a second single called "Hornet's Nest" b/w "Knock Your Self Out." Chalpin also supplies Simon with other Knight/Hendrix tracks: "The U.F.O.," "I'm a Fool for You Baby," "The Ballad of Jimmy," "Gotta Have a New Dress," and "Your Love."

Mid-June
The Blood Brothers
Uptown Theater, Philadelphia, Pennsylvania
Hendrix teams up with former Squires sax player Lonnie Youngblood and forms the Blood Brothers.

Lonnie Youngblood
Abtone Studios, New York
Hendrix and Youngblood record two singles, "Go Go Shoes" b/w "Go Go Place" and "Soul Food (That's a What I Like)" b/w "Goodbye, Bessie Mae." The pair also records "Wipe the Sweat," a song that debuts Hendrix's lead vocal. Both Youngblood's and Hendrix's vocals are not used by producer Johnny Brantley.

The Icemen
Abtone Studios, New York
Working with producer Johnny Brantley and Lonnie Youngblood, Hendrix records two sides for the Icemen: "(My Girl) She's a Fox" b/w "(I Wonder) What It Takes." The Icemen are aspiring singers Gino Armstrong and James Stokes.

Jimmy Norman
Abtone Studios, New York
While producing a session for the Icemen, Johnny Brantley has

Hendrix record two sides for singer Jimmy Norman: "You're Only Hurting Yourself" b/w "That Little Old Groovemaker."

Tuesday, 6/21
RSVP Records, New York
Hendrix signs a publishing contract with RSVP Records for the tracks "Station Break" and "Flying on Instruments."

Thursday, 6/23
Al Hendrix marries Ayako "June" Fujita in Seattle.

Sunday, 6/26
The Ronettes
Ondine, New York
Hendrix and an unknown band back up the female vocal trio the Ronettes. Hendrix's first public performance of "Wild Thing" takes place on this date.

Wednesday, 29
Bob Dylan's *Blonde on Blonde* LP is released, and Hendrix purchases a copy at Colony Records in Manhattan. He insists that his friends listen to the record.

JULY
Saturday, 7/2
Jimi James and the Blue Flames
Ondine, New York
After their show at Forest Hills Tennis Stadium, members of the Rolling Stones venture into Ondine nightclub and witness for the second time Hendrix playing guitar. Hendrix is said to have composed "3rd Stone from the Sun" while working at Ondine.

Tuesday, 7/5
Cafe Wha?, Greenwich Village, New York
Hendrix passes his audition at the tiny underground nightclub.

Hendrix temporarily uses drummer Chas Mathews and bassist Tommy Butler.

Thursday, 7/6
Manny's Music, New York
Hendrix meets fifteen-year-old guitarist Randy Wolfe and asks him to sit in with his band that evening.

Mid-July
Jimi James and the Blue Flames
Cafe Wha?, Greenwich Village, New York
Hendrix's new band features Randy Wolfe (rhythm guitar), Danny Casey (drums), and Randy Palmer (bass). Their gig at the Wha? lasts through most of August.

Late July
Jimi James and the Blue Flames
Connie's Ballroom, Harlem, New York
House bassist at the Cafe Wha? Tommy Butler organizes one gig for Hendrix, a drummer, and himself.

AUGUST
Tuesday, 8/2
Jimi James and the Blue Flames
Cafe Wha?, Greenwich Village, New York
Keith Richard's girlfriend, Linda Keith, sees Chas Chandler at the entrance of Ondine and invites him to watch Hendrix perform at the Cafe Wha?

Thursday, 8/4
Jimi James and the Blue Flames
Cafe Wha?, Greenwich Village, New York
One day after the Animals play two sold-out shows at the Rheingold Central Park Music Festival, Chas Chandler goes down to the Cafe Wha? with Linda Keith to watch Hendrix perform

an afternoon set. After seeing him play "Hey Joe," Chandler sets up a series of business meetings with Hendrix at the Kettle of Fish.

Danny Taylor replaces Blue Flames drummer Danny Casey, and Hendrix adds sixteen-year-old Mark "Moogy" Klingman on organ and harmonica for the remainder of his time at Cafe Wha?

Early August
Night Owl Cafe, Greenwich Village, New York
Hendrix auditions for club owner Joe Marra, who is impressed but decides to pass on hiring Hendrix in favor of crowd pleaser James Taylor.

Still playing at the Wha? Hendrix's act attracts John Hammond Jr., who invites Hendrix to sit in with his band.

Saturday, 8/20
Curtis Knight and the Squires
Lighthouse Cafe, New York
Hendrix plays his final gig with Curtis Knight and the Squires.

Saturday, 8/27
The Screaming Nighthawks
Cafe Au Go Go, Greenwich Village, New York
Hendrix joins John Hammond Jr.'s two-week-old band, the Screaming Nighthawks.

SEPTEMBER
Sunday, 9/4
John Hammond Jr.
Cafe Au Go Go, Greenwich Village, New York
Hendrix sits in with John Hammond Jr. at the Cafe Au Go Go's Blues Bag show. The lineup also features Judy Roderick, Eric Andersen, Tom Rush, Patrick Sky, David Blue, Richie Havens, and the Butterfield Blues Band.

Monday, 9/5
The Animals perform at Steel Pier in Atlantic City, New Jersey, the final date on their American tour.

Friday, 9/9
John Hammond Jr.
Cafe Au Go Go, Greenwich Village, New York
Hendrix and Randy California join in on John Hammond Jr.'s set. Tim Hardin and the Times Square Two are also on the bill.

Monday, 9/12
Hendrix applies to the Seattle Records Office for a copy of his birth certificate.

Tuesday, 9/13
John Hammond Jr. and the Blue Flame
Cafe Au Go Go, Greenwich Village, New York
Hendrix is advertised as the Blue Flame on the bill with John Hammond Jr.

Monday, 9/19
A copy of Hendrix's birth certificate arrives in New York from Seattle, and arrangements are made to obtain a passport for Jimi.

Tuesday, 9/20
Scott English, a New York writer and publisher, helps the passport process move along by agreeing that he's known Hendrix for eight years and that Hendrix is of good character.

Friday, 9/23
John F. Kennedy International Airport, New York
Passport NO G-1044108 is issued in New York City to James Marshall Hendrix.

At 9:00 p.m. Hendrix, his new manager, Chas Chandler, and Terry McVay, the Animals' road manager, sit in first class on a Pan

Am jet and leave America for London, England. Hendrix brings only his guitar, a change of clothes, and a jar of Valderma face cream. Hendrix will not return to America until June 1967.

Saturday, 9/24
London, England
Two hours after landing in Britain, Hendrix jams for about three hours at Zoot Money's house. Later that evening, Chandler takes Hendrix to the Scotch of St. James Club for a jam, where Hendrix meets his future girlfriend, Kathy Etchingham. Hendrix will share room 301 at the Hyde Park Towers Hotel with Chandler and his girlfriend, Lotte.

Monday, 9/26
Birdland, London
Hendrix attends auditions for Eric Burdon's New Animals and later jams with the band.

Tuesday, 9/27
Hendrix jams with the VIPs at the Scotch of St James Club. Hendrix does not have an official work permit yet. Kit Lambert tries to sign Hendrix for his new Track label.

Wednesday, 9/28
Hendrix phones his father to tell him he is in England. A nonwork residence permit, valid until December 28, 1966, is issued to Hendrix.

Thursday, 9/29
Birdland, London
At auditions for his new band, Hendrix asks guitarist Noel Redding to return the next day. Later, Chandler takes Hendrix to Blaises Club for a jam with the Brian Auger Trinity. French singer Johnny Hallyday sees Hendrix perform and asks Chandler to let Jimi accompany Hallyday on a French tour, where no work permit is required.

Friday, 9/30
Michael Jeffery offers Noel Redding the job as bassist in the Jimi Hendrix Experience.

OCTOBER
Saturday, 10/1
Cream
Regent Street Polytechnic, London
Hendrix sits in with the newly formed group Cream, featuring one of his heroes, Eric Clapton, as well as Jack Bruce and Ginger Baker, on Howlin' Wolf's "Killing Floor" and one other number.

Monday, 10/3
Chandler calls Redding and confirms he has been hired as the bass player for the Jimi Hendrix Experience.

Tuesday, 10/4
Chas Chandler is informed that a jazz drummer by the name of John "Mitch" Mitchell, formerly of Georgie Fame's Blue Flames, is available. Jimi and Redding begin rehearsing in London.

Wednesday, 10/5
Birdland, London
Mitch Mitchell joins Hendrix and Redding for the audition. Over the course of two hours, the group plays many R&B standards, including the 1964 track Hendrix was involved with, titled "Mercy, Mercy." Mitchell passes the audition, and the Jimi Hendrix Experience is formed.

Thursday, 10/6
Aberbach Publishing House, London
Hendrix, Redding, and Mitchell begin a week of rehearsals for their upcoming tour of France.

Tuesday, 10/11
The Jimi Hendrix Experience receives new Marshall equipment.

Wednesday, 10/12

The Jimi Hendrix Experience flies from London to Paris for its first tour with Johnny Hallyday.

Thursday, 10/13

The Jimi Hendrix Experience

Le Novelty, Evereux, France

The Experience plays a fifteen-minute set that includes "In the Midnight Hour," "Mercy, Mercy," "Land of a Thousand Dances," and "Hey Joe."

Friday, 10/14

The Jimi Hendrix Experience

Le Rio, Nancy, France

The Experience is on tour with Long Chris, the Blackburds, and Johnny Hallyday.

Saturday, 10/15

The Jimi Hendrix Experience

La Salle Des Fêtes, Villerupt, Lorraine, France

The Experience is on tour with Long Chris, the Blackburds, and Johnny Hallyday.

A review for this concert refers to Jimi as "Tommy Hemdrix": "Of the two parts of the show, the first was the 'calmest.' Long Chris opened the show, followed by a black man, Tommy Hemdrix, who, after a bit of trouble with his guitar strap, put on a good display, contorting then playing his instrument . . . with his teeth."

Tuesday, 10/18

The Jimi Hendrix Experience

L'Olympia, Paris

The Experience adds "Wild Thing" to its set.

Wednesday, 10/19

The Jimi Hendrix Experience

Scotch of St. James Club, London
Hendrix jams with Viv Prince, the new guitarist with the New Animals.

Sunday, 10/23
De Lane Lea Studios, London
During its first recording session, the Jimi Hendrix Experience records
three takes of "Hey Joe" with the Breakaways on harmony vocals.

Monday, 10/24
The Knuckles Club, London
Hendrix jams with the Deep Feeling. The group features Dave
Mason and Jim Capaldi, who later form Traffic.

Tuesday, 10/25
The Jimi Hendrix Experience
Scotch of St. James, London
The London debut of the Jimi Hendrix Experience takes place.

NOVEMBER
Wednesday, 11/2
De Lane Lea Studios, London
"Stone Free" and a rough demo of "Can You See Me" are recorded.

Tuesday, 11/8–Friday, 11/11
The Jimi Hendrix Experience
Big Apple Club, Munich
Hendrix ends up smashing his guitar, to the German audience's
approval.

Thursday, 11/24
De Lane Lea Studios, London
The Experience records "Love or Confusion" and "Here He Comes."

Friday, 11/25
The Jimi Hendrix Experience
Bag O' Nails Club, London

Chandler sells most of his guitars to pay for an extravagant press reception after the group's performance at the club. Also in attendance are members of the Beatles, the Who, the Rolling Stones, and the Hollies. Hendrix gives his first press interview, for the *Daily Mirror*.

Saturday, 11/26
The Jimi Hendrix Experience
Ricky Tick Club, Hounslow, England
The Experience opens for the New Animals.

Sunday, 11/27
Jimi Hendrix turns twenty-four.

DECEMBER
Thursday, 12/1
London
Hendrix signs a contract with Yameta.

Tuesday, 12/6
Hendrix, Chandler, and his girlfriend, Lotte, move to a flat at 34 Montague Square, London. The previous tenant was Ringo Starr of the Beatles.

Wednesday, 12/7
Hendrix is issued a further residence permit, valid through January 15, 1967, that officially allows him employment in the UK.

Saturday, 12/10
The Jimi Hendrix Experience
Ram Jam Club, London
The Experience opens for John Mayall's Bluesbreakers.

Sunday, 12/11
Rembrandt Hotel, London
Hendrix and Kathy Etchingham visit Little Richard after his concert

at the Saville Theatre. Hendrix asks Richard for fifty dollars and gets it.

Tuesday, 12/13
The Jimi Hendrix Experience
Rediffusion Studios, Kingsway, London
The Experience makes its television debut, on *Ready Steady Go!*
The group performs a live version of "Hey Joe," during which Hendrix plays the solo with his teeth. The show airs the following day.

CBS Studios, London
The Experience records multiple takes of "Foxy Lady," "Red House," "Can You See Me," "Love or Confusion" and "3rd Stone from the Sun."

Friday, 12/16
The Jimi Hendrix Experience
Chislehurst Caves, Bromley, Kent, England
Polydor Records releases the first single in the UK by the Jimi Hendrix Experience: "Hey Joe," b/w "Stone Free."

Wednesday, 12/21
The Jimi Hendrix Experience
Blaises, London

De Lane Lea, London
"Remember" and "Red House" are recorded.

Thursday, 12/22
The Jimi Hendrix Experience
Guildhall, Southampton, England

Monday, 12/26
The Jimi Hendrix Experience
Upper Cut, London

Hendrix writes "Purple Haze" in his dressing room prior to his performance.

Thursday, 12/29
The Jimi Hendrix Experience
BBC TV, Lime Grove Studios, London
The Experience performs "Hey Joe" on *Top of the Pops*.

Saturday, 12/31
The Jimi Hendrix Experience
Hillside Social Club, Folkestone, England
"Hey Joe" enters *Record Mirror*'s UK charts at number thirty-eight in the Top 50 singles and number eleven in the Top 20 R&B singles.

Folkestone, England
Hendrix, Etchingham, Mitchell, and Redding attend a New Year's Eve party at Redding's mother's house. According to Margaret Redding, it was cold that night and Hendrix asked if he could stand next to the fireplace, which leads to the idea for his song "Fire."

Index